179th y...

Ra...

Astrological

and

Predictive

Almanac

1999

edited by
Edwin Raphael

Published by W. Foulsham & Co. Ltd., Bennetts Close, Cippenham, Slough, Berks, SL1 5AP.
©Copyright 1998 ISBN 0-572-02326-X
Printed in Great Britain by Cox & Wyman Ltd., Reading.

CONTENTS

RAPHAEL'S WORLD PROPHECY FOR 1999

In Cabbalistic astrology the year 1999 equates with the tarot symbol of the 'Wheel', a period symbolising the forces of destined change and the need to respond positively to it. In particular, the theme of multi-culturalism continues to deepen, affecting groups with strong nationalistic interests. The challenge is theirs to realise and accept that the world is no longer the same, and certainly not as small as they would wish! Likewise, financial markets now expand within not merely Europe, America or Japan, but reach the limits of a more inclusive, global based economy.

This is all very much in keeping with Uranus and Neptune's continued journey through the sign of Aquarius, the sign of collective involvement. While one cannot fail to notice the emphasis on 'corporate' this or 'multinational' that in business, it also signifies the slow emergence of the ideals of genuine universal 'brotherhood'. We can see its slow birth, too, in recent peace summits involving warring nations or groups. This Aquarian shift does not signify utopian peace, nor is it any guarantee of success, but it does indicate a gradual awakening to the fact that the old divisions simply won't work, and that getting together around the negotiating table just might do some good. As Churchill once put it, 'jaw-jaw is better than war-war'!

Neptune and Uranus in Aquarius will no doubt contribute to some pretty enthusiastic pre-millennial fever, too. Though expectations will be high, hopes for an Eden-like, peace-filled universe will obviously be dashed. However, we will, in years to come, see ever more innovative progress in science and technology (such as developments with alternative means of powering cars). And certain 'New Age' subjects will emerge more into the mainstream, especially those with an ecological basis, as people awaken more to the need for a healthy environment. No longer will the 'eco-warriors' be seen as woolly minded hippies! Their ideas will be turned to practical account.

As for the supposedly doom-laden solar eclipse in August 1999, this is more likely to signify a crisis in the European parliament, rather than Armageddon.

Virgo the Leading Sign for 1999

Leading the World Horoscope for 1999 is the sign Virgo, under whose traditional rulership comes Canada, Kurdistan, Vietnam, Switzerland and Turkey. These are areas of the world which may well see turning-points in their major affairs. Virgo is the sign of the discriminating, hard worker, carelessly trying to improve her affairs. Virgo is also the Sun sign on the Middle East peace process chart, indicating further struggles in attempts at a settlement.

Virgo rules the workforce, health, public services, the armed forces and ecological matters. It's likely we'll see a greater emphasis on public health world-wide, alerting us to matters of dietary intake and the like. Virgo rules the things often taken for granted, such as 'green issues', and the emphasis on how we treat the planet as a whole will become more focused. Interestingly, Virgo rules rural and domestic animals too, thus we can expect some effective pressure from animal rights groups, for instance over the treatment of livestock or the effects of pollution on fish in our rivers. Again, this concern for the environment at large falls perfectly within the context of the Aquarian Age.

Saturn is the main ruler in 1999, emphasising more of the need to learn from the past while maintaining successes in the present. Contrary to any utopian expectations, Saturn as ruler this year delivers a cool, clear message: 'Wake up to what's really going on'. And the influence of Virgo as leading sign only emphasises the very sober fact that the world doesn't improve without *working* at it. For some folks, in particular those with a fervent religious or extreme right wing bent, this simple message has not yet been understood. One day, though, hopefully!

Horoscope Analysis by Liz Greene

ASTRO✳INTELLIGENCE

Currently available reports are:
— **The Psychological Horoscope Analysis**
— **The Child's Horoscope**
— **The Relationship Horoscope**

The Astro*Intelligence reports are an entirely new type of Horoscope reading written by the celebrated astrologer and psychologist, Liz Greene. As a renowned author on astrology and a practising Jungian Analyst, Liz Greene brings her unique psychological approach to Horoscope Interpretation. In a manner that surpasses most other astrologers, Liz Greene probes the very depths of your unconscious or hidden nature. Through the planets she uncovers the archetypal characters of your inner drama; the interplay between who you think you are, and the character that lies in your subconscious; between masculine and feminine, and other contrasting sides of your nature, adding practical suggestions on how to express each part in a creative way. Furthermore Alois Treindl, an expert in Artificial Intelligence and astrology has structured computer programs so that Liz Greene's remarkable text can be woven together in a way that actually mirrors her unique and powerful methods of interpretation.

What do other astrologers say?

"Liz Greene has no peers where psychological astrology is concerned and this program really does capture her mind and insights to an astonishing degree. It is said that the computer can never replace an individual astrologer, but it is difficult to imagine an astrologer producing a report of this depth and quality by hand for less than ten times the cost. I recommend A*I reports to most of my clients and often use them as an invaluable preliminary to my consultative work." — Charles Harvey, DFAstrolS, President of the Astrological Association.

Liz Greene

Liz Greene, astrologer, author and Jungian Analyst, has written or co-written over ten major astrological titles including 'Relating', 'Saturn', 'Astrology for Lovers', 'The Astrology of Fate', 'Luminaries' and 'Inner Planets'

Special Notes for Ordering
Relationship Horoscope

The **Relationship Horoscope** is addressed to one partner only. However, a second report from the other party's point of view is available. The cost of both reports is £45 (plus £1.50 p&p). There is of course considerable overlap between the two analyses and in most cases the single report of £30 (plus £1.50 p&p) will be adequate. If you order one report on behalf of one person only, please make it clear whom it is for, by underlining the appropriate name on the order form. You can always order the other half of the **Relationship Horoscope** at a later stage. The charge for the second report will be £15 (plus £1.50 p&p).

Time of Birth

To prepare an Analysis the time of birth must be known to within 1 hour. Please give the local time of birth, i.e. the time on the clock. If you were born 'around Midnight', make it clear whether it was at the start or the end of the day.

Postage and Packing

Rates per package, whether it is one chart over several including the video.
UK: £1.50   Europe: £2.00   Outside Europe: £3.00
Either telephone your order on 0171 497 1001 – have your credit card handy or fill in the coupon and send it to:
Astro*Intelligence, 78 Neal Street, London WC2H 9PA.

6

BRITAIN'S HOROSCOPE
FOR 1999

What of the relatively new Labour Government then? In a first year punctuated by only minor gaffes and some backtracking over benefit policy, Labour have at least fulfilled their own astrological pledge to create a dynamic – some would say smug – image with the Sun on the MC! With Tony Blair at the helm, as predicted last year relations with abroad have been essentially positive – and with Jupiter on the Descendant of this chart, they continue to be so in 1999. But while American and European opinions of this government tend, on the whole, to be favourable, it is closer to home that Labour will hear the voices of dissatisfaction. The annual chart shows Capricorn rising (with Sun conjunct Saturn opposed to the MC), signifying pressure from the grassroots element – what we might term the old guard socialists. This may ultimately lead to factions and splits as traditional Labourites make their voices heard. Obviously this will be grist to the mill for the Conservatives, ready to insist that New Labour is nothing more than Old Labour in new clothes. But what it really means is that the party as a whole is quite divided between two ideologies. With Saturn strong on all relevant charts to England, this year can expect 'New Labour', to pursue further what have been labelled the policies of the last Tory Government. In short, the ruling powers now have their minds set on preserving the status quo, especially in monetary policy. The outlook for the Government in 1999 may be summarised as a party in love with its own image as progressive modernisers which, in fact, conceals many old, entrenched ideas.

Radical ideas, either within Labour itself or 'rights' groups may be in the air in January – not the smoothest start to the year. There may be heavy criticism in March regarding education measures (especially regarding universities), though the overall trend here is towards improvement. The year is characterised by hard-headed and consequently unpopular political decisions, which we may see in both May and June as Saturn contacts sensitive points. An increase in national self-congratulation occurs in July as Britain looks to its past – naturally connected to the millennium. In fact much of the year has this theme of 'British is best' and we can expect much in the news regarding the nation's heritage and identity, with the Government making PR capital of it (as if what's great about Britain is symbolised by New Labour!). This we can expect to see in the summer months, though by October radical voices are heard again, possibly proving embarrassing to the Government. This may well come from the Liberal Democrats, whose chart this year shows even more of the progressive, reforming spirit. However, they also make their mark via co-operation in Government think-tanks, unlike the Tories who will have another rather ineffective year in opposition.

European Union

Throughout 1999 the prospect of attracting Britain into the single European currency remains as vital as ever. At the time of writing, the possibility for full membership on January 1st seems less than slim – indeed, the Chancellor has made it known that we will not join the single currency for the lifetime of this Government. The annual chart for Britain suggests caution, despite warnings from Europhiles about staying out. But this caution will prove wise.

The Economy

Serious tests of the Government's popularity encompasses employment in 1999. The jobless total will fail to decrease, with many casualties owing to lack of exports in manufacturing. The idealistic 'welfare to work' programme is shown in Neptune's position on the chart, and its lack of practical application will become evident now. We can thus expect some draconian measures in June, July and August. Much the same applies to the economy with the finance and banking sector under pressure, though foreign investments may see a rise in the second half of the year. The overall picture for most folk seems to be of little real growth.

The Royal Family

With so many strong planetary contacts to the area of the chart related to the monarchy this year, we shouldn't be surprised to see yet further pressure on the Royal family. This is in connection with the continued question of its relevance to modern Britain. Strong criticism may be in the air in February, August, July and November. Prince William may be in the news in June regarding the strain of his role as a Royal.

Home Affairs

Millennium fever sets the ground for innovation in the arts, fashion and popular entertainment in May, June and September, with Uranus's link to Venus, when there is a sense that Britain has become a kind of culture capital of the world. But where more serious matters are afoot, the Government's inability to deliver on pledges continues to rankle. The issue of increased class sizes in schools may surface again in April, with bad feeling expressed by teachers and parents. Yet tougher measures for dealing with crime may be in the news in May and July, though with little attention to underlying social problems. Though we may see a minor tonic for the job market in June (probably as a result of foreign investment) the health service may be in the news regarding the still-too-high hospital waiting lists. February, April and November are the worst months for our roads, as the problem of traffic congestion continues. Yet, it's a good year for the media, with our film industry and book trade having something to smile about (March, July and December look favourable). Within TV and cinema we may even see an easing of certain kinds of censorship. But there is an overall sense this year that while the nation is out enjoying itself, so to speak, things are getting no better at home.

THE ASTROLOGY SHOP
COVENT GARDEN

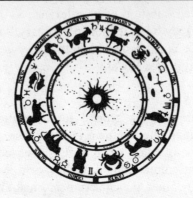

Astrology Books
Over One Thousand Astrological Titles
UK and International Mail Order service available from the Shop.

Astrological Video & Audio Cassette Tapes

Astro*Intelligence
Astrologer Liz Greene's
Psychological Horoscope, Child Horoscope & Synastry Analyses.
Available in English, German, French, Spanish, Italian, Dutch or Norwegian.

Astro*Carto*Graphy
A3 Colour World Relocation Maps + 3 City Analysis

Chart Calculation Service

Equinox Chart Interpretations
Choice of Character Profile, Year Transit Forecast, Child Profile or
Compatibility Profile. Each report is annotated with astrological symbols.

Chart Blanks, Posters & Unusual Gifts

THE ASTROLOGY SHOP
78 Neal Street, Covent Garden, London WC2H 9PA.
Telephone: 0171 497 1001   Fax: 0171 497 0344
E-Mail: equinox@equinox.uk.com

GLOBAL AFFAIRS IN 1999
A PROPHETIC PREVIEW

UNITED STATES

For Bill Clinton, 1998 was quite a year with the re-emergence of allegations of sexual misconduct. At the time of writing these have failed to dent his general popularity, possibly on account of the improved economic performance. We've also seen the US taking on the role of 'peacemaker'; note the Irish and Palestinian issues, which arise from the Pluto factor in the 'marriage' house of the Clinton administration chart. On other charts pertinent to America, this Pluto factor continues throughout 1999, yet strong Saturn energies indicate a weakening of its powers abroad, and possibly a blotting of its image. On the whole, it is time (the seeds of which were sown in last year's chart) when America must face up to the fact of having to fall further into line with the international community. Rather like Britain this year it must look to home, and here we can expect further tensions from right wing religious and terrorist elements who see Clinton as a too-soft liberal. Culturally, America will focus yet more on its own past, and even its failings (expect to see a greater emphasis on the historical novel or movie, for example). The Saturn factor shows America as more 'muted' this year, somehow making less of a stir on the global stage.

Though February indicates defeats in negotiation over international policy, probably in UN talks, there is a sense of general optimism at home as Jupiter crosses America's IC, presaging an improvement in property markets and general infrastructure. There may be further supportive measures for native American-Indian communities too. March may see a deeply divided Senate, with divisions in both parties, possibly over international defence and the plans for NATO expansion eastwards. April may see a senior White House figure exposed in a wrongdoing, again fulfilling the pattern of scandals throughout this administration. In June, racial issues and protests arise; this may manifest as further condemnation from the UN Human

Rights Commission on US capital punishment policy. We can expect further talks on the potential political abuse of the death penalty. In August there may be political gaffes as America reckons with its chequered past. With prominent Mars and Pluto, this may also be a period at risk from the 'lone terrorist' element or controversy from the armed militia who have 'opted' out of mainstream society. However, the year ends on a much more hopeful note with Jupiter's transit to Venus. Opinion polls in October are likely to show a high percentage in Clinton's popularity rating. (This happy news may be marred in November by pronouncements from apocalyptic sects about the end of the world.) There may also be a major drugs scandal involving a prominent public figure at this time.

EUROPE
The singular focus of attention in Europe this year is obviously the issue of the single currency, and in Britain – as we might expect – there is divided opinion on its potential merits. In theory, its introduction should lead to harmonisation of the economies throughout Europe, a kind of super economic society with – it is supposed – each member having an equal standing. (More echoes of the Aquarian Age!) The reality is, however, that no one really knows how to present a single monetary policy for a group of countries with varying unemployment levels, inflation and interest rates. Naturally, there is much consumer concern about rising prices as the natural consequence of the single currency. Again, in theory, prices shouldn't rise and fall, but this is almost certain to happen when the Euro gets underway on 1st January 1999.

The Euro's origins go back to the Hague Summit of the late 60s. What then of its official launch in the late 90s? The chart I have constructed for the 'birth' of the single currency ably indicates the almost utopian idealism that underpins it, and the obvious potential pitfalls about its implementation. Firstly, a lack of positive planetary contacts to the sun indicates the 'wrong' time at which to proceed. The Euro's Sun is 'unhealthy' and needs more time to 'get better'. The strongly placed Neptune (opposite MC) denotes lack of practical realism, confusion and mishandling, suggesting that any optimism about standardised economies will run into trouble. Euro-sceptics opine that it's too soon for certain member states to enter the single currency. This is nicely indicated by Mars – impatient energy – on the Ascendant opposite Saturn. It also indicates division, strife and disagreement, and with Saturn square MC, the continual presence of stumbling-blocks.

Interestingly though, the will is present to overcome them and a significant transit of Jupiter (to the Descendant) in May suggests the dust settling after a rocky start. Responses to economic performance tend to be more positive than the doubters expect after a year in operation, January 2000. However, the real test of future credibility arises in April when serious taskmaster Saturn crosses into the Euro's eighth house of big business, banks and international finance.

FRANCE

As we have seen above, the progress of the Euro is by no means smooth in 1999. And far from France and Germany being united in European policy, divisions are likely over their disagreement over the role of the European Central Bank. Germany wants the bank to be independent with a strong anti-inflation policy, and that may mean further job losses. France wants a central bank with more political hegemony. This latter is well reflected in the 1997 chart for the French prime minister, with prominent Mars and Pluto. If one may loosely distinguish between the underlying philosophies of both France and Germany at present, the former has its eye on national and social reform while the latter seems wholly concerned with monetary policy. In February, Jupiter crosses France's IC (domestic and 'national' affairs) heralding good news for campaigners on citizen's rights and the environment. Further political tensions are signalled in May as Saturn squares Uranus, possibly leading to a constitutional crisis. At the root of this will be the tense situation of 'cohabitation' between a conservative president and left wing prime minister. June shows a brief period of celebration via the arts and leisure industry – now is the month for French culture! However, as Saturn enters the sixth house (work) this month, too, we may see further packages aimed at getting unemployment down, not that the prospects look at all rosy. Commentators rightly note that the advent of the EMU may mean rising jobless totals, and this could be the beginning of a testing period for France. Indeed, August (with a tense angle between Jupiter and Pluto) may see some political backlash and loud voices from the extreme right. Support for the National Front may show an increase, for example. The second half of the year certainly indicates pressure on the government to introduce a more flexible labour market, and by December there is good news for the government in this respect.

GERMANY

At the time of writing, Germany is ready for a national election in September 1998 when the current chancellor, Helmut Kohl (Christian Democrats), will run against the Social Democrat challenger, Gerhard Schroder. But whatever the outcome (and remember that both the Christian and Social Democrats support the Euro) there are discrepancies and crises ahead regarding involvement in Europe. With transiting Uranus opposed to Neptune on Germany's national chart (in its 'marriage' house), we should not be surprised to see its position undermined in some way by European partners. Though 1999 seems to be marred by the spectre of rising unemployment, possibly as a result of the Euro, and certainly in the eastern regions, the first half of the year up until May shows minor economical improvement with Jupiter still passing through Germany's second house (money) on the national chart. However, with Saturn as one of the chief 'ruling' planets for Germany, its passage through the third house indicates the presence of entrenched ideas in the country's fabric and the determination to stay on course with already implemented policies.

Challenges to this occur in May and June when there may be pressure in Europe, with more disagreements in summits, possibly with the French president. Politically and economically, July and August is a loss-cutting time as the government takes on a hard-headed approach to domestic problems.

Additionally, there may be further demands from the

14

Bundesbank to reduce wages for EU officials. In October, a particularly sensitive transit from Mars may put racist issues in the news, with the neo-Nazis fomenting unrest and possible violence in the east. The astrological house on Germany's chart where this transit occurs is significant: the twelfth, ruling both subversive activity and the 'underclass'. This problem doesn't seem to be addressed very effectively this year in Germany.

RUSSIA

Russia is undergoing a period of political turmoil. President Yeltsin has undergone extensive pressure in the Duma while seeing his country pushed further into economic troubles. As with other countries during the Aquarian Age, Russia is attempting to reform and modernise itself, and of course a crippled economy doesn't help. Difficulties here have been renewed by the Far East monetary crises, or at least that's where Russia is content to put the blame. One of the other reasons is the declining value of oil and gas, which provide half of Russia's hard currency income. It is factors such as these which constitute continuing periods of pressure, and the tense angles to modern Russia's chart (set from 5.45 GMT on 25th December 1991). In particular there is the presence of the 'quincunx' aspect, associated with sudden crises requiring drastic change.

Also, the traditional chart reveals several opposition aspects, signifying divisiveness and the need for compromise. As early as January we're likely to see more power struggles in the Duma. At the time of writing, Boris Yeltsin is struggling to gain approval for his chosen candidate for prime minister (another 'young reformer'), while the Communist-dominated parliament is proving resistant. Here again we witness a paradigm of the Aquarian spirit of reform and change trying to manifest, and Russian politics in 1999 is beset by strife arising from this reform versus orthodoxy. This theme runs through the chart this year, and is most focused in January, March and November. In particular, March may well see deepening financial troubles with Saturn and Uranus in tense aspect (in the 'money houses' of the chart). For one, the issuing of short-term bonds has become difficult and expensive, and rising wage arrears in the public sector continues to be a problem. These issues may be in the news in March and August.

Further opposition aspects in July, August and November (involving Saturn and Pluto) may provoke some ire from the ultra-nationalists over NATO's eastward expansion. This has already caused controversy in the American Senate, where both Democrats and Republicans are anxious that such will increase the chances of renewed Russian nationalism in the post-Yeltsin era. It is of note that the president is able to survive in the midst of such adversity, though this seems just as much the result of a passive Russian people preferring a strong figure in the Kremlin. One theory abounds that Yeltsin may decide to call early presidential elections (though this defies the constitution). But 1999 seems to be the wrong time to take up a such Communist-nationalist challenge.

IRELAND

The Northern Ireland peace process encompasses so many complex issues that one is almost at a loss as to where to begin. With both religious and political matters (in many cases inseparable) splitting the country (and having done so for most of the century), hopes for a lasting solution to Ireland's manifold troubles would be foolishly optimistic. The birth chart for the Loyalist acceptance of Republican bona fides (31st August 1994) illustrates the deep political divisions between these two elements, with three planets in stubborn Scorpio. However, a ray of hope appeared on Good Friday 1998 when the peace agreement – involving most of the parties round the conference table – finally concluded. Significantly, planetary influences on this day show the clash of wills (with four major planets in Aries) despite the initial willingness to talk (Moon in Libra). The main factors, however, depict the old, entrenched ideas (Pluto) behind the show of diplomacy (contact with Venus).

Of course, the crucial matter regarding any resumption of continued violence is not what is accepted at the conference table, but whether the separatist paramilitaries (such as splinter groups from the IRA) will continue their own campaigns. (On the Unionists' side, many are unhappy with what they see as largesse shown to Sinn Fein with the release of political prisoners.) As mentioned, the chart for the Good Friday peace agreement has Venus in hard aspect to Pluto, signifying the ever-present danger of shadowy, subversive activity. In 1999, January, March, June and October are periods of tension in this respect, not to mention the marching season in July when tempers are particularly frayed. The latter three months shows the involvement of Uranus, the planet of sudden unexpected happenings. In particular, mid-March seems at risk from aggressive, violent energy with a prolonged contact from Mars. Again, we can expect to see either Loyalist or Republican paramilitaries in the news. June seems to indicate another deadlock in the healing process, whether concerning border divisions or tensions between Protestants and Catholics. Even so, Uranus can mean not merely sudden flare up, but also a breakthrough in stasis, and this is the most optimistic note one can sound so far. For history has so far shown that division and strife in Ireland tends not to be the exception, but the rule. While there has indeed been some move towards resolution, it is the underlying will for constructive compromise that seems to be lacking. As noted in last year's Raphael's Almanac, the best hope for a real practical settlement doesn't occur until 2002.

ISRAEL

Will the Aquarian Age of hoped-for humanitarian advancement make its mark on the ongoing 50-years war in the Middle East? At the time of writing (May 1998) there is news of the recent failure of peace talks. This I predicted last year, pointing to intense breakdowns in communication for that month. Will things get any better then? Much obviously depends on Israel, or rather prime minister Binyamin Netenyahu who has, since taking power in May 1996, done little to further the peace process. Indeed, commentators note that he has proven even more resistant to Palestine than his predecessor, Shimon Peres. Though peace agreements have been signed with Egypt, Jordan and Palestine, the crisis continues. Perhaps we should not be so surprised, in view of the triple conjunction on Israel's chart involving the Moon, Saturn and Pluto – at best a safeguarding of national interests, at worst blind resistance to change. As far as

17

astrological indications go, there are in fact several charts one must inspect to gain an overall picture, in particular the Washington and Oslo agreements and the national charts for Israel and Palestine (even though no Palestinian state was actually formed!).

We may, however, take note of the PLO chart to illustrate the progress of Yasser Arafat. Here we see a firm resolve not to take no for an answer with strong Uranus and Pluto near the Ascendant, while its Libran Moon demands to be treated as an equal. (This push-forward initiative on the part of Palestine, and blocking on the part of Israel, was aptly symbolised when Yitzak Rabin almost refused to shake Arafat's hand to conclude the Washington Declaration back in 1993. Appropriately, Arafat made the first move!)

Pluto activity on the Palestine chart in January 1999 indicates a stepping up of pressure on Israel, while Netenyahu's chief concern remains with security demands – thus, another tense period. However, with generous Jupiter at large on the 'peace process' chart in March, hopes must be raised for a far more positive manifestation on implementing agreements. There may be further summits that now raise expectations. This trend towards resolution and practical action does actually seem to gain momentum, with Jupiter crossing the Descendant (dealings with 'others') in May. This happens on the Israeli national chart, and so it's possible we may see the prime minister giving more ground. This seems to be the best chance for compromise over contested territory like the West Bank. Of course, the area is continually at risk from terrorism, and Pluto activity in the months of January, May, June and November show tension and thus possible violence.

IRAN

The progressive ideals of the Aquarian Age (remember, now with two significant planets moving through that sign) seem to be gathering momentum in Iran, as President Khatami seeks to establish his 'civil society' (another Aquarian phrase!). However, the struggle ahead lies in having to work within the limitations of the traditional clergy, for under the constitution Iran is a theocracy and supreme power lies in the hands of a religious leader, regarded as God's representative on earth. Yet the society is gradually undergoing changes: there are attempts at modernisation and reform with Khatami's government, greater freedom of the press, and religious intellectuals seeking more relaxed interpretations of the Koran. Of course, the more conservative powers are understandably very wary.

There are several 'correct' birth times for modern Iran in the wake of the 1978 revolution and the consequent ousting of the Shah. While the Ayatollah Khomeini had already arrived in Tehran on 1st February 1979, the existing regime did not officially surrender power until 11th February, which is the date on which I have based the chart of contemporary Iran. Firstly, the 'new' planet Chiron falls in the twelfth house (the 'unconscious') showing that secret forces are continually at work to bring about changes to the status quo. Indeed, the chart depicts a country divided between those in power and the feelings of its citizens, with Sun and Moon in opposition, further exacerbated by a square from Uranus, leading to instability and unrest. But this Uranus factor also spells challenges to the old order, something which we can expect to see in some form in April, May and June 1999. The April clash between Chiron ('new order') and Saturn ('old order') suggests a clamping down by the traditionalists on progressive reforms. The link between Uranus and Mars (in May and June) is potentially explosive, and may mean the government goes too far in implementing reformist measures – thus stoking the ire of the conservatives. Indeed, this year, we see a government that comes very close to trying the patience of the present Ayatollah, Ali Khamenei. Civil issues, especially women's rights, return to the news in September (and November) with the Uranus-Moon opposition. This is likely to be another period of protest among prominent spokespeople. In fact, the chart as a whole illustrates the potential for radical progress, with even some improvement in its human rights record. There may be some enlightened discussion among the conservative judiciary in July, for example. On the subject of the reforms, Khatami's culture minister has commented that 'they will not break. They have the support of the entire nation; they are like a waterfall'.

IRAQ

As predicted for 1998, America's military installations in the Gulf appeared in March's news. This was the consequence of Iraq's expulsion of UN inspectors investigating the suspected arsenal of biological weapons, and the question remains as to whether Iraq is still a threat to the West. (The short answer is: potentially yes, so long as Saddam Hussein remains in power.) The chart for Iraq, based on the military coup of 1958, demonstrates perfectly the modern regime, with aggressive Mars at the top of the chart, the strong Sun (indicating its self-righteous face to the world) and Saturn opposing two planets in the twelfth (the house of shady, secret machinations). In 1999 some significant movements occur; Jupiter crossing Iraq's chart in March may result in further audacities, possibly presaging more UN pressure (again, the issue of stockpile weapons may arise) in May. Though sanctions are likely still to weaken the Iraqi infrastructure, the president himself remains unaffected. Indeed, throughout the year there are helpful aspects to Saddam's birth chart, which far from suggesting any sort of uprising against him (for example, from Shia forces) tends to indicate some further nose-thumbing to the western powers. This is most likely to occur in June, November and December, with possible sabre-rattling in December as Mars is brought into play on the Iraq chart. Anyone hoping for a hasty overthrow of the president is likely to be severely disappointed.

CHINA

China's ascendancy as a major economic force in 1999 was indicated in last year's *Raphael's Almanac*, indeed it seems to have surpassed all expectations. The combination of financial and export know-how with widespread cheap labour has enabled China to become a major international trading power with its 'socialist market economy'. (The trend is slowing down, however, as China is about to reach a critical point in its affairs.) While fears of its handling of the former British colony of Hong Kong have subsided, reunification with Taiwan nevertheless remains an issue. Some commentators express fear of a military invasion, even though in the past US intervention has proved effective. What is more likely is that we will witness the ever-increasing efficiency of financial leverage, forcing Taiwan into concessions through direct trade links. Indeed, it is China's status as a formidable economic force that has spared it the calamitous fate of neighbouring South-east Asian countries. (For example, the so-called Asian flu has meant the collapse of the Indonesian economy, and at the time of writing Japan's economy is reported as being on the brink of collapse, while unemployment in South Korea is quoted as rising by 10,000 per day).

There are three major planetary movements on China's national chart in 1999, denoting both its strength as a major player on the global stage and favourable responses from abroad. The first is a hopeful transit by Neptune in February (repeated again in August), pointing to ever-improving relations with the international community – particularly Europe. China's human rights record should demonstrate further progress, though its position on Tibet is likely to remain ambivalent, with little real change. The second is Jupiter's crossing of China's rising sign in April, traditionally associated with the spirit of change and fresh initiatives. China will be in an expansive mood now and this will be a favourable month for the business community. The third important transit is the Saturn return in June, which will step up China's determined economic reform package. The writing has been on the wall for a year, since it was announced by the then prime minister Li Peng. (Significantly, it was outlined in Saturnian terms: the drive, it was promised, would be handled 'prudently, patiently and carefully'!) The downside of all of this during the summer months will be redundancies in state-owned enterprises. The Saturn return will now coincide with a sharp rise in unemployment figures.

Economically, we can expect some slight fall off in growth around June, though overall performance is good. Some commentators state that, in the long term, China's economy is slowly running out of steam. Such pundits may be proven right by spring 2000 when Saturn moves into the second house of the chart (money). At any rate, this is a new test for China's overall economic structure. Much depends on how the Saturn return is handled and whether the promised 'modern enterprise system' succeeds.

1999 – The Year of the Rabbit

Chinese astrology works on a slightly different time scale than the more familiar Western branch of the study and the actual commencement of the Chinese New Year differs from year to year. It is not therefore until February 16th that the Year of the Rabbit officially begins. Between the beginning of January and the middle of February the world is still under the rulership of the strange, unusual and totally independent Tiger, and so the peculiar qualities of the Tiger rulership are perpetuated.

Beyond February 26th life in the world should become more predictable generally, though there is bound to be an air of the mysterious and in a way there could be no better introduction to the Millennium than that which is presented by the Rabbit. Rabbit years offer new solutions to old problems and are probably more peaceful than most. It isn't that things fail to get done, but the Rabbit often brings an interlude where thought and meditation are preferable to impulsive action. Rabbit years are ones during which spirituality often prevails.

The Element associated with the Rabbit during 1999 is Earth and this is likely to 'firm up' some of the more nebulous qualities of the Rabbit year, making for a practical approach that is not usually represented by this timorous animal. The combination of the Rabbit and Earth is certainly interesting and might bring about subtle changes in the beliefs and attitudes of many states, regions and individuals.

On the world stage as a whole it is likely to be the case that leaders will be more willing to talk and then go away and think about what has been said, showing a willingness to return and mull over details once again. If the pen is mightier than the sword, then communication, born of a deep, spiritual insight, is greater than both – a fact proved by the Year of the Rabbit. Not all situations will turn out equally favourable but there should be a definite air of co-operation, understanding and compassion. However, financial confidence might by somewhat lacking.

If you were born under the sign of the Rabbit, which generally speaking would mean your birthday fell in 1915, 1927, 1939, 1951, 1963, 1975 or 1987, you can expect an extra boost in the year ahead and a little more in the way of success. You are a thoughtful individual who will always do your best to help those round you. Although you may not be the most dynamic person in the world you have a tremendous capacity for intuition and usually know the right way to behave under any given circumstance.

RAPHAEL'S CALENDAR
Background Notes

A calendar is a system of subdividing the year into days, weeks and months. For early civilisations, just as today, a practical calendar was an important element in social and religious life as well as in agriculture.

A natural unit of time is the *day*, which is the time taken for the Earth to turn once on its axis. The day has not always been measured from midnight to midnight as we do now. For the ancient Babylonians, Jews and Greeks the day was from sunset to sunset; for the ancient Egyptians and Hindus it was from dawn to dawn. The Romans demarcated their day from midnight to midnight.

Another natural unit of time is the *month*, calculated by the passage of the Moon around the Earth. The earliest calendars were based on the Moon. Each month began with the observation of the New Moon in the western sky. Such a month, from New Moon to New Moon, is termed a 'synodic' month, and is about 29½ days long. The general custom was to have months of 29 and 30 days alternately.

Twelve synodic months made up the cycle of the year, which consisted of 354 days, i.e. 11 days short of a solar year (365 days). A discrepancy of this order soon mounts up. This was troublesome because the seasons are related to the Earth's journey around the Sun. In order to harmonise the lunar with the solar reckonings, about every three years an extra – 'intercalary' – month was inserted into the calendar.

The calendars of the ancient Babylonians, Hebrews, Chinese, Greeks and the Arabs were all lunar based. Quite early on, however, the ancient Egyptians used a year of 365 days. This was divided into months of 30 days with five extra days to bring the lunar year into line with the seasonal year.

To calculate the true length of the year, the Egyptians made observations on the rising of the star Sirius (Sothis) in relation to the Sun. They would look for the first rising of the star after its period of invisibility due to the conjunction of the Sun. This so-called 'heliacal rising' of Sirius always coincided with the beginning of the Nile flood, and this was the time the Egyptian civil year began.

24

The Tropical Year (counted from solstice to solstice, or from equinox to equinox) in actual fact is not exactly 365 days but close to 365¼ days. So every year the Egyptians' calendar fell about six hours behind the Sun. In four years it was 24 hours, a full day, behind. In 1,460 years it would be behind by 365 days – back where it started in the solar-lunar cycle.

The Julian Calendar

The republican Roman calendar was a lunar one, and suffered hopelessly from the confusion caused by the discrepancy with the solar year. Julius Caesar took the advice of an astronomer from Alexandria in Egypt, a Greek named Sosigenes, to abandon the lunar calendar. Sosigenes duly drew up a solar calendar, based on his calculation of 365¼ days for the Tropical Year. At the time, the Roman lunar calendar was 80 days behind the Sun, so Caesar decreed that the year 46 BC should have 445 days, to bring it into line with the solar calendar.

The months were much the same as those of the old republican calendar though slightly modified to give a more even pattern of numbering. An extra day was intercalated in February every fourth year.

The Julian calendar was established on 1st January 45 BC, by order of Caesar, over the entire Roman Empire. In 8 BC, the Emperor Augustus made some adjustments to the lengths of some of the months.

The Roman calendar year had originally commenced in March, which was when the new consul took office. From 153 BC this took place on the 1st *(Kalendae)* January, and January then became the first month of the year. In the original Julian Calendar there were no weeks – a seven-day week was introduced by the Emperor Constantine I in the fourth century AD.

Because the Julian Calendar was still imperfect it was eventually replaced by what is known as the Gregorian Calendar, which we use today. Dates in the former are referred to as Old Style (OS) and in the latter as New Style (NS).

The Gregorian Calendar

Sosigenes had over-estimated the Tropical Year by 11 minutes 14 seconds. Although a comparatively small figure, over the centuries a discrepancy of several days accumulated. In the sixteenth century, on the advice of astronomers, Pope Gregory XIII introduced a calendar correcting the length of the solar day. He decreed that 5th October 1582 (OS) should be 15th October 1582 (NS), and that century years should not be leap years unless they were divisible by 400. For example, the year 2000 will be a leap year, but 2100 will not. By modern computation, the Gregorian Calendar is still 25 seconds longer than the Tropical Year, but it will not need to be revised for many years to come.

In the New Style Calendar, 1st January was firmly established as the date of the New Year. (In early mediaeval times, 25th March was considered as New Year's Day, though in Anglo-Saxon England it was 25th December until William the Conqueror decreed it to be 1st January.) The Gregorian Calendar was immediately adopted in the Roman Catholic countries of Spain and Portugal (and their colonies), the Italian states, Luxembourg and most of France. By 1584 most of the Roman Catholic German states and Belgium had done so, followed by Hungary in 1587. However, because of the division of Protestants and Roman Catholics, and of the Eastern and Western churches, the adoption of the Gregorian Calendar tended to be very slow elsewhere, in spite of its advantages. Denmark, Holland and the German Protestant states adopted the New Style during 1699–1700.

Britain, and her colonies (which included America), embraced the Gregorian Calendar at noon on 2nd September 1752. By then the Julian Calendar was 11 days ahead of the Sun, so this number of days had to be dropped. The day after 2nd September became the 14th. Sweden followed in 1753, then Japan (1872), Egypt (1875) and China (1912). The Russians did not adopt it until 1918, and Greece not until 1923.

The calendar changes from OS to NS dates are important not only for historians but for astrologers dealing with historical personages and events. To calculate a horoscope, an OS date must first be converted to NS. There is a simple conversion table showing how many days should be added for specific centuries (see page 31).

Dates for events quoted in books often specify OS or NS in brackets, so there is no doubt as to which calendar is being used. Very often, however, OS dates are automatically converted to NS without mention of it.

Time Systems

For an astrologer wanting to construct a historical chart, ascertaining the correct date is the first hurdle. Then, to calculate an accurate horoscope, it is necessary to know the time of a birth as accurately as possible. Here more problems arise. Until the last quarter of the nineteenth century time was a very local affair, and people set their watches and clocks in various rough-and-ready ways. For example, a person might set his watch by the church clock, which in turn was set by the sundial.

The trouble with sundial time is that the Sun does not travel at a uniform rate round the Earth. One of the reasons for this is that the Earth's orbit is not circular but slightly elliptical, so the Earth's distance from the Sun varies. When it is nearer to the Sun it travels faster than when it is farther from it, and therefore the Sun appears to travel across the sky at varying speeds.

The time we watch on a sundial is called 'true' or 'apparent' solar time. It is the True Local Time for that particular place. When the sundial shows *noon* the Sun is crossing the *meridian*. The meridian is an imaginary line across the dome of the sky from the north point on the horizon, through the point vertically above the observer (the zenith) and down to the south point on the horizon. The interval between two consecutive crossings of the meridian by the Sun at noon is a 'true' or 'apparent' solar day (counted from midnight to midnight, to avoid changing the date at noon).

For practical purposes, time systems are based on the average speed of the Sun as it goes round the Earth – the 'mean Sun'. The *mean solar day* is divided into intervals of equal length. Its 24 hours, subdivided into minutes and seconds, are the ones shown on our clocks.

Apart from the solar day, there is another kind of day important to astronomers and astrologers. This is the *sidereal day*, which is the period of rotation of the Earth in relation to the stars. Put in another way, it is the time taken by two consecutive crossings of the meridian by the same star.

The sidereal day is nearly four minutes shorter than the day measured by the clock. Why is this so? One has to remember that the Earth, in addition to rotating on its axis, is travelling through space round the Sun. When it has turned on its axis once, it has to turn an additional degree to point to where the Sun is compared

27

to where it was the day before. By the same ratio, a sidereal hour, minute and second are also shorter than in a clock day. If the stars took *exactly* 24 hours to go round the Earth, we should see them in exactly the same position immediately overhead at the same hour every night. Instead, they get there four minutes earlier every night.

The Earth's true revolution period (365 days 6 hours 9 minutes 9.5 seconds) is known as a *Sidereal Year*. It is about 20 minutes longer than the Tropical Year. In fact, in every observatory there is a special clock for measuring *sidereal time*. It is set at 0 hours when 0° Aries is culminating on the meridian of that place.

The Precession of the Equinoxes

Because the Earth is not quite a perfect globe, as it rotates there is a slight wobble of its axis. The resulting gradual swing of the axis gives rise to the phenomenon known as the *precession of the equinoxes*.

Due to the precession, there is a gradual backwards (retrograde) motion of the vernal equinox along the ecliptic against the background of the stars. The ecliptic is the apparent path of the Sun around the Earth, seen against the stars. The twelve signs of the zodiac are 30° divisions of the plane of the ecliptic. Within this plane, or band, the planets have their orbits. The vernal point is when the Sun enters 0° of the 'tropical' sign of Aries. Because of the precession, amounting to approximately 1° every 70 years, the vernal point is actually no longer in the *constellation* of Aries but has fallen back to that of Pisces.

So in the Sidereal Year the equinoxes and solstices, which mark the beginning of the seasons, are very slowly shifting backwards. But in the Tropical Year (365 days 5 hours 48 minutes 4.5 seconds), i.e. the period between two returns of the Sun to the spring equinox, the seasons will always remain in the correct months – summer will never fall in December!

Greenwich Mean Time

In the eighteenth century, Greenwich Observatory established the mean solar day by astronomical and mathematical calculation. Its clock was corrected every day to conform to it, though the public at large had no means of knowing the Greenwich 'standard' time. Their time was still based on the local meridian. For every 13 miles a person travelled either east or west made a difference of one minute of True Local Time (Sun time). But life then was comparatively simple and the means of travel slow, so if the time in one town was different from that in another part of the country it didn't matter a lot.

In the early nineteenth century, developments in communications changed people's attitudes to time and time-keeping. The first passenger train ran in 1825, the first crossing of the Atlantic by steamship was in 1827. Bradshaw's railway time-tables (in local time) began in 1839, and the public telegraph in 1843. Obviously, for organisations like the railways, telegraph companies and the Post Office, having different times all over the country was a great inconvenience.

In 1840, the Great Western Railway ordered that London time should be kept at all its stations and in its timetables, and in the next few years many other railways followed suit. By 1852, Greenwich time signals were being transmitted automatically from the Royal Observatory by electric telegraph to railway stations and the Electric Telegraph Company, for distribution throughout Great Britain.

By 1855, 98 per cent of the public clocks in Great Britain were set to GMT. As late as 1880, GMT became the legal time in Britain. It is sometimes referred to as *Universal Time* (UT).

World Standard Time Zones
In 1884, delegates from 25 nations attended the Washington Meridian Conference. The aim was to select a common zero for longitude and time reckoning throughout the whole world. After considering various places, including Bethlehem and the Great Pyramid, a majority vote set 0° longitude at Greenwich.

Following the Washington Conference, a time-zone system was adopted, country by country, based on the Greenwich meridian. Some countries resisted the new system but one by one conformed over the following years. One of the last, Holland, was forced to use Central European Time during the German occupation, the usage being confirmed in 1956.

A table of standard time zones in use today is to be found on pages 151–52. Those east of Greenwich are 'minus zones'. Their local time is converted into Greenwich time by subtracting the number of hours indicated. The 'plus zones' are west of

Greenwich, and their local time is converted to GMT by adding the given number of hours.

In Raphael's Calendar (pages 32–56), birthdays and special events are in GMT or local time except when otherwise indicated.

NB: *The birth times given are ones that are considered well attested. Such data are regularly published in the journal of the Astrological Association (396 Caledonian Road, London, N1 1DN).*

The Ecclesiastical Calendar

The beginnings of the calendar of the western Christian churches go back to the Jewish calendar, whose roots run down to the civilisations of Babylon and ancient Egypt. The names of the days of the week, however, are derived from pagan religions. The word Easter, according to the Venerable Bede, is derived from Eostre, the Teutonic goddess of springtime.

Easter Day takes its time from the Jewish feast of the Passover, because the Crucifixion occurred three days before it. The Passover festival begins on the 14th day of the month of Nisan in the Jewish religious calendar. Easter Day is officially designated as the first Sunday after the Full Moon that falls on or after 21st March, unless the Full Moon falls on a Sunday, when Easter Day is the Sunday after. However, the 'Moon' in these calculations is not the real Moon in the heavens but a hypothetical calendar one with alternating cycles of 29 and 30 days. Tables used in determining the date of Easter can be found at the beginning of the *Book of Common Prayer*.

Although the Orthodox Churches calculate Easter in the same way, it falls on a different date owing to the fact that they use the Julian Calendar to do this.

A series of other commemorations connected with the life of Christ depends on the date of Easter. *Lent*, beginning on Ash Wednesday, is a period of 40 days that ends on Easter Eve (Holy Saturday), the day before Easter Day. It has six Sundays, the last two being known as Passion and Palm Sunday. *Ascension Day* falls 40 days after Easter Day. The Sunday before it is called Rogation Sunday. *Pentecost (Whit Sunday)* is seven weeks after Easter, and the Sunday that follows is *Trinity Sunday*. The Thursday after Trinity Sunday is *Corpus Christi*. *Advent Sunday* is the Sunday nearest 30th November.

Unlike the moveable feasts mentioned above, Christmas and

Epiphany have a fixed date. In addition, the Church consecrated certain fixed days of the year to particular saints – some of these appear on Raphael's Calendar pages. The days in bold type denote Principal Holy Days, Festivals and Greater Holy Days of the Church of England as given in the *Alternative Service Book 1980*.

CALENDAR CONVERSION TABLE (OS TO NS)

Century	Years	Days	Century	Years	Days	Century	Years	Days
21st	2000-99	13	14th	1300-99	8	7th	600-99	3
20th	1900-99	13	13th	1200-99	7	6th	500-99	2
19th	1800-99	12	12th	1100-99	7	5th	400-99	1
18th	1700-99	11	11th	1000-99	6	4th	300-99	1
17th	1600-99	10	10th	900-99	5	3rd	200-99	0
16th	1500-99	10	9th	800-99	4	2nd	100-99	−1
15th	1400-99	9	8th	700-99	4	1st	0-99	−2

The Seasons in 1999 (GMT)

Spring Quarter commences March 21st at 01h. 46m.
Summer Quarter commences June 21st at 19h. 49m.
Autumn Quarter commences September 23rd at 11h. 31m.
Winter Quarter commences December 22nd at 07h. 44m.

JANUARY

The month dedicated by the ancient Romans to the god Janus, who kept the gate of heaven. He was also the guardian of all gateways and doors, including the entrance to the year. Janus was represented with two faces, one looking forwards, towards the future, the other looking behind, to the past.

Day of		Remarkable Days.
M	W	Birth data of the famous, etc.
1	F	**The Naming of Jesus.** New Year's Day. Republic of China founded 1912
2	S	Iraq invaded Kuwait 1990 (2 a.m., Kuwait City). Death duties introduced 1894
3	⑤	**2nd Sunday after Christmas.** 'Lord Haw Haw' hanged 1946. John Thaw b. 1942
4	M	Don Bradman made his first Test century against England at Melbourne 1929
5	Tu	Twelfth Night. Wassail Eve. France regained Calais 1558. Mozart d. 1791
6	W	**Epiphany.** Twelfth day. Angus Deayton b. 1956. Sonny Bono d. 1998
7	Th	First Rugby League football matches played (Northern Union Rules) 1895
8	F	Kegworth air disaster 1989 (8.25 p.m.). Evacuation of Gallipoli 1916
9	S	1st Earl of Avon (Anthony Eden) resigned 1957 following Suez crisis
10	⑤	**1st Sunday after Epiphany.** Cleopatra's tomb was discovered 1890
11	M	British penny post introduced 1840. Women over 30 given the vote 1918
12	Tu	Michael Aspel b. 1933 (4 a.m., London). Des O'Connor b. 1932. St Benedict
13	W	Dallas airport opened 1974. Stephen Hendry b. 1969 (9.25 p.m. BST, Edinburgh)
14	Th	Edmund Halley d. 1742. Humphrey Bogart d. 1957. Warren Mitchell b. 1926
15	F	British Museum opened 1759. First telephone directory published 1880
16	S	Admiral David Beatty (1st Earl) b. 1871. Ivan the Terrible crowned 1547
17	⑤	**2nd Sunday after Epiphany.** Lloyd George b. 1863 (8.39 a.m., Manchester)
18	M	Capt. Robert Falcon Scott reached South Pole 1912. Rudyard Kipling d. 1936
19	Tu	James Watt b. 1736. Zeppelin Raid 1915. Earl of Surrey executed 1547
20	W	George V d. 1936. Matt Busby d. 1994. Terry Waite kidnapped 1987
21	Th	Jack Lord (*Hawaii Five-O*) d. 1998. Cleopatra's Needle arrived 1878
22	F	Queen Victoria d. 1901. Falkland Islands ceded to Britain by Spain 1771
23	S	William Pitt d. 1806. Anna Pavlova d. 1931. Lord Denning b. 1899
24	⑤	**3rd Sunday after Epiphany.** Sir Winston Churchill d. 1965
25	M	**The Conversion of St Paul.** Burns Night. Idi Amin coup 1971
26	Tu	India became a Republic 1950 (10.18 a.m. IST, New Delhi)
27	W	Turkish attack on Suez Canal 1915. Mozart b. 1756 (8 p.m. LMT, Saltzberg, Austria)
28	Th	Henry VIII d. 1547. Sir Francis Drake d. 1596. Acker Bilk b. 1929
29	F	Victoria Cross instituted 1856. Sasha Distel b. 1933 (1.45 p.m. WET, Paris)
30	S	Hitler appointed German Chancellor 1933 (11.15 a.m. MET, Berlin). St Basil
31	⑤	**9th Sunday before Easter (Septuagesima).** Bonnie Prince Charlie d. 1788

*Unless otherwise stated, times mentioned above may be assumed to be in
GMT or the local time*

JANUARY

The Voice of the Heavens

As the year gets under way, education and communication matters are brought into focus with the Full Moon on the 2nd (suggesting good things in the technological revolution). Other radical ideas prevail this month, possibly with some backlash against the Government from protest groups. Economically, there is likely to be less confidence in sterling towards the end of January. There may be fundamentalist elements on the rise in the Middle East in the early phase of this month, while we can also expect significant power clashes in the Russian parliament. This is also a tense month in Ireland owing to action by separatist paramilitary groups.

Political scheming may be exposed in South Africa – one of its leader's future is in jeopardy. There is even risk of earthquakes in Japan or America's West Coast after the New Moon of the 19th. Italy will enter the European single currency with great optimism, though it may be blinding itself to certain economic facts. There may be renewed concern over China's military intentions with regard to its neighbours, particularly Taiwan. An increase of pressure on Israel by Palestine over disputed territory may mar the peace process.

Second favourites may be worth following at National Hunt meetings.

NATIONAL DAYS
1st – Haiti; Cuba; Sudan *(Independence Day)*; Western Samoa *(Independence Day)*. *4th* – Myanmar, formerly Burma. *11th* – Albania. *13th* – Togo *(National Liberation Day)*. *26th* – Australia *(Australia Day)*; India *(Republic Day)*.

RAPHAEL'S WEATHER GUIDE FOR JANUARY 1999
Generally cold and freezing with some heavy snowfalls. High winds and blizzards will occur 19th–23rd, but mainly in the North. It will be somewhat brighter from the 20th.

FEBRUARY

Probably named after the Etruscan god Februus, it was the month of purification among the ancient Romans. Candlemas Day, on the 2nd, was formerly the feast day of the Purification of the Blessed Virgin Mary. If the weather is dry and frosty about this day, it is said there will be more winter ahead than behind. But if it is wet, winter is more than half over.

| Day of | | Remarkable Days. |
M	W	Birth data of the famous, etc.
1	M	Boris Yeltsin b. 1931 (4.30–5 p.m., Butka, nr Talitsa). St Brigid
2	Tu	**Presentation of Christ in the Temple.** Gene Kelly d. 1996. Sir David Jason b. 1940
3	W	T.W. Robertson, dramatist/actor, d. 1871. *Luna IX* moon landing 1966
4	Th	George Herbert, poet, d. 1633. Sweet rationing ended 1953
5	F	J.P. Dunlop, inventor of the tyre, b. 1840. George Arliss d. 1946
6	S	Accession of Queen Elizabeth II, 1952. Jimmy Tarbuck b. 1940. St Dorothy
7	☉	**8th Sunday before Easter (Sexagesima).** Dora Bryan b. 1926
8	M	Earthquake in London 1750. Jules Verne b. 1828 (noon LMT, Nantes)
9	Tu	Mia Farrow b. 1945 (11.27 a.m. PST, Los Angeles). Soap rationed 1942
10	W	New Delhi became capital of India 1931. Victoria and Albert married 1840
11	Th	Regiment of the Welsh Guards founded 1915. Thomas Edison b. 1847
12	F	London Customs House burnt 1814. Abe Lincoln b. 1809. Darwin b. 1809
13	S	Richard Wagner d. 1883. Dresden bombing raid began 1945 (10.13 p.m. MET)
14	☉	**7th Sunday before Easter (Quinquagesima).** St Valentine's Day
15	M	Decimal currency introduced 1971. King George VI's funeral 1952
16	Tu	Shrove Tuesday. Tutankamun's tomb opened 1923. Nylon patented 1937
17	W	**Ash Wednesday.** Patricia Routledge b. 1929 (12.30 a.m., Birkenhead, Cheshire)
18	Th	Michelangelo d. 1564. John Travolta b. 1954. Martin Luther d. 1546
19	F	Duke of York b. 1960 (3.38 p.m., London). David Garrick, actor, b. 1717
20	S	Glen's earth orbit 1962. Edward VI crowned 1547. Voltaire b. 1694
21	☉	**1st Sunday in Lent.** Battle of Verdun 1916. Robert Southwell hanged 1595
22	M	Duchess of Kent b. 1933. F.W. Woolworth opened 'nothing over 5c shop' 1879
23	Tu	French Revolution began 1848. The first Rotary Club founded in Chicago 1905
24	W	First commercial nylon product (a toothbrush) went on sale in the USA 1938
25	Th	Pope Pius V excommunicated Queen Elizabeth I 1570. George Harrison b. 1943
26	F	Sir Christopher Wren d. 1793. £1 notes first issued 1797. Buffalo Bill b. 1846
27	S	Paddy Ashdown b. 1941 (4.30 p.m. IST, New Delhi). Elizabeth Taylor b. 1932
28	☉	**2nd Sunday in Lent.** Relief of Ladysmith 1900. Robin Cook b. 1946

Unless otherwise stated, times mentioned above may be assumed to be in
GMT or the local time

FEBRUARY

The Voice of the Heavens

We may see further criticism of the Royal Family this month, with 'radicals' making their voices heard – though the general consensus will hold their views as unwelcome. This seems to be a particularly tense month where transport is concerned, and further instances of 'road rage' may be in the news. The eclipse that begins the month points to possible radical change in world politics. Regions of the world sensitive to this are Europe, Libya, Africa and countries of the Pacific rim. We're likely to see a marked show of 'attitude' from America in its relations with abroad. However this may lead to its suffering defeats in UN negotiations. Back home though, America sees improvements in its property markets. Much is the same for France this month, where there is a rise in 'people power' with favourable developments for campaigners for citizens' rights.

Further scuffles are to be expected in the Middle East, with some difficulties for the Israeli government. In Europe, with the single currency off to a difficult start, there will be talk of overturning the entire project. Even so, an eventual return to previous high expectations is indicated. China improves its dealings with international partners, especially in Europe.

The Tote Gold Trophy at Newbury may be won by a 6-year-old carrying 11 st 5 lb.

NATIONAL DAYS

4th – Sri Lanka. *6th* – New Zealand *(Waitangi Day)*. *7th* – Grenada *(Independence Day)*. *11th* – Iran. *16th* – Lithuania. *18th* – Gambia *(Independence Day)*; Nepal. *23rd* – Brunei. *24th* – Estonia. *25th* – Kuwait. *27th* – Dominican Republic *(Independence Day)*.

RAPHAEL'S WEATHER GUIDE FOR FEBRUARY 1999

A fair start, but a cold spell is due 10th–25th when there will be frost and snow in eastern counties and inland over high ground. The South-east will stay fairly mild.

MARCH

The month is named after Mars, the Roman god of war. There is a saying, 'a bushel of March dust is worth a king's ransom'. This is because dry, windy weather in March produces a good tillage. In 1999 on the 21st of the month the sun enters the vernal equinox (the first point of Aries).

| Day of | | Remarkable Days. |
M	W	Birth data of the famous, etc.
1	M	St David's Day. Lindbergh baby kidnapped 1932. Joe Louis retired 1949
2	Tu	John Wesley d. 1791. Rhodesia a republic 1970. Australia Bill 1986
3	W	Alexander Graham Bell b. 1847. Barbican Arts Centre opened, London, 1982
4	Th	John Dunn, broadcaster, b. 1934 (9.50 p.m., Glasgow). Forth Bridge op. 1899
5	F	Covent Garden Theatre fire 1856. Rex Harrison b. 1908 (9.30 a.m., Glasgow)
6	S	Elizabeth Barret Browning b. 1817. Zebrugge disaster 1987. St Felicity
7	☉	**3rd Sunday in Lent.** Sir Ranulph Fiennes b. 1944 (11.30 p.m., Windsor, Berks)
8	M	Commonwealth Day. William III d. 1702. Hector Berlioz d. 1869
9	Tu	Alexander Graham Bell patented first telephone 1876. George Burns d. 1996
10	W	Prince Edward b. 1964 (8.20 p.m., London). Bakerloo Line opened 1906
11	Th	Baghdad captured from Turks by British 1917. Mount Etna erupted 1974
12	F	*Izvestia* founded 1917. Thomas Arne, composer of *Rule Britannia*, b. 1710
13	S	Uranus discovered 1781. Scottish F.A. founded 1873. Dunblane massacre 1996
14	☉	**4th Sunday in Lent** (Mothering Sunday). The New English Bible pub. 1961
15	M	Nicholas II, last Czar of Russia, forced to abdicate 1917. Ides of March.
16	Tu	Jerry Lewis b. 1926 (12.15 p.m., EST, Newark, NJ). Egypt Independence 1922
17	W	St Patrick's Day. Benjamin Franklin d. 1790. Elastic band patented 1845
18	Th	*Torrey Canyon* wrecked 1967. Ivan the Terrible d. 1584. Chamberlain b. 1869
19	F	**St Joseph of Nazareth.** Edgar Rice Burroughs, creator of Tarzan, d. 1950
20	S	John Lennon married Yoko Ono in Gibralter 1969. Dame Vera Lynn b. 1917
21	☉	**5th Sunday in Lent** (Passion Sunday). Vernal Equinox (1.46 a.m.)
22	M	National Gallery founded 1824. Nicholas Monsarrat *(The Cruel Sea)* b. 1910
23	Tu	Pakistan declared an Islamic Republic 1956 (7.05 a.m., Karachi)
24	W	Steve McQueen b. 1930 (12.15 p.m. CST, Indianapolis). Queen Mary d. 1953
25	Th	**The Annunciation.** Lady Day. King Faisal of Saudi Arabia assass. 1975
26	F	William Hague b. 1961 (4.50 a.m., Rotherham, Yorks). Beethoven d. 1827
27	S	Nikita Krushchev became Soviet leader 1958. Tenerife jet disaster 1977
28	☉	**6th Sunday in Lent** (Palm Sunday). Constantinople became Istanbul 1930
29	M	John Major b. 1943 (2 a.m.–4.30 a.m. BST, Brixton). Richmond Park op. 1904
30	Tu	Vincent van Gogh b. 1853 (11 a.m. LMT, Zundert, the Netherlands). Goya b. 1746
31	W	Franz Joseph Haydn b. 1732 (4 p.m., Rohrau, Austria). Charlotte Brontë d. 1855

Unless otherwise stated, times mentioned above may be assumed to be in
GMT or the local time. Clocks forward 1 hour 28th March (BST)

MARCH

The Voice of the Heavens
Reforms in the education system may lead to serious criticism
from spokespeople. One view will be that such changes do little
to modernise curricula in schools and colleges, even though the
overall trend is good. (It may be that the proposed changes are not
in fact implemented.) There's good news for the media this
month, and especially for moguls in the film and book industries.
There may be local elections showing an upsurge of support for
the Liberal Democrats. Due to a lengthy Mars transit, Ireland
looks unstable and at risk from aggressive factors trying to
scupper the peace process – though the main parties will make
positive progress. In the USA, we may see divisions in the Senate
over the international defence issue, and even terrorist action by
right wing factors in the mid-West.

Russia is likely to undergo more monetary problems as a
consequence of its issuing of short-term bonds. We should see
optimistic news related to the Middle East peace process
involving Israel and the Palestinians. Iraq seems to be feeling
highly confident (if not downright arrogant) and may overstep the
mark in some way in foreign dealings. This may result in pressure
from the UN security council.

*The Grand National at Liverpool may be won by the second
favourite.*

NATIONAL DAYS
1st – Bosnia-Hercegovina; Wales *(St David's Day)*. *3rd* – Bulgaria; Morocco. *6th* –
Ghana. *11th* – Denmark. *12th* – Mauritius. *17th* – Irish Republic *(St Patrick's Day)*.
21st – Namibia *(Independence Day)*. *23rd* – Greece *(Independence Day)*; Pakistan
(Pakistan Day). *26th* – Bangladesh *(Independence Day)*. *28th* – Azerbaijan
(Independence Day).

RAPHAEL'S WEATHER GUIDE FOR MARCH 1999
In the main the weather will be springlike, though rather breezy and cloudy at times.
A change around the 15th–16th will be followed by sunnier days with rising
temperatures.

APRIL

The name April means the 'opening' month, from the Latin *aperire*, to open. It is the time when buds unfold, and the earth opens to receive seed – helped along by April showers. Between midnight and noon on the 1st of the month, anyone is liable to be made a fool of.

Day of		Remarkable Days.
M	W	Birth data of the famous, etc.
1	Th	**Maundy Thursday.** First day of Passover. All Fool's Day. VAT began 1973
2	F	**Good Friday.** Falklands invaded 1982. US mint established 1792
3	S	**Easter Eve.** Doris Day b. 1922 (4.30 p.m., CST, Cincinnati). BUPA f'd 1947
4	�	**Easter Day.** 1st day of Passover. Oscar Wilde arrested, Cadogan Hotel 1895
5	M	**Easter Monday.** IRA stopped Grand National 1997. Jane Asher b. 1946
6	Tu	USA declared war on Germany 1917. Eden became Prime Minister 1955
7	W	World Health Organisation formed 1948. Mary Pickford b. 1893
8	Th	Sandie Shaw won Eurovision Song Contest for Britain *(Puppet on a String)* 1967
9	F	Severiano Ballesteros b. 1957. Bobby Fischer b. 1943. Paul Robson d. 1976
10	S	Omar Sharif b. 1932 (5.30 p.m. EET, Alexandria, Egypt). William Booth b. 1829
11	☉	**1st Sunday after Easter** (Low Sunday). The film *Gandhi* won eight Oscars 1983
12	M	The Russians made the first manned space flight with Yuri Gagarin 1961
13	Tu	London to Australia airline service begun by Quantas/Imperial Airways 1935
14	W	Highway Code issued 1931. Sir John Guilgud b. 1904. Lincoln assass. 1865
15	Th	Belsen liberated 1945. Hillsborough disaster 1989. *Titanic* sank 1912
16	F	Sir Peter Ustinov b. 1921 (11 a.m. BST, London). Spike Milligan b. 1918
17	S	Islamic New Year. Linda McCartney d. 1998. Benjamin Franklin d. 1790
18	☉	**2nd Sunday after Easter.** San Francisco earthquake 1906 (5.13 a.m. PST)
19	M	Pierre Curie, who discovered radium, killed in Paris 1906. Ruby Wax b. 1953
20	Tu	Capt. Cook discov. New South Wales 1770. Hitler b. 1889. Canaletto d. 1768
21	W	Queen Elizabeth II b. 1926 (2.40 a.m. BST, London). St Anselm d. 1109
22	Th	£1 coins introduced 1983. Sir Yehudi Menuhin b. 1916 (11.30 p.m. EST, NY)
23	F	St George's Day. Dennis Compton d. 1997. William Shakespeare b. 1564
24	S	Duchess of Windsor b. 1986. *Bismark* sunk *Hood* 1941. Easter Rising 1916
25	☉	**3rd Sunday after Easter. St Mark the Evangelist.** Anna Sewell d. 1878
26	M	Trial of Oscar Wilde began at the Old Bailey 1895. Chernobyl disaster 1986
27	Tu	Golden Gate Bridge, San Francisco, opened 1937. London Zoo opened 1828
28	W	Mussolini shot by partisans 1945. Edward IV b. 1239 (11.30 p.m., London)
29	Th	Lonnie Donegan b. 1931 (3 a.m. BST, Glasgow). Zipper patented 1913
30	F	Telephone line UK to Australia opened 1930. Vietnam War ended 1975

Unless otherwise stated, times mentioned above may be assumed to be in
GMT or the local time

APRIL

The Voice of the Heavens

Disaffected teachers may be in the news again this month, possibly to do with large class sizes or unsatisfactory wages. Economic institutions around the world are prone to some instability this month, though news from the City seems optimistic. In America, we may see a senior politician exposed in a misdemeanour (invoking public condemnation from religious figures). A recent political crisis in India may deepen, though this may be diverted by terrorist activity in the south. In the business world, we may witness the further merging of the multinationals, possibly with French companies showing favourable prospects. Figures related to Germany's economic performance look good, though the trend may soon fall off.

In Iran, conflicts between the liberal-minded government and the religious status quo may arise as the former seeks to implement more progressive reforms. China is now in an expansive if not ebullient mood. While this looks favourable for initiatives in the business sphere, there may be conflict with Vietnam and the Philippines regarding the huge oil reserves in the South China Sea. Switzerland may take further steps towards EU membership.

At Newmarket the Craven Stakes may be won by the favourite.

NATIONAL DAYS
4th – Senegal. *13th* – Chad. *16th* – Denmark *(Queen Margarethe II's birthday)*. *17th* – Syria. *18th* – Zimbabwe *(Independence Day)*. *23rd* – England *(St George's Day)*. *26th* – Tanzania *(Union Day)*. *27th* – Afghanistan *(Revolution Day):* Sierra Leone *(Independence Day)*. *30th* – The Netherlands *(Queen Juliana's Birthday)*.

RAPHAEL'S WEATHER GUIDE FOR APRIL 1999
There will be a fairly pleasant start to the month, with a few seasonal showers. A rise in temperature around the 18th will be followed by longer bright spells.

MAY

In Latin *Maius*, which is probably derived from Maia, the goddess of growth and increase. On the *Kalendae* of May, i.e. the 1st May, the traditional May Day, Roman youths sang and danced in the fields in honour of Flora, the goddess of fruits and flowers.

Day of		Remarkable Days. Birth data of the famous, etc.
M	W	
1	S	**St Philip and St James.** David Livingstone d. 1873. Una Stubbs b. 1937
2	☉	**4th Sunday after Easter.** New Labour Government 1997 (11.30 a.m. BST, London)
3	M	May Day Bank Holiday. Festival of Britain opened by George VI 1951
4	Tu	*Daily Mail* published 1896. Michael Barrymore b. 1952 (8 a.m., London)
5	W	Napoleon d. 1821. Britain's first satellite launched California 1967
6	Th	Tony Blair b. 1953 (6.10 a.m. Edinburgh). *Hindenburg* disaster 1937
7	F	First Isle of Man TT race held 1907. *Lusitania* sank 1915. Eva Peron b. 1919
8	S	VE Day 1945. Harry S. Truman b. 1884. Sir David Attenborough b. 1926
9	☉	**5th Sunday after Easter** (Rogation Sunday). Howard Carter b. 1873
10	M	Mother's Day first celebrated, in Philadelphia, 1907. Fred Astair b. 1899
11	Tu	Prime Minister Spencer Perceval assassinated in House of Commons 1812
12	W	Labour leader John Smith d. 1994. Coronation of George VI 1937
13	Th	**Ascension Day.** Stevie Wonder b. 1950. Tim Pigott-Smith b. 1946
14	F	**St Mathias the Apostle**. Blackpool Tower opened 1894. Warsaw Pact 1955
15	S	Frank Sinatra d. 1998. Britain dropped first H-bomb in the Pacific 1957
16	☉	**Sunday after Ascension Day.** 'Dam Busters' raid 1943. Home Guard formed 1940
17	M	Queen Victoria laid Victoria & Albert Museum foundation stone 1899
18	Tu	First Wimpey Bar opened in London 1955. Pope John Paul II b. 1920
19	W	Anne Boleyn executed 1736. Victoria Wood b. 1953. Gladstone d. 1898
20	Th	Cher b. 1946 (7.31 a.m. PST, El Centro, CA). John Pertwee d. 1996
21	F	Manchester Canal opened 1894. Daylight saving time introduced 1916
22	S	Sri Lanka proclaimed a republic 1972. Blackwall Tunnel opened 1897
23	☉	**Pentecost (Whit Sunday).** Bonnie and Clyde killed in Louisiana 1934
24	M	West German Federal Republic came into existence 1949 (00 a.m., Bonn)
25	Tu	Donald McClean, diplomat and spy, b. 1913 (2.30 p.m. GMT, London)
26	W	John Wayne b. 1907 (1 p.m. CST, Winterset, IA). George Formby b. 1904
27	Th	Henry Kissinger b. 1923. Golden Gate Bridge op. 1937. *Bismark* sunk 1941
28	F	Dame Thora Hird b. 1913. Duke of Windsor d. 1972. Anne Brontë d. 1849
29	S	Oak Apple Day. Edmund Hillary and Sherpa Tenzing conquered Everest 1953
30	☉	**1st Sunday after Pentecost (Trinity Sunday).** Joan of Arc burnt at stake 1431
31	M	Spring Bank Holiday. Clint Eastwood b. 1930. Battle of Jutland 1916

Unless otherwise stated, times mentioned above may be assumed to be in GMT or the local time

MAY

The Voice of the Heavens

Government popularity may weaken in the face of hardline policy decisions this month. This trend should now be illustrated in local elections which reveal the opposition parties in the ascendancy. However, the economy should point towards a decrease in interest rates. In Europe we may see improvement in the performance of the single currency, though it's possible this favourable trend will fail to last. Prospective second-wave members may thus be in the thrall of some misplaced optimism. In France, political conflicts indicate a possible constitutional crisis. In-fighting among members of the European Parliament may show in clashes between Germany's chancellor and France's president. In particular, the New Moon of the 15th indicates frayed tempers. There's every indication, though, that this is merely a storm in a teacup.

Pressures in the finance community in Japan are likely to weaken its economy even further, causing widespread tension and panic. While in Israel a trend indicating positive momentum in the peace process occurs, there is a possibility of civil unrest among the Palestinians. Singapore and Vietnam also have a tense, strife-ridden month.

At Newmarket the 2000 Guineas may be won by the favourite and the 1000 Guineas by the second favourite.

NATIONAL DAYS

3rd – Poland. *11th* – Laos. *15th* – Paraguay *(Independence Day)*. *17th* – Norway *(Constitution Day)*. *20th* – Cameroon. *22nd* – Republic of Yemen. *23rd* – Germany. *24th* – Eritrea *(Independence Day)*. *25th* – Argentina; Jordan *(Independence Day)*. *26th* – Georgia *(Independence Day)*; Guyana *(Independence Day)*. *28th* – Armenia *(Independence Day)*; Ethiopia. *30th* – Croatia *(Statehood Day)*. *31st* – South Africa.

RAPHAEL'S WEATHER GUIDE FOR MAY 1999

Generally sunny and warm with some muggy overcast periods between the 10th and 15th. In the North-east there will be wind and rain, with the odd local thunderstorm.

41

JUNE

The month is possibly named after a Roman family name, Junius, related to the Latin word *juvenis,* meaning 'young'. Alternatively it may have been named after the goddess Juno, the queen of heaven, wife of Jupiter, protector of women and marriage. June marriages are said to be lucky.

Day of		Remarkable Days.
M	W	Birth data of the famous, etc.
1	Tu	L-plates introduced 1935. TV licences issued 1946. John Masefield b. 1878
2	W	Elizabeth II crowned at Westminster Abbey 1953 (12.32 a.m. BST)
3	Th	**Corpus Christi.** The Duke of Windsor married Mrs Wallis Simpson 1937
4	F	US-Mexico War 1845. 'Suffragette' Derby 1913. George III b. 1738
5	S	Lord Kitchener was lost at sea when HMS *Hampshire* hit a mine 1916
6	☉	**2nd Sunday after Pentecost.** D-Day landings 1944. Bjorn Borg b. 1956
7	M	Virginia McKenna b. 1931. First Northern Ireland Parliament 1921
8	Tu	Norway and Sweden separate 1905. Duke and Duchess of Kent married 1961
9	W	The Queen opened Gatwick Airport 1958. Charles Dickens d. 1870
10	Th	Prince Philip, Duke of Edinburgh, b. 1921 (9.46 p.m. EET, Kerkira, Corfu)
11	F	**St Barnabas the Apostle.** *Endeavour* wrecked 1770. Constable b. 1776
12	S	Earl of Avon (Anthony Eden) b. 1897. President George Bush b. 1924
13	☉	**3rd Sunday after Pentecost.** W.B. Yeats b. 1865 (10.40 p.m. LMT, Dublin)
14	M	J. Logie Baird, Scottish pioneer of television, d. 1946. St Dogmael
15	Tu	Magna Carta 1215. Nelson Mandela sentenced 1964. Edvard Greig b. 1843
16	W	Enoch Powell b. 1912. Harrow school founded 1572. RSPCA founded 1824
17	Th	Barry Manilow b. 1943 (9 a.m. EST, Brooklyn, NY). Earhart flight 1928
18	F	Napoleon defeated at the Battle of Waterloo 1815. Delia Smith b. 1941
19	S	Bessie Wallace Warfield who became the Duchess of Windsor b. 1896
20	☉	**4th Sunday after Pentecost.** Father's Day. Access. Queen Victoria 1837
21	M	Summer solstice (7.49 p.m.). Prince William b. 1982. Tobruk fell 1942
22	Tu	First cricket match played at Lord's 1814. George V crowned 1911
23	W	Nasser became first president of Egypt 1956. Adam Faith b. 1940
24	Th	**The Birth of St John the Baptist.** New Foundland discovered 1497
25	F	Korean War began 1950. Custer's Last Stand 1876. J. Cousteau d. 1997
26	S	UNO Charter signed 1945. First colour TV pictures, New York 1951
27	S	**5th Sunday after Pentecost.** Charles Parnall, Irish Republican b. 1846
28	M	Victoria crowned 1838. Henry VIII b. 1491. Polish uprising 1956
29	Tu	**St Peter the Apostle.** Trade Unions legalised 1871. David Niven d. 1983
30	W	Hong Kong returned to China 1997. Mike Tyson b. 1966

Unless otherwise stated, times mentioned above may be assumed to be in
GMT or the local time

JUNE

The Voice of the Heavens

'British is best' is the message in this month's news, particularly in the entertainment, arts and fashion business. But this favourable trend extends also to the job market when we can expect a minor boost due to investors from abroad. However, the National Health Service remains a controversial topic, especially with regard to lengthy waiting lists. We may hear news too that Prince William is under strain in his capacity as a Royal. Also, Labour may be having a major reshuffle, with some surprising new faces appearing in the Cabinet. In America, there may be human rights issues in the news (particularly related to capital punishment policy). In Ireland there may be another stalemate regarding the basis of peace settlements.

In France, this is also a month of celebration via the arts and leisure industry. Paris now competes with London for the title of 'style capital'! However, France is struggling in vain to get unemployment down. Iran's government may be too audacious now, progressing with impatience in reformist measures, thus risking a backlash from the traditionalists. This is an important month for China as it concentrates on an economic reform package. Public sector companies will suffer though.

At Epsom the Derby could be won by the second favourite and the Oaks by a French-trained filly.

NATIONAL DAYS
2nd – Italy. *5th* – Seychelles *(Liberation Day)*. *6th* – Sweden. *10th* – Portugal. *12th* – The Philippines *(Independence Day)*; Russia *(Independence Day)*. *17th* – Iceland. *23rd* – Luxemburg. *25th* – Mozambique *(Independence Day)*; Slovenia *(Statehood Day)*. *26th* – Madagascar *(Independence Day)*; Somalia. *27th* – Djibouti *(Independence Day)*.

RAPHAEL'S WEATHER GUIDE FOR JUNE 1999
Rather cool and unsettled to begin with, but becoming warm and sunny with temperatures in the 70s. There will be scattered showers in the West and South-east.

JULY

Formerly called *Quintilis*, the fifth month of the Roman year. Mark Anthony renamed it in honour of Julius Caesar. Based on a legend, it is said that if it rains on St Swithun's Day (15th July) there will be rain for 40 days afterwards. But the saint died in 862, so this should apply only to the old Julian Calendar.

Day of		Remarkable Days.
M	W	Birth data of the famous, etc.
1	Th	Diana, Princess of Wales b. 1961. Robert Mitchum d. 1997
2	F	David Owen b. 1938 (2.30 p.m. BST, Plympton, Devon)
3	S	**St Thomas the Apostle.** B. of Gettysburg 1863. Food rationing ended 1954
4	☉	**6th Sunday after Pentecost.** American independence 1776 (2.17 a.m., Philadelphia)
5	M	P.T. Barnum b. 1810. Bjorn Borg won at Wimbledon for the 5th time 1980
6	Tu	Dave Allen b. 1936. Last London tram ran 1952. Henry II d. 1189
7	W	Live Aid concert 1985. Tony Jacklin, golfer, b. 1944. Ringo Starr b. 1940
8	Th	NSPCC founded 1884. Vivien Leigh d. 1967. Sarah Kennedy b. 1950
9	F	Dame Barbara Cartland b. 1901 (11.40 p.m. GMT, Edgebaston, Birmingham)
10	S	*Telstar I* launched 1962. Greenpeace ship *Rainbow Warrior* explosion 1985
11	☉	**7th Sunday after Pentecost.** Aga Khan d. 1957. George Gershwin d. 1937
12	M	Bank Holiday, NI (Orangeman's Day). Crimea evacuated 1856
13	Tu	Harrison Ford b. 1942. First TV broadcast 1930. Ruth Ellis hanged 1955
14	W	Parliament legalised abortion 1967. Emily Pankhurst b. 1858
15	Th	St Swithun's Day. Rembrandt b. 1606. National Insurance Act 1912
16	F	Ginger Rogers b. 1911. Nicholas II shot 1918. Barbara Stanwyck b. 1907
17	S	First edition of *Punch* published 1841. Hundred Years War ended 1453
18	☉	**8th Sunday after Pentecost.** Spanish Civil War began 1936. N. Mandela b. 1918
19	M	Spanish Armada defeated 1588. J.M. Barrie d. 1937. Degas b. 1834
20	Tu	Euston, the first railway station in London, was opened in 1837
21	W	Neil Armstrong took first steps on the moon 1969 (10.56 p.m. EDT).
22	Th	**St Mary Magdalen.** First Mormons reached Salt Lake City site 1847
23	F	Prince Andrew married Lady Sarah Ferguson at Westminster Abbey 1986
24	S	The British captured Gibraltar from the Spanish 1704. Peter Sellars d. 1980
25	☉	**9th Sunday after Pentecost. St James the Apostle.** Mussolini arrested 1943.
26	M	Mick Jagger b. 1943 (6.30 a.m. BDS, Dartford, Kent). G.B. Shaw b. 1856
27	Tu	Korean armistice signed at Panmunjom 1953. Atlantic cable laid 1866
28	W	Austria-Serbia War 1914. Jackie Onassis b. 1929. Beatrix Potter b. 1866
29	Th	Prince Charles married Lady Diana Spencer 1981. Van Gogh d. 1890
30	F	Penguin paperbacks pub. 1935. Kate Bush b. 1958. Henry Ford b. 1863
31	S	Evonne Cawley b. 1951. Franz Liszt d. 1886. Crippen arrested 1910

Unless otherwise stated, times mentioned above may be assumed to be in
GMT or the local time

JULY

The Voice of the Heavens

It may now be evident that trends in falling unemployment are about to reverse and the announcement of further cost-cutting measures in the benefits system will certainly not be welcomed by all. Later in the month we may see a fairly large backlash in public opinion, even from those not directly affected. Other measures, in this case to combat crime, may be prominent news as the Home Secretary is under pressure from various sections of society such as welfare groups. This seems to be the month for change and reform at home and there may even be announcements of a change to the electoral system. Economically though, pressures within the system may lead to some restructuring within the banking sector. This is the month when Germany tightens its money belt in an attempt to cut further losses. There may be pressure from the Bundesbank regarding wages for EU officials.

The United Nations peace-keeping force may be successful in quelling unrest in war-torn countries, like those in Eastern Europe. In South-east Asia, problems continue to pile up, with Indonesia undergoing continued crises. In Iran, we can expect some wise moves on the part of the conservative judiciary.

At Goodwood favourites may be worth following in the non-handicaps. The Stewards Cup may be won by a 4-year-old carrying 9 st 1 lb.

NATIONAL DAYS

1st – Canada *(Dominion Day)*; Burundi; Rwanda. *4th* – United States *(Independence Day)*. *5th* – Venezuela. *6th* – Comoros *(Independence Day)*; Malawi *(Independence Day)*. *10th* – The Bahamas. *11th* – Mongolia. *14th* – France *(Bastille Day)*. *17th* – Iraq *(Revolution Day)*. *18th* – Spain. *20th* – Colombia. *21st* – Belgium. *23rd* – Egypt. *26th* – Liberia *(Independence Day)*. *27th* – Belarus, formerly Byelorussia *(Independence Day)*. *28th* – Peru.

RAPHAEL'S WEATHER GUIDE FOR JULY 1999

A sizzling month with the highest temperatures of the summer (reaching the mid-80s). Humidity will be high, and intermittent thunderstorms can be expected.

AUGUST

This month was once called *Sextilis*, as it was the sixth from March, the beginning of the Roman year (pre-Julian Calendar). In 8 BC the name was changed to *Augustus*, in honour of the Roman emperor of that name (63 BC–AD 14). The month had always been a lucky one for him.

Day of		Remarkable Days.
M	W	Birth data of the famous, etc.
1	♌	**10th Sunday after Pentecost.** Slavery abolished in all British dominions 1834
2	M	Bank Holiday (Scot). Death duties introduced 1894. T. Gainsborough d. 1788
3	Tu	Rupert Brooke b. 1887. Jack Straw b. 1946. Hudson Bay discovered 1610
4	W	Queen Mother b. 1900 (11.31 a.m., St Pauls, Waldenbury). World War I began
5	Th	Oyster season opens. Richard Burton d. 1984. Marilyn Monroe d. 1962
6	F	**The Transfiguration of our Lord.** A-bomb on Hiroshima 1945 (8.16 a.m. JST)
7	S	Alan Leo, astrologer, b. 1860 (5.49 a.m. London). Mata Hari b. 1876
8	♌	**11th Sunday after Pentecost.** Dustin Hoffman b. 1937 (5.07 p.m. PST, Los Angeles)
9	M	A-bomb on Nagasaki 1945 (11.02 a.m. JST). Edward VII crowned 1902
10	Tu	Greenwich Observatory founded 1675. Automobile Club (RAC) founded 1897
11	W	Atlantic Charter 1941. First Ascot races 1711. Anna Massey b. 1935
12	Th	Grouse Season starts. Ian Fleming d. 1964. US annexed Hawaii 1898
13	F	H.G. Wells d. 1946. Berlin Wall construction began 1961. Fidel Castro b. 1927
14	S	India independent from the British 1947 (midnight IST, Delhi)
15	♌	**12th Sunday after Pentecost.** Princess Royal b. 1950 (11.50 a.m. BST, London)
16	M	Madonna b. 1958 (7 a.m. EST, Bay City, MI). Elvis Presley d. 1977
17	Tu	Robin Cousins b. 1957 (12.15 a.m. BST, Bristol). Ted Hughes b. 1930
18	W	Genghis Khan, ruler of Mongolia, d. 1227. South Africa Olympics ban 1964
19	Th	Bill Clinton b. 1946 (8.51 a.m. CST, Hope, AR). Sir Henry Wood d. 1944
20	F	George Adamson, conservationist, murdered by bandits in Kenya 1989
21	S	Princess Margaret b. 1930 (9.22 p.m. BST, Glamis Castle, Scotland)
22	♌	**13th Sunday after Pentecost.** B. of Bosworth Field 1485. Steve Davis b. 1957
23	M	Paris liberated 1944. Rudolph Valentino d. 1926. Blitz began 1940
24	Tu	**St Bartholomew the Apostle.** Vesuvius erupted, burying Pompeii, AD79
25	W	Johann Strauss d. 1849. Duke of Kent killed 1942. St Louis d. 1270
26	Th	Capt Cook set sail 1768. Alison Steadman b. 1946. Battle of Crécy 1346
27	F	Mountbatten killed 1979. First oil-well drilled, in Pennsylvania, 1859
28	S	Charles Boyer b. 1899 (5.15 p.m. Paris Time). David Soul b. 1944
29	♌	**14th Sunday after Pentecost.** The Beatles' last live concert 1966
30	M	Bank Holiday (except Scotland). Cleopatra committed suicide 30BC
31	Tu	Diana, Princess of Wales killed 1997. Henry Moore, sculptor, d. 1986

Unless otherwise stated, times mentioned above may be assumed to be in GMT or the local time

AUGUST

The Voice of the Heavens

Extreme planetary factors this month indicate turbulence in many of the world's major countries. Britain is no exception towards economic reform. There may now be what some see as rather draconian measures. The Prime Minister's quest to modernise Britain may coincide neatly with further voices opposing the monarchy. A Government PR drive not unrelated to millennium fever will not impress everyone. France may see some political backlash regarding the EU and there may be a further upsurge from the extreme right, with increased support for the National Front. The wage arrears in public sector jobs in Russia is brought into focus, though President Yeltsin's popularity seems not to be significantly threatened. America is at risk from violence, but it is the 'enemy within' variety – the lone terrorist situation.

Political corruption may dominate the news in South Africa this month as serious investigations get under way. There may be renewed conflict in India with its neighbour Pakistan as some old ill-will resurfaces. Spain, however, sees a good month from an economic point of view – its business exports may be especially newsworthy.

At York races the Ebor Handicap may be won by a 4-year-old carrying 8 st 1 lb.

NATIONAL DAYS
1st – Switzerland. *6th* – Bolivia. *9th* – Singapore. *10th* – Ecuador. *14th* – Pakistan *(Independence Day)*. *15th* – Congo; South Korea *(Independence Day)*. *17th* – Gabon *(Independence Day)*; Indonesia. *19th* – Afghanistan. *24th* – Ukraine *(Independence Day)*. *25th* – Uruguay *(Independence Day)*. *27th* – Moldova *(Independence Day)*. *31st* – Kyrgyzstan *(Independence Day)*; Malaysia; Trinidad and Tobago *(Independence Day)*; Uzbekistan *(Independence Day)*. *First Monday in August* – Jamaica.

RAPHAEL'S WEATHER GUIDE FOR AUGUST 1999
Following a warm and sunny start, the weather will slowly deteriorate around the 17th and will remain very changeable until the last two or three days.

SEPTEMBER

The name of our ninth month is actually derived from the Latin *septem*, meaning seven. In ancient Roman times, the year commenced with March, so it was the seventh month. The Full Moon nearest the autumnal equinox, which rises for several days at about sunset, is known as the Harvest Moon.

Day of		Remarkable Days.
M	W	Birth data of the famous, etc.
1	W	German invasion of Poland 1939. Lord (Cecil) Parkinson b. 1931. St Giles
2	Th	Great Fire of London 1666. Lord George Brown b. 1914. Tolkein d. 1973
3	F	Sweden switched to driving on the right 1967. World War II began 1939
4	S	Edvard Greig d. 1907. The Queen opened the Forth road bridge 1964
5	☉	**15th Sunday after Pentecost.** Mother Teresa d. 1977. Louis XIV b. 1638
6	M	Australia first played at the Oval 1880. The *Mayflower* set sail 1620
7	Tu	Elizabeth I b. 1533 (2.30 p.m. LMT, Greenwich). Italy surrendered 1943
8	W	**Blessed Virgin Mary.** First V-2 hit Britain 1944. Richard I b. 1157
9	Th	Desmond Tutu enthroned 1986. The first air mail service started 1911
10	F	Dusseldorf bombing 1942. Colin Firth b. 1960. Arnold Palmer b. 1929
11	S	Jewish New Year (5760). Jessica Mitford b. 1917 (4.30 p.m. BST, Gloucester)
12	☉	**16th Sunday after Pentecost.** MOT tests introduced 1960. H.G. Wells d. 1946
13	M	Roald Dahl b. 1916. Claudette Colbert b. 1905 (7.45 a.m. Paris Time, Paris)
14	Tu	Holy Cross Day. Duke of Wellington d. 1852. Dante buried 1321
15	W	Battle of Britain Day. Agatha Christie b. 1890 (4.30 a.m., Torquay)
16	Th	Two-tier postal system began in Britain 1968. Maria Callas d. 1977
17	F	Laura Ashley d. 1985. Pat Phoenix d. 1986. Desmond Lynam b. 1942
18	S	Greta Garbo b. 1905 (7.30 a.m. MET, Stockholm). Jimmi Hendrix d. 1970
19	☉	**17th Sunday after Pentecost.** Twiggy b. 1949. Michael Elphick b. 1946
20	M	Day of Atonement (Yom Kippur). *QE2* launched 1967. Sibelius d. 1957
21	Tu	**St Matthew the Apostle.** Edward II killed at Berkeley Castle 1327
22	W	Viscount Tonypandy (George Thomas) d. 1997. Michael Faraday b. 1791
23	Th	Autumnal equinox (11.31 a.m.). Neptune discovered by Johann Galle 1846
24	F	George Cross inst. 1940. London Polytechnic opened 1882. St Paul
25	S	1st day of Tabernacles. Michael Douglas b. 1944 (10.30 a.m. EDT, Brunswick, NJ)
26	☉	**18th Sunday after Pentecost.** Anne Robinson b. 1944. George Gershwin b. 1898
27	M	The first train ran on the Stockton and Darlington Railway 1825
28	Tu	Louis Pasteur d. 1895. Brigitte Bardot b. 1934 (1.15 p.m. WET*, Paris)
29	W	**St Michael and All Angels.** Leslie Crowther d. 1996. Elizabeth Gaskell b. 1810
30	Th	Pinewood Studios opened 1936. BBC's Radio 1 launched in 1967

Unless otherwise stated, times mentioned above may be assumed to be in
GMT or the local time (indicates summer time)*

SEPTEMBER

The Voice of the Heavens

We can expect a continuation of the celebratory air in Britain this summer, with our past heritage (our 'greatness') at the forefront of the media. While this species of 'feel good factor' looms large, Neptune's influence at this time suggests it to be no more than a mass delusion! Also, in keeping with the influence of this planet, a major celebrity may be the subject of a minor scandal. In America, meteorological conditions may dominate the headlines, and Alaska is at high risk of earthquakes. Pakistan may reappear in the news, embroiled in conflict with India, though by the New Moon of the 25th the global mood seems to move towards peace-making and co-operation. And at last we may now see a more relaxed approach by the IMF and World Bank with regard to debts of Third World countries.

This trend towards conciliation should extend to the Far East, with Europe showing concern for faltering 'tiger' economies like South Korea and Indonesia. In Iran, there may be good news for civil issues and women's rights, as the government steps up its move towards a modern democracy.

At Doncaster races the St Leger may be won by the favourite and the Portland Handicap by a 4-year-old carrying 9 st 7 lb.

NATIONAL DAYS

1st – Libya. *2nd* – Vietnam. *6th* Swaziland *(Independence Day)*. *7th* – Brazil *(Independence Day)*. *8th* – North Korea *(Independence Day)*. *9th* – Tajikistan *(Independence Day)*. *15th* – Costa Rica *(Independence Day)*; El Salvador *(Independence Day)*; Guatemala *(Independence Day)*; Honduras *(Independence Day)*; Nicaragua *(Independence Day)*. *16th* – Mexico *(Independence Day)*; Papua New Guinea *(Independence and Constitution Day)*. *18th* – Chile. *21st* – Belize *(Independence Day)*; Malta *(Independence Day)*. *22nd* – Mali. *23rd* – Saudi Arabia. *24th* – Guinea-Bissau *(Independence Day)*. *30th* – Botswana.

RAPHAEL'S WEATHER GUIDE FOR SEPTEMBER 1999

There will be fine and sunny periods to about the 11th, when it will turn cooler. Mixed weather will prevail until the 21st, when it will brighten again.

OCTOBER

The name of the tenth month is actually derived from the Latin *octo*, meaning eight, as it was the eighth month from March, the commencement of the Roman year (pre-Julian Calendar). In the old Celtic calendar, 31st October was the last day of the year – when witches were abroad (it is now called Hallowe'en).

Day of M	W	Remarkable Days. Birth data of the famous, etc.
1	F	Jimmy Carter b. 1924 (7 a.m. EST, Plains, GA). *Picture Post* published 1938
2	S	German reunification 1990 (midnight MET, Berlin). Sting b. 1951
3	☉	**19th Sunday after Pentecost.** SOS signal established 1906. St Francis
4	M	Susan Sarendon b. 1946 (2.25 p.m. EST, New York). *Sputnik I* launched 1957
5	Tu	Tea rationing ended 1952. The Jarrow March began 1936. St Placid
6	W	Promenade Concerts began 1895. *The Jazz Singer* première, New York 1927
7	Th	The *Independent* published 1986. Clive James b. 1939. Marie Lloyd d. 1922
8	F	First British breathaliser test took place 1967. Britain joined ERM 1990
9	S	Duke of Kent b. 1935 (2.05 a.m. GMT, London). Brian Blessed b. 1936
10	☉	**20th Sunday after Pentecost.** Judith Chalmers b. 1936. Edith Piaf d. 1963
11	M	The *Mary Rose* was raised in 1982. The Anglo-Boer War began in 1899
12	Tu	Luciano Pavarotti b. 1935 (1.40 a.m. MET, Modena). Aleister Crowley b. 1875
13	W	Edwina Currie b. 1946 (11.30 p.m. Liverpool). Beryl Reid d. 1996
14	Th	Battle of Hastings 1066. Bud Flanagan b. 1896. Lillian Gish b. 1896
15	F	Amnesty International formed 1962. H. Goering committed suicide 1946
16	S	The Great Storm of 1987. *The People* pub. 1881. Moshe Dayan d. 1981
17	☉	**21st Sunday after Pentecost.** Harry Carpenter b. 1925. Chopin d. 1849
18	M	**St Luke the Evangelist.** Russia sold Alaska to USA for $7.2m 1887
19	Tu	BP announced first North Sea oil find 1970. Johathan Swift d. 1745
20	W	Sir Christopher Wren b. 1632. Lord Montague of Beaulieu b. 1926
21	Th	Lord Nelson killed in a naval battle off Cape Trafalgar, Spain 1805
22	F	Metropolitan Opera House opened in New York 1883. Trotsky b. 1877
23	S	Diana Dors b. 1931. W.G. Grace d. 1915. Battle of Alamein 1942
24	☉	**22nd Sunday after Pentecost.** Tito Gobbi, baritone, b. 1913. St Raphael
25	M	Charge of the Light Brigade 1854. *Private Eye* first published 1961
26	Tu	Jeffrey Archer resigned as Chairman of the Conservative Party 1986
27	W	Simon Le Bon b. 1958. Cuba discovered 1492. China admitted to UN 1971
28	Th	**St Simon and St Jude, Apostles.** David Dimbleby, broadcaster, b. 1938
29	F	The New York Stock Exchange in Wall Street crashed 1929
30	S	John Logie Baird produced first TV pictures at his London workshop 1925
31	☉	**23rd Sunday after Pentecost.** Hallowe'en. Battle of Britain ended 1940

Unless otherwise stated, times mentioned above may be assumed to be in GMT or the local time. Clocks back 1 hour 31st October.

OCTOBER

The Voice of the Heavens

Despite concern over the economy this month, with poor prospects for trade and commerce later on (after the Full Moon of the 24th), we should see a government relatively in favour with the electorate. However, there are indications of muddles and mix-ups in Parliament over new legislative measures, clearing the ground for one of the Opposition parties – probably the Liberal Democrats – to make capital from Government mistakes. President Clinton's public image not only remains unscathed but there's every chance of an increase in popularity estimates via recent polls. In Germany, an active Mars may mean that racist issues dominate the news, with right wing elements possibly causing violence in the east. Considerable German job losses now seem more than likely.

Political and economic tensions in Italy may cast a shadow on its role in the European Union, and a popular government figure may be humiliated. There may be a renewal of concern for ethnic Albanians in Kosovo, arising from clashes with Serbian authorities. Freak weather will afflict Armenia, Georgia, Turkey, Iraq, Yemen, Ethiopia, Indonesia, Japan and Brazil.

At Newmarket the Cambridgeshire may be won by a horse carrying 8 st 6 lb and the Cesarewitch by a 5-year-old carrying 7 st 12 lb.

NATIONAL DAYS

1st – China; Cyprus *(Independence Day)*; Nigeria *(Republic Day)*. *2nd* – Guinea. *4th* – Lesotho. *9th* – Uganda *(Independence Day)*. *10th* – Taiwan *(Double Tenth Day)*. *12th* – Equatorial Guinea *(Independence Day)*; Spain *(Day of the Hispanidad. Columbus' discovery of the western hemisphere)*; Fiji. *23rd* – Hungary. *24th* – Zambia *(Independence Day)*. *26th* – Austria. *27th* – Turkmenistan *(Independence Day)*. *28th* – Czech Republic. *29th* – Turkey *(Republic Day)*.

RAPHAEL'S WEATHER GUIDE FOR OCTOBER 1999

A mainly dry and lovely Indian Summer in most areas. From the 22nd temperatures will drop slightly, with fog and mist affecting visibility in some parts.

NOVEMBER

The name of this month is a contraction of the Latin *Novem ab imbre,* meaning the ninth month from winter – it was the ninth month from March, the beginning of the Roman year (pre-Julian Calendar). The Gunpowder Plot aimed to destroy James I, the Lords and Commons, at the opening of Parliament, November 1605.

Day of		Remarkable Days. Birth data of the famous, etc.
M	W	
1	M	**All Saints' Day.** First radio licences went on sale in Britain 1922
2	Tu	All Souls. Channel 4 launched 1982. Jenny Lind, soprano, d. 1887
3	W	David, Lord Linley b. 1961 (10.45 a.m., London). Henri Matisse d. 1954
4	Th	Ronald Reagan elected US president 1980. Alamein victory 1942
5	F	Guy Fawkes night. First automatic traffic lights, Wolverhampton, 1927
6	S	Nigel Havers b. 1949 (3 a.m., London). Henry VI crowned 1429
7	𝕾	**7th Sunday before Christmas.** Steve McQueen d. 1980. St Engelbert
8	M	Enniskillen bomb at Remembrance Day service 1987 (10.45 a.m.)
9	Tu	Edward VII b. 1841 (10.48 a.m., London). Jill Dando b. 1961
10	W	The Tyne Bridge at Newcastle opened 1930. Hirohito crowned 1928
11	Th	Stevenage was designated the first New Town in Britain 1946. St Martin
12	F	*Ark Royal* sunk 1941. Dionne Warwick b. 1941. Mariella Frostrup b. 1962
13	S	Robert Louis Stevenson b. 1850. Planet Pluto discovered 1930
14	𝕾	**Remembrance Sunday.** Prince of Wales b. 1948 (9.14 p.m., London)
15	M	Peter Phillips b. 1977 (10.46 a.m., London). Petula Clark b. 1933
16	Tu	Henry III d. 1272. Oklahoma became the 46th state of the Union in 1907
17	W	Suez Canal opened 1869. Theosophical Society founded 1875 (8 p.m., New York)
18	Th	Push-button telephones introduced by the Bell Telephone Company 1963
19	F	Tennyson appointed Poet Laureate 1850. Gettysburg Address 1863
20	S	Princess Elizabeth married Lt. Philip Mountbatten 1947. Bo Derek b. 1956
21	𝕾	**5th Sunday before Christmas.** Darwin's *Origin of the Species* pub. 1859
22	M	John F. Kennedy shot in Dallas (1.31 p.m. CST). Tom Conti b. 1941
23	Tu	Petrol rationed during the Suez crisis 1956. Boris Karloff b. 1887. St Felicity
24	W	Sir Hiram Maxim, machine gun inventor, d. 1916. Ian Botham b. 1955
25	Th	Thanksgiving (USA). Agatha Christie's *The Mousetrap* op. in London 1952
26	F	Brinks Mat robbery (£25 million worth of gold bars) 1983
27	S	John Major elected PM 1990. John Alderton b. 1940. Ernie Wise b. 1925
28	𝕾	**Advent Sunday.** Enid Blyton d. 1968. Sinn Fein founded in 1905
29	M	Mary Whitehouse formed the National Viewers and Listeners Association 1965
30	Tu	**St Andrew the Apostle.** Crystal Palace destroyed by fire 1936

Unless otherwise stated, times mentioned above may be assumed to be in GMT or the local time

NOVEMBER

The Voice of the Heavens

Travel difficulties may be in the news again as congestion worsens, and this is a high risk time for accidents – especially on motorways. This is given more weight by retrograde Mercury, which also signifies that the Government may have to abandon recent decisions and set about examining again ideas formerly discarded. The transport minister may come in for some rather heavy brickbats now. There is a possible major drugs brouhaha in the United States this month and a new controversy over smuggling and lapses in customs security. Also a religious sect preparing for Armageddon may hit the headlines. Unemployment may well worsen in France, despite a previous measure to try and stem the tide. There may be tensions expressed by Russia's ultra-nationalist elements regarding NATO's expansion in the east, particularly regarding the Baltic states.

In the Middle East, tension may arise owing to violence and atrocities carried out by terrorists. Other areas of the world under strain this month are Central Africa, including Rwanda and Burundi, and South East Asia, in particular Indonesia. A Pluto effect may mean difficulties in OPEC as exports plunge (crisis meetings will therefore be on the agenda).

The November Handicap at Doncaster may be won by the second favourite.

NATIONAL DAYS
1st – Algeria. *3rd* – Dominica *(Independence Day)*; Panama *(Independence Day)*. *9th* – Cambodia *(Independence Day)*. *11th* – Angola *(Independence Day)*. *18th* – Latvia; Oman *(Birthday of the Sultan)*. *19th* – Monaco *(St Devote's Day)*. *22nd* – Lebanon *(Independence Day)*. *25th* – Suriname *(Independence Day)*. *28th* – Mauritania. *29th* – Yugoslavia. *30th* – Scotland *(St Andrew's Day)*; Benin.

RAPHAEL'S WEATHER GUIDE FOR NOVEMBER 1999
A fair start will give way to easterly gales between the 6th and 10th. From mid-month snow can be expected in the North, with the South tending to be wet.

DECEMBER

The name of the twelfth month, and last month of our year, is derived from the Latin *Decem ab imbre,* meaning the tenth month from the winter. It is the tenth month from March, the commencement of the Roman year (pre-Julian Calendar). The shortest day of the year (winter solstice) is on 22nd December in 1999.

Day of		Remarkable Days.
M	W	Birth data of the famous, etc.
1	W	Lee Trevino b. 1939 (4.35 p.m. CST, Dallas, TX). Queen Alexandria b. 1844
2	Th	The new St Paul's Cathedral opened 1697. Marquis de Sade d. 1814
3	F	Eamonn Holmes b. 1959. Mel Smith b. 1952. P.-A. Renoir d. 1919
4	S	The *Dandy* comic first published 1937. Ronnie Corbett b. 1930
5	☉	**2nd Sunday in Advent.** W.A. Mozart d. 1791. Claude Monet d. 1926
6	M	Irish Free State officially proclaimed 1922 (5 p.m. GMT, Dublin)
7	Tu	Pearl Harbour 1941. Captain Bligh d. 1817. Edmondo Ros b. 1910
8	W	Sammy Davis Jnr b. 1925 (1.20 p.m. EST, New York). Clifton Bridge op. 1864
9	Th	1st day of Ramadan. Danny Blanchflower d. 1993. Judi Dench b. 1934
10	F	Edward VIII abdicated 1936. Kenneth Branagh b. 1960. Aswan Dam op. 1864
11	S	George VI accession 1936. First Motor Show opened in Paris 1894
12	☉	**3rd Sunday in Advent.** Frank Sinatra b. 1915 (3 a.m. EST, Hoboken, NJ)
13	M	Abel Tasman sighted New Zealand 1642. Battle of River Plate 1939
14	Tu	Stanley Baldwin, three times PM, d. 1947. George Washington d. 1799
15	W	Piccadilly underground line opened 1906. Sitting Bull killed 1890
16	Th	Noel Coward b. 1899 (2.30 a.m., Teddington). Boston Tea Party 1773
17	F	*Graf Spee* scuttled in Montevideo 1939. Wright's powered flight 1903
18	S	Rosemary Leach b. 1935. Robson Green b. 1964. Betty Grable b. 1916
19	☉	**4th Sunday in Advent.** Edith Piaf b. 1915 (5 a.m. WET, Paris). St Timothy
20	M	Uri Geller b. 1946 (2 a.m. EET, Tel Aviv). Jenny Agutter b. 1952.
21	Tu	Pilgrim Fathers landed at Plymouth Rock, MA, 1620. Jane Fonda b. 1937
22	W	Winter solstice (7.44 a.m.). Patricia Hayes b. 1909. George Elliot d. 1880
23	Th	Vincent Van Gogh cut off his ear 1888. J. Arthur Rank b. 1888
24	F	Christmas Eve. John Osborne d. 1994. London Coliseum opened 1904
25	S	**Christmas Day.** William the Conqueror crowned, Westminster Abbey 1066
26	☉	**1st Sunday after Christmas. St Stephen the first Martyr.** Boxing Day
27	M	**St John the Evangelist.** Bank Holiday. Louis Pasteur b. 1822
28	Tu	**Holy Innocents.** Bank Holiday. Nigel Kennedy, violinist, b. 1956
29	W	Lord Stockton (Harold Macmillan) d. 1986. Bernard Cribbins b. 1928
30	Th	First performance of Cole Porter's *Kiss Me Kate* in New York 1948
31	F	New Year's Eve. Sir Anthony Hopkins b. 1937 (10.30 a.m., Port Talbot)

Unless otherwise stated, times mentioned above may be assumed to be in
GMT or the local time

DECEMBER

The Voice of the Heavens

Planetary alignments early in the month indicate stresses between the interests of democracy and dictatorships. But this also entails the forces of liberalism versus conservatism, with the traditionalists in the ascendancy at this time. Fundamentalist religious groups in America, Egypt and Iran may thus be in the headlines. At home, public services may be in the news, with possible concern over the NHS or sections of the workforce demanding fairer employment legislation. End of the millennium fever continues, especially in America with everyone who has something to prophesy getting in on the act. The fears regarding world-wide computer systems may abate, with some reassuring voices now from the experts.

In Europe, there may be hopeful news for the labour market in France as the prime minister sticks to his employment reform packages. Germany may have cause for optimism in the economy, though unemployment continues to rise. Iraq may yet again be thumbing its nose to the western powers with either vague threats or actual sabre-rattling. There may be tragedy in the Arab Gulf, and possibly the death of a leading political figure in Saudi Arabia. Further unrest in Central Africa will be a cause of great concern.

At Kempton Park races the King George VI Chase may be won by the favourite.

NATIONAL DAYS

1st – Romania. *2nd* – Laos; United Arab Emirates. *5th* – Thailand *(birthday of the King).* *6th* – Finland *(Independence Day).* *7th* – Côte d'Ivoire. *11th* – Burkina Faso. *12th* – Kenya. *16th* – Bahrain *(anniversary of the accession of the Emir, Shaikh Isa);* Kazakhstan *(Republic Day).* *17th* – Bhutan. *18th* – Niger. *23rd* – Japan *(birthday of the Emperor).*

RAPHAEL'S WEATHER GUIDE FOR DECEMBER 1999

An unsettled month, with gales during the second week, some danger of high seas off the East coast and local flooding. But it will turn quite mild as the Millennium nears.

YOUR 200-YEAR PERPETUAL CALENDAR

Many types of perpetual calendars for finding the day of the week upon which particular dates in the past fell or upon which particular dates in the future will fall have been published in numerous reference books, but most of them are extremely confusing and difficult to use. Usually it takes a mathematician of high calibre to carry through the computations necessary to obtain the day of the week desired. The accompanying calendar, which is a drastic revision, extension and rearrangement of an old method, is the simplest one that the editor has been able to find to date, requiring only the addition of two simple numbers mentally, namely, a key number and date in question. Simple instructions for the use of the calendar are given in the lower right-hand corner. Those who may be curious as to the day of the week upon which they were born or upon which some particular event occurred in the past will find the calendar quite interesting and informative. Included also are the calendars for the next 50 years, in case anyone should be interested.

Table 1

								Jan.	Feb.	Mar.	Apr.	May	June	July	Aug.	Sept.	Oct.	Nov.	Dec.
1850	1878		1918	1946	1974	2002	2030	2	5	5	1	3	6	1	4	0	2	5	0
1851	1879		1919	1947	1975	2003	2031	3	6	6	2	4	0	2	5	1	3	6	1
*1852	1880		1920	1948	1976	2004	2032	4	0	1	4	6	2	4	0	3	5	1	3
1853	1881		1921	1949	1977	2005	2033	6	2	2	5	0	3	5	1	4	6	2	4
1854	1882		1922	1950	1978	2006	2034	0	3	3	6	1	4	6	2	5	0	3	5
1855	1883		1923	1951	1979	2007	2035	1	4	4	0	2	5	0	3	6	1	4	6
*1856	1884		1924	1952	1980	2008	2036	2	5	6	2	4	0	2	5	1	3	6	1
1857	1885		1925	1953	1981	2009	2037	4	0	0	3	5	1	3	6	2	4	0	2
1858	1886		1926	1954	1982	2010	2038	5	1	1	4	6	2	4	0	3	5	1	3
1859	1887		1927	1955	1983	2011	2039	6	2	2	5	0	3	5	1	4	6	2	4
*1860	1888		1928	1956	1984	2012	2040	0	3	4	0	2	5	0	3	6	1	4	6
1861	1889	1901	1929	1957	1985	2013	2041	2	5	5	1	3	6	1	4	0	2	5	0
1862	1890	1902	1930	1958	1986	2014	2042	3	6	6	2	4	0	2	5	1	3	6	1
1863	1891	1903	1931	1959	1987	2015	2043	4	0	0	3	5	1	3	6	2	4	0	2
*1864	1892	1904	1932	1960	1988	2016	2044	5	1	2	5	0	3	5	1	4	6	2	4
1865	1893	1905	1933	1961	1989	2017	2045	0	3	3	6	1	4	6	2	5	0	3	5
1866	1894	1906	1934	1962	1990	2018	2046	1	4	4	0	2	5	0	3	6	1	4	6
1867	1895	1907	1935	1963	1991	2019	2047	2	5	5	1	3	6	1	4	0	2	5	0
*1868	1896	1908	1936	1964	1992	2020	2048	3	6	0	3	5	1	3	6	2	4	0	2
1869	1897	1909	1937	1965	1993	2021	2049	5	1	1	4	6	2	4	0	3	5	1	3
1870	1898	1910	1938	1966	1994	2022	2050	6	2	2	5	0	3	5	1	4	6	2	4
1871	1899	1911	1939	1967	1995	2023		0	3	3	6	1	4	6	2	5	0	3	5
*1872		1912	1940	1968	1996	2024		1	4	5	1	3	6	1	4	0	2	5	0
1873		1913	1941	1969	1997	2025		3	6	6	2	4	0	2	5	1	3	6	1
1874		1914	1942	1970	1998	2026		4	0	0	3	5	1	3	6	2	4	0	2
1875		1915	1943	1971	1999	2027		5	1	1	4	6	2	4	0	3	5	1	3
*1876	1900	1916	1944	1972	2000	2028		6	2	3	6	1	4	6	2	5	0	3	5
1877		1917	1945	1973	2001	2029		1	4	4	0	2	5	0	3	6	1	4	6

Table 2

Sunday	1	8	15	22	29	36
Monday	2	9	16	23	30	37
Tuesday	3	10	17	24	31	
Wednesday	4	11	18	25	32	
Thursday	5	12	19	26	33	
Friday	6	13	20	27	34	
Saturday	7	14	21	28	35	

*All years in the lines to the right of the asterisks are Leap Years

Instructions

Find the year in question in Table 1. On the same line, to the extreme right, find the key number under the month in question. Add the key number to the date in question, then find the total in Table 2. On that line, to the left, will be found the day of the week desired.

CAMILLA PARKER-BOWLES

Camilla Parker-Bowles' reputation as the 'other-woman', along with her tendency to shun publicity, has made her one of the most enigmatic figures in English life today. Her story, in many ways, is as old as English royal history, replete with royal privilege, marital manipulations, and dangerous liasons. But what is she really like, and what personal qualities have helped her friendship with Prince Charles endure for a quarter of a century?

Camilla was born on 17th July 1947 at 7 a.m. in London. This makes her a double Cancerian – that is, both her Sun and her Moon are in the sign of Cancer. It is significant that both the key women in Prince Charles's life have been Cancerians, women ruled by the mysterious, feminine Moon, the planetary deity whose province is the world of feeling, imagination and kinship ties. This is not altogether surprising when we recall that the Moon is the most elevated planet in the Scorpio prince's chart: it is placed in the tenth house (signifying maternal power), is in its exaltation sign, Taurus (enhancing the lunar influence), and is conjunct the North Node (indicating the importance of relationships with females).

As a double Cancerian, Camilla is profoundly emotional, ultra-sensitive and extremely private. With four planets in this watery sign, Camilla has a strong need to nurture something, be it her children, the world of nature, her own creativity or the creativity in others. Cancerians also have a lovable playful nature, but this side is seen only by those intimates she truly trusts. Although her emotions may fluctuate greatly, there is a steadfast devotion underneath her mood swings, and she is not one to give up on relationships. Close friends have described her as 'witty, warm and wise', and she is respected for her calm strength in the face of crises and for her unwavering loyalty to Prince Charles. She has never spoken to the press about her relationship with the prince, and the Royal Family (on numerous occasions) have shown their appreciation of her discretion. Some would say she has proved her loyalty to the 'firm', but astrology gives us a deeper understanding – her powerful angular Saturn reinforces a strongly traditional, conventional nature.

Camilla's bond with Prince Charles is enhanced by her earthy, goonlike sense of humour, and by a shared passion for the countryside, music and painting. Camilla's Cancerian nature is also shrewd, and no doubt she feels safe behind the mask of the unglamorous rich country bumpkin. Remembering Cancer's mascot the Crab, we know that Camilla has a strong need for emotional security and an instinct for self-protection. But within her self-protective shell there will be a very active emotional and imaginative life going on. Camilla's need for privacy is even more emphasised by the placement of her Sun in the twelfth house, showing that she is a natural 'behind the scenes' person, someone who prefers staying out of the limelight but who can nevertheless play the role of the 'power behind the throne'. It is true that, many years ago, she declined the prince's marriage proposal because she did not wish to live her life in a fishbowl. But another characteristic of this twelfth house solar position is that of the 'strategist' who plots in unseen ways to ensure her own emotional needs will be met. Camilla would have felt that her place in the prince's affections would not be jeopardised by his marriage to the young, idealistic Lady Diana Spencer who she felt was as 'quiet as a mouse'.

The twelfth house is also connected with sacrifice, and psychologically with having had an inaccessible father. It is interesting to note that while Camilla was beginning to risk and even enjoy more positive public notice, especially around the time of her fiftieth birthday celebration, this attention was abruptly eclipsed by Princess Diana's death and all that this meant for the world. Her identity suddenly had to go back-stage again, for Diana's memory was being deified and embraced by the public. Negative public feeling for Camilla intensified – she was the 'other woman' who was linked with the ruination of the royal marriage. We can look to Camilla's Leo Ascendant with its rising

© Barry Batchelor, PA

Saturn-Pluto conjunction to understand her capacity to attract disapproval. This is the signature of a very proud, stubborn, intense personality, who has enormous will-power and the stamina to endure public humiliation and to allow her personality to be reborn time and time again. But there is a deeper irony at work here. Leo is a regal sign which needs adoration and which loves the limelight, a quality distinctly at odds with her reclusive twelfth house Cancerian Sun and with both self-doubting Saturn and secretive Pluto. In choosing not to marry Prince Charles, Camilla had to watch the growing popularity and privilege of the royal couple, and especially of Princess Diana. It could be conjectured that Camilla's unacknowledged envy of the princess's status made it easier for her to despise Diana's naivety and to betray a fellow 'lunar sister'. Diana's own need to play the role of the 'lamb to the slaughter' undoubtedly contributed to this dynamic between them, but her demise can only have darkened Camilla's reputation further – at least, temporarily. In reality, both were victims of the age-old double standard of the monarchy: marry a virgin, but keep the woman you love as your mistress.

It needs to be said, however, that although Camilla's role in the royal marriage is readily seen as having been subversive, it is not easy to bear the heavy energies of Saturn and Pluto. They are the mark of a deep thinker, the 'outsider' or the personality who is a catalyst, whose behaviour can bring great change and reform. Society resists these changes because our deepest prejudices are evoked by these two planets. A more considered view of Camilla's choices might reveal that, in fact, she has also played the role of the scapegoat for the changes that need to occur in the privileged royal circle. Camilla's identity will continue to go through many transformations, and her resilient Sun trine Jupiter in Scorpio indicates that she will survive very well.

Camilla's Moon is exactly conjunct Venus in Cancer, and in this we see the feminine as mother (Moon) and the feminine as lover (Venus) come together to act as one. It is a signature of great tenderness, sympathy and popularity. Her Moon-Venus is squared by Neptune, the planet of inspiration, romance, glamour, sacrifice and deception. This configuration is very romantic; it is that part of Camilla which is warm and affectionate, and which could be described as the 'muse' or even the 'siren'. Psychologically, this aspect can create tremendous hopes and longings for romantic perfection. But some degree of disillusionment always follows, which – in time – allows for a needed adjustment to the actual limits of reality. This configuration also signifies artistic sensitivity and a love of the arts in general. Artistic creativity and flair is further emphasised by her Mars in Gemini in a trine aspect with Neptune. In the 'Venus department', Camilla and Prince Charles are kindred souls, for he has a close Venus-Neptune conjunction, and we have seen how this has manifested in him as a love of beauty, the Mysteries and artistic talent. This mutual aspect – in fact, forming aspects between their charts – reinforced the tendency within each of them to live double lives, to feel that their emotional longings could somehow only be fulfilled by an unattainable 'other' outside of marriage.

Will Camilla and Charles marry? Astrology cannot give a definite answer to this question. However, the astrology of both their charts indicates some positive and startling changes in the coming two years, and this applies especially in the area of relationships as they both have Leo rising and therefore Uranus is sojourning through their Aquarian seventh houses. This brings an influence which can be liberating and revitalising, but it can also be suddenly disruptive and alienating. This transit will bring Camilla increasingly into contact with the public, and it will also demand a very high degree of honesty and versatility. Uranus's opposition to her Pluto in February and October shows that she then has the opportunity to rebuild her life in a very constructive way. Saturn's long sojourn through her tenth house, beginning in late April 1998 and continuing until 2001, suggests a time of public responsibility, a time when her role will be redefined and often tested. If Camilla and Charles do marry, there is no doubt that she has many strong qualities – artistic sensitivity, altruism, staying power – to bring to what would be a demanding, and very different, life.

BILLY CONNOLLY

'Versatile' is most certainly a word applicable to this hugely popular entertainer. 'Feisty', 'irreverent', 'outspoken', 'restless', those too – but 'versatile' heads the list. Consider the varied occupations before reaching the heights of stardom – messenger, shipyard welder, oil rig worker, paratrooper, itinerant busker and folk singer. (In the late sixties he was half of a folk duo with Gerry Rafferty, though, ominously, was unable to take folk seriously.) Soon he would become famous as a ribald comic in his native Scotland – before anyone south of the border had heard of him. Several years later his career took off with success as a recording artist, finally entailing stage and film roles, television travelogues, and perhaps unusually (but remember that versatility) the title role in an ubiquitous American TV sitcom. Thus, his career CV depicts a variety of seemingly contradictory guises, and in such proportions as to practically amount to collector's mania. But what's the real man like?

Billy Connolly was born in Glasgow on 24th November 1942 (though we don't have his birth time, sufficient planetary information is available), giving him a Sagittarian Sun, and Gemini Moon. These placements give him that loveable, wide-eyed quality, where everything freshly discovered out there has a sense of wonder and magic – or is turned into something funny. Hence, the stand-up comedy. Of note here are the hilarious recollections of his rather tough childhood (my favourite is the one about being forced to swim in the icy North Sea: 'Get in there ya big jessie!'), for Billy has a Moon-Saturn hard aspect, indicative of a sense of deprivation where life's little luxuries are concerned. (It hasn't, however, debarred him for a thorough education in the School of Life and its attendant setbacks.) Sun conjunct Venus imbues him with artistic, creative leanings, a

© Peter Jordan, PA

usually affable nature and a love of beauty, while elsewhere the Mercury factor is strong. Together with Mars it is placed in Scorpio – no doubt contributing to the ribald humour, the penchant for getting down to the nitty-gritty of everyday life, added to which the Mercury-Jupiter trine gives him a wide perspective, a broad mind and the ability to 'humour' life, as it were.

What we've seen so far is the Billy Connolly we're acquainted with, the public image, yet the chart reveals inner stresses, too. It may surprise some Connolly watchers to learn he's not the most inwardly self-confident of human beings (Sun-Saturn opposition) and is, in many ways, quite a shy man. There's a freedom-limitation conflict here: the Sun-Venus conjunction opposes Uranus and Saturn at the other end of the chart. On many occasions he's felt constrained by circumstance, unable to 'be himself' as the world bears down with responsibilities. This has likewise affected personal relationships where love and affection is so often restricted by practical considerations (Venus opposite Saturn). Thus, the pleasure-loving, indulgent Sun-Venus personality is hampered by external circumstance, assuming either the form of heavy duty (Saturn) or sudden, upsetting change (Uranus). He's handled this chart conflict quite well (indeed, these days he's a contented family man following his second marriage at the start of this decade), by channelling energies into career goals. In sum, this is a most untypical Archer, for that ascension to the Olympian heights (stardom, Hollywood, etc.) has always invoked memories of being a mere 'ordinary' mortal after all. Indeed, he's known to return to gritty Glasgow quite often. Going back to his roots is thus something vital to his soul!

In 1999, with progressed Mercury hitting Saturn, we may see the 'other' Billy Connolly appear in career projects, possibly in more sombre and dramatic film roles or serious TV reportage of some kind. January, May and November are all critical points too, suggesting a major shift in direction or personal upheavals – clearing the ground for new development as Pluto hits his natal Saturn.

RAPHAEL'S ASTROLOGICAL STUDIES

ROBSON GREEN

Robson Green is one of the most familiar faces on British television, and has already achieved remarkable success in music with his partner Jerome. Born in Hexham in Northumberland on 18th December 1964, he's definitely a northern boy with lots of heart. As a Sun Sagittarian with his Moon in Gemini, he is also a very adventurous soul who wants to range the whole world and try almost everything at least once. Although we do not know his time of birth, which determines the Ascendant and the placing of the planets around the chart, we can see from using a chart set for noon that he was born with the Midas touch, and that he is also a bit of a philosopher.

Robson's Sagittarian nature is essentially fiery, impulsive and optimistic. This positive outlook and a gutsy appetite for excitement led him out of his early shipbuilding career to follow his heart's desire, which had always been to act. Sagittarians are good at risking and landing themselves in the right place at the right time. After training for three years at the Live Theatre in Newcastle upon Tyne, where his potential was recognised, he got his first role on TV as part of the cast for *Casualty*. His Sagittarian character is also very aspiring – he needs to be moving, learning, enjoying the journey as he aims his sights on a new experience or conquest. With Mercury conjoined his Sun, he is an especially expressive Sagittarian, and can be quite talkative, even blunt. This aspect definitely gives him the gift of the gab, and strengthens his memory and capacity to mimic. True to his fiery nature, he loves wide open spaces and lots of sport.

Robson was born at a full moon. This gives him a very extrovert personality, but also contributes to his sensitivity and tendency to be 'nervy'. He also has the personality of the jokesmith (Moon in Gemini). His mind is quick and his intuition

strong. He sees the connections between things, the levity and the profundity all in the same twinkling of an eye. Social and moral issues affect him deeply. His Gemini Moon makes him a collector of information, people and experiences – an eternal child asking 'why?' and 'what for?'. But his Sagittarian essence helps him become capable of discerning the nugget of meaning and value from it all.

Role models would have been particularly important for his open, impressionable nature, especially female role models – as indicted by the Moon with the ascending node. His grandmother was especially important during his youth. She was '… a great entertainer, teacher, a lover of people, a socialist through and through'. This expresses Robson's own humanitarian feelings, which not only Sagittarius bestows but also his Jupiter opposition Neptune. This combination, a signature of idealism and generosity, is also linked with his Mars, the planet of personal energy and sexuality. This gives him great charisma, sex appeal and the ability to play a romantic lead successfully (and it also increases his Sagittarian luck!). Mars is also configured with electrifying Uranus and subversive Pluto, indicating that there are darker energies at work within him – the energies of the fanatic reformer, the rebel who fights untiringly on the side of justice. His role as the maverick officer who narrowly escapes death in *Touching Evil* for Anglia TV could have been tailor-made for him. It could be that some of his own private struggles with violence or dysfunctional family relationships have enabled him to identify passionately with the northern soul, with people who have 'surmounted adversity from the past, present and future'.

Saturn and Chiron in Pisces indicate that there is a side of him which struggles in seclusion to keep his spirits high. Saturn square Venus gives a niggling lack of confidence, but it also gives a serious, committed attitude to relationships.

Jupiter's sojourn through Pisces during 1998 brings an expansive and emotional period for him, but with so many opportunities there'll be the danger of taking on more than he can manage over the next two-year period.

MO MOWLAM

'She's the same with everybody, no airs and graces ... it's the same with kids, she never talks down to them.' 'She's pushy ... bloody-minded and determined ... a tough customer ... the hardest working MP in the country.' Thus spake a variety of close observers of the Northern Ireland Secretary, a politician who – to those not in the know, as it were – may appear largely unremarkable. In any case, Cabinet ministers seldom receive as much attention as a PM (unless due to some scandal or other), being generally a dreary collection of party mouthpieces. In Mo Mowlam's case however, we can make an exception. Here is perhaps the most eye-opening vignette, allegedly overheard while talking to Gerry Adams: 'You bloody well get on and do it, otherwise I'll headbutt you.' Even detractors admit to her almost superhuman courage and tenacity, for it must be said that the current Labour MP for Redcar is a force to be reckoned with.

Dr Marjorie Mowlam (the 'Mo' is in fact an abbreviation of her surname), was born in Watford, on 18th September 1949. Destined for a successful education and academic career, Mo finally appeared on the Opposition front bench in the late eighties. Ten years later, of course, we find her as Secretary of State for Northern Ireland in the new Blair Government, making jocular threats of physical violence to Sinn Fein leaders. This last is instructive: while we have Mo's Sun in conscientious Virgo, the proud Leo Moon is conjunct fiery, gutsy Mars. (Moon = emotion; Mars = desire; hence the 'bloody-minded' tag.) Striking too is the concentration of major planets in the same hemisphere, indicating a powerful focus of energy – with none wasted – into only one (or a few) important priorities. Also, the chart is motivated mainly by planets in fire (energy) and earth (practicality) creating a kind of relentless locomotive effect, if

© *Ben Curtis, PA*

you'll pardon the metaphor. Here there is little room for woolly idealism, abstractions or sentiment. Is it any wonder then that, as Mo herself says, she 'just wants to get results' and that her favourite self-description is 'pragmatic'?

Her Virgoan Sun trine to Jupiter (in Capricorn) makes 'getting results' all the more enjoyable too, and on a deeper level brings good luck on the material plane. We should also take the opportunity to explode the myth of Virgo as the 'chaste, tidy, ashtray emptier'. Even with strict Saturn occupying her Sun sign, Mo is known to be almost pathologically untidy (a policeman once having seen her living-room believed she'd been burgled, until it was pointed out that that was how she kept it!), but the Virgoan *mind* is always organised. Typically, Mo is an inveterate 'list maker' outlining her duties for the day in careful detail. And yet Mo's earlier love life has been 'spectacularly untidy' (her own words) though this is hardy surprising with passionate Venus (in Scorpio) square to Mars. At best this combination goes into 'all or nothing' mode in love, producing the fiercely loyal lover, at worst the individual who is too emotionally 'heavy' for others. Mercury in Libra is always fair minded, and square to Jupiter gives her an unshakable optimism, a feeling that almost anything is possible. Indeed, there are many who feel the Irish peace agreement would not have happened without her.

In many ways 1999 seems to be an emotional roller-coaster of a year with significant Neptune transits (to Venus) in April and May. This may result in some confusion and possibly disillusionment in personal relationships, especially if others fail to live up to high ideals. In July, matters here may come to a head with the progressed Moon, but whatever happens this is likely to undermine her confidence. (However, August is a much happier period in love, with Jupiter transiting Venus.) In her career her strengths continue due to the lengthy progressed Jupiter (to her Sun) though late August and early September show stresses behind the scenes at Westminster, when she'll be under pressure to change her mind on a crucial issue.

GERRY ADAMS

It is early 1996 when newsflashes report the explosion of a huge bomb in London's Canary Wharf. Two are dead. The IRA are obviously responsible. Only a few months later a similar one devastates central Manchester (though with no fatalities). Again it is the work of the IRA. The president of Sinn Fein (the IRA's political arm) is called on in the media to denounce the bombings. No direct condemnation can be heard over the airwaves. The critics, hostile in any case to him, repeat their denunciations, saying that behind the façade of politico-talk he is nothing more than a terrorist. Surely, it can't be as simple as all that?

Gerry Adams was that man, surely the most singular (at any rate in recent times) controversial figure in Irish politics. Interned twice for suspected terrorist activity, imprisoned in the notorious Long Kesh compound, attacked by commentators and politicians (including actual physical harm from loyalists), he is no stranger to the headlines. For a time we even witnessed the risible spectacle of seeing his words lip-synched on TV news reports due to a broadcast ban. Any lesser individual would have abandoned such a career long ago. Just what is it that's sustained him, then?

He was born in Belfast on 6th October 1946, giving him Sun in Libra, Moon in Sagittarius, Venus in Leo, Mercury and Mars in Scorpio. To gain our picture of the inner man, we shall examine four powerful aspects made to these 'personal planets'. Firstly, the Moon-Saturn square reflects the early privations of his childhood. Rarely does one 'have it easy' during upbringing with this aspect. But it also colours his inner personality with a sober, if melancholy, approach to the world. In particular, it gives him a determination to resist the vicissitudes of life.

Saturn again figures in the conjunction with Venus. Here is

© *Peter Jordan, PA*

someone rather emotionally reserved and withdrawn, prepared to forego pleasure and comfort in the pursuit of aims and ambitions. This attitude, this inner resilience, has played its part in his crusade to give a voice to the Republican movement and all the tragedies it has entailed. In this context the Mars-Pluto square is vital, usually associated with a life of strife, brutality and being up against difficult odds. In a birth chart it gives one a ruthless capacity and the *desire to achieve ends at all costs*. Whatever one thinks of Gerry Adams, there is no denying his utter, unshakable commitment to Republicanism and the refusal to back down in the face of colossal opposition. This has made him many enemies, but Mars-Pluto is *fearless*. Together with the Sagittarian Moon, his Sun-Neptune conjunction makes him a 'seeker' discontented with the status quo. It also gives him a huge need to believe in a higher cause – and here we have what really makes Gerry Adams tick. In his case the 'higher cause', the Ideal, is the reunification of Ireland (even though that seems well nigh impossible). However, one must understand Neptune to see what drives an individual like Adams. Sun-Neptune indicates a commitment of almost spiritual fervour to the 'cause', often submerging one's ego into the bargain. The individual thus sees it as altruistic, self-sacrificial, though others may see it as blindness – a self-delusion in the face of other realities. His Libran Sun also makes him a romantic of sorts, which his autobiography spells out: he obviously sees his own part in the Troubles in a rather mythologised way. A terrorist? Certainly not. A *freedom fighter*.

The year 1999 looks to be a much calmer one for Gerry Adams, indicating greater fulfilment in his private life. However, there may be severe challenges in professional dealings as Uranus transits opposite his natal Pluto in both May and June. This period will probably call into question Sinn Fein's strength as a political force in the peace process and prove quite a stressful time for its president. Likewise, August has weighty challenges from those in the corridors of power. But as Venus is definitely the dominant planet this year on the progressed chart, it's certain he has peace and reconciliation on his mind.

74

YOUR PERSONAL ASTRO READING FOR 1999

In the 36 pages following you will find three pages devoted to your own birth period. There are 12 astrological Sun 'signs' and they change about the 21st or 22nd of each month. A 'sign' refers to one of the 30-degree divisions of the ecliptic (the apparent path traced by the Sun around the Earth).

For example, if you were born between 22nd December and 20th January, the Sun would have been in the sign of Capricorn and you will come under the influence of that sign. You will then find in the pages devoted to your birth period that your ruling planet is Saturn and Saturday is your most fortunate day. The special dates given will show you the good and not-so-good influences that come out of the general horoscope of the month.

Every person is affected to some degree by an astrological sign under which he or she was born. It is, of course, readily admitted that a monthly horoscope chart of this general nature cannot be as accurate as one that is worked out from the actual time and place of birth. But by and large, it is something that will be found useful.

ARIES

The Ram: a cardinal, fire sign
March 21st–April 20th

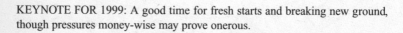

Your ruling planet: Mars
Special day: Tuesday
Gem: diamond
Colour: red
Mental expression: enterprise
Celtic tree affiliation: alder
Nature: impulsive, courageous, self-centred

KEYNOTE FOR 1999: A good time for fresh starts and breaking new ground, though pressures money-wise may prove onerous.

FAVOURABLE AND CHALLENGING DATES

	Social	Business	Travel	Challenging
Jan.	4th–5th, 20th–21st	7th, 10th–11th, 23rd–24th	2nd–3rd, 26th–27th	8th–9th
Feb.	2nd–3rd, 12th, 13th, 16th	8th–9th, 19th–20th	21st–22nd, 23rd	4th–6th
Mar.	2nd–3rd, 25th–27th	18th–19th, 21st–23rd	9th–10th, 23rd–24th	4th–5th
Apr.	3rd–4th, 13th–14th, 24th–25th	14th–15th, 20th–21st	18th–19th, 26th–27th	1st–2nd, 27th–29th
May	3rd–4th, 21st–22nd, 29th–30th	12th–13th, 17th–18th	10th–11th, 16th, 29th	25th–26th
Jun.	5th–6th, 23rd–24th	8th–9th, 19th–20th	12th–13th, 21st–22nd	21st–22nd
Jul.	1st–3rd, 21st–23rd, 30th–31st	5th–7th, 12th–13th	9th–10th, 25th	18th–20th
Aug.	11th–12th, 17th–18th	2nd–3rd, 29th–30th	10th–11th, 23rd–25th	15th–16th
Sep.	5th–8th, 16th–17th, 23rd–24th	9th–10th, 25th–26th	2nd–3rd, 14th–15th	11th–12th
Oct.	1st–3rd, 27th–29th	5th–6th, 17th–18th, 25th–26th	14th–15th, 28th	8th–10th
Nov.	7th–9th, 15th–16th	9th–10th, 19th–20th	1st–2nd, 22nd–24th	4th–6th
Dec.	11th–12th, 17th–18th	5th–7th, 22nd–23rd	13th–14th, 27th–29th	2nd–3rd

MONTHLY FORECASTS

January: A month providing stimulus and encouragement in your career, and the Full Moon of the 2nd may see a crucial matter coming to fruition. Around the 4th–5th, social life really takes off, though someone may let you down by the 8th–9th. The second half of the month sees improvement all round socially, especially by the 20th–21st. However, another Full Moon on the 31st is a warning not to take the goodwill of others for granted, in particular with romantic partners.

February: Largely a period of improvement and co-operation, and this applies to both work and social encounters. Pressure around the 4th–6th may leave you in doubt over a proposal, though by the 9th you should see some progress. The New Moon on the 16th may lead to surprising events with social newcomers –a time to get out and about. Likewise, during the 21st–22nd you may find you need as many breaks from obligations as possible. For one, this is not the most favourable time for going ahead with big projects.

March: Don't allow the planetary low of the 4th–5th to mar your dealings with others following the boost of the previous two days when there's light at the end of the tunnel. Even so, there may be hold-ups. The New Moon on the 17th may put a personal matter into an entirely new perspective, possibly assisting the planetary shift of the 19th (when practical affairs should improve). From the 20th onwards, confidence and vitality are yours owing to the new solar shift. Now, self-promotion works wonders only too well – as you should soon see.

April: Making a big impression on folk is what you're good at this month and both friendships and business go your way. The early hump of the 1st–2nd is something you can put behind you quickly, especially by the 12th–13th when a tête-à-tête may point you in a completely new direction. You may find your luck is in on the 14th–15th if you're prepared to gamble. From the 20th–21st you should see good things coming your way on the material level. Hedge your bets in important decisions when it comes to work and professional issues, for by the Full Moon of the 30th matters here may be reaching fruition. This will be the time to capitalise.

May: The 5th–6th may see a slight downside to personal relationships and give and take is necessary if you're not going to feel left out in the cold. In business matters things improve around the 12th–13th when your decision making shows excellent judgement and will bring favourable results. Also, by the New Moon of the 15th, there may be even more scope for advancement. By the 21st–22nd, though the pace of life may be hurried, there's plenty to keep you interested! The latter part of the month may see you on a losing streak if you're not careful – just play things safe on the 25th–26th and 30th.

June: The 5th–6th is a period of greater freedom for you. There seems to be many good things happening socially, so soak up the limelight while you can. You should have the best of both worlds mid-month. The New Moon on the 13th keeps you properly in touch with what's going on and what you need to know, while domestic matters are ever more rewarding. This is especially so by the 23rd–24th when you can probably afford to let the rest of the world go by. Not so for the Full Moon of the 28th, when a professional matter needs your undivided attention.

July: Socially you should be well in demand round the 1st–3rd and romantically you should be delighted with what happens now. By the 12th–13th (the latter of which is a New Moon) you should find 'someone up there' indicating the way forward, and it's now that your intuitions prove correct. The 18th–20th has its drawbacks and your energies may be somehow in short supply, though by the 21st–23rd you'll be back in the social spotlight making entertaining company for others. On the Full Moon of the 28th though, perhaps it's best not to take every little thing for granted!

August: As early as the 2nd–3rd there are favourable social trends when others enjoy the sunny side to your personality. These happy influences continue into mid-month, though the 15th–16th are days perhaps when you should give the prima donna role a rest! From the 23rd–24th there are improvements all round in work and practical issues, and the more ambitious your plans are now the better. The Full Moon on the 26th may make life rather dreary, though by the 29th–30th you should be back on tip-top form once more.

September: The 2nd–3rd is quite a restless period when you need to break free from restrictions, but effectiveness at work is still in the ascendant. The New Moon on the 9th should make this quite obvious, and any plans up your sleeve should now be initiated. These forward moving trends may have slowed down by the 11th–12th, though there are fulfilling social encounters on the horizon by the 16th–17th. By the 23rd–24th the focus is on what you can get out of relationships, and this should prove to be quite a lot! Thinking big pays off around the 25th–26th – this is not a time to be concerned with minor, petty details.

October: The 5th–6th is definitely a period for going to the nub of any personal problems, and partners will seem more than co-operative. There is, however, a lull patch on the 8th–10th when you may be in the dark over a recent matter. The 17th–18th is likely to be rather eventful on the career front as a new dynamic trend begins. But beware of making enemies! From the 23rd–24th you may have to think hard about jettisoning something from your life. It's time to get rid of any dead wood! This will at least pave the way for possible exciting new initiatives on the Full Moon of the 24th when you should be raring to go.

November: The month is underpinned by topsy-turvy influences, and you must beware of being all at sea with current objectives on the 4th–6th. However, the 7th–9th shows rapid improvement to your social diary. Mid-month shows favourable influences for travel and getting about, and by the 22nd–24th your sense of adventure knows no bounds. You can now broaden interests and generally get more from life (the Full Moon on the 23rd may unearth some vital information for you). The 27th–29th ought to see you at the peak of your abilities, both socially and in business. Risky ventures may well now turn out in your favour.

December: During the early part of the month there may be overriding uncertainty that hampers your actions. Play it safe on the 2nd–3rd. By the 5th–7th you should find far more in the way of friendly support from those around you, with the New Moon of the 8th providing a personal tonic to your spirits. You should find your popularity is stronger than ever around the 17th–18th. From the 22nd–23rd you will benefit from keeping as high a profile as possible, and you'll want to be on the go for much of the festive period.

TAURUS

The Bull: a fixed, earthy sign
April 21st–May 21st

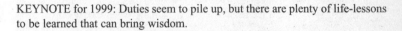

Your ruling planet: Venus
Special day: Friday
Gem: emerald
Colour: red-orange
Mental expression: steadfastness
Celtic tree affiliations: willow, hawthorn
Nature: stubborn, conservative, artistic

KEYNOTE for 1999: Duties seem to pile up, but there are plenty of life-lessons to be learned that can bring wisdom.

FAVOURABLE AND CHALLENGING DATES

	Social	Business	Travel	Challenging
Jan.	1st–2nd, 9th–10th	4th–5th, 20th–21st, 24th–26th	7th–8th, 15th–16th	11th–12th
Feb.	5th–6th, 19th–20th	10th–12th, 21st–23rd	2nd–3rd, 25th–26th	7th–8th
Mar.	2nd–4th, 18th–19th	8th–9th, 20th–21st	21st–22nd, 27th–28th	6th–8th
Apr.	2nd–3rd, 25th–27th	5th–6th, 12th–13th 20th–21st	9th–10th, 25th–26th	3rd–4th
May	3rd–4th, 8th–10th	5th–6th, 14th–15th	18th–19th, 6th–7th	1st, 27th–29th
Jun.	5th–7th, 22nd–23rd, 28th–29th	8th–9th, 17th–19th	7th–8th, 19th–20th	23rd–25th
Jul.	3rd–4th, 12th–13th	9th–10th, 18th–20th	10th–11th, 22nd–23rd	21st–22nd
Aug.	3rd–5th, 23rd–24th	4th–5th, 13th–14th	10th–12th, 26th–27th	17th–18th
Sep.	4th–5th, 17th–18th	1st, 16th–17th, 27th–28th	13th–14th, 24th–25th	13th–15th
Oct.	5th–7th, 16th–17th, 23rd–24th	9th–10th, 25th–26th	3rd–4th, 16th–18th	11th–12th
Nov.	1st–2nd, 10th–12th	9th–10th, 21st–22nd	14th–15th, 29th–30th	7th–8th
Dec.	7th–8th, 11th–12th	9th–10th, 19th–20th	1st–2nd, 22nd–23rd	4th–6th

MONTHLY FORECASTS

January: A month when planetary influences favour travel and being on the move. As early as the 1st–2nd, getting about should bring you into contact with interesting folk – look out for the weird and wonderful! The Full Moon at this time, however, may stop you in your career tracks if you've gone ahead without careful planning. Don't let a setback in your aims leave progress at a total standstill. From the 20th–21st, career matters look set for bigger gains and the chance to step up the ladder of success now appears. By the 24th–26th there should be an outbreak of good luck for Taureans, so make the most of it.

February: The first part of the month may show challenges to overcome, especially on the 7th–8th when getting ahead shouldn't be your main concern. However, the New Moon on the 16th may present new opportunities for career advancement, with social highlights occurring around the 19th–20th. So this is a time of happy co-operative effort in both political and social encounters. The 21st–22nd may well be a fortuitous period personally when risk-taking goes in your favour and success arrives that little bit easier. However, the 24th–25th shows that your love life may be the one area where you have to tread rather carefully.

March: Getting together in group encounters seems to be the real way forward now, though on the 2nd you may feel just a little left out. Mid-month trends may see your happiest time socially, especially on the New Moon of the 17th – be on the lookout for new faces. From the 22nd–23rd you may find that career progress is much slacker, though the preceding two days should bring a little personal luck. On the whole the latter part of the month may find you keeping a low profile. But then again personal and emotional concerns seem to be quite a preoccupation, though nonetheless very rewarding.

April: Though the month begins with a lunar low on the 3rd–4th (when minor setbacks may occur), the 5th–6th should see practical matters going your way (definitely a time to be busy). Things only get better, for by the 12th–13th financial prospects seem rosier and by the 20th–21st you're in a much more powerful position to influence others – especially higher-ups. However, the Full Moon on the 30th may require a serious compromise.

May: There should be brand new focus on exciting initiatives by the 5th–6th (just avoid trouble on the 1st), when you're far better equipped for success and competition. Around the 8th–10th and through to the New Moon on the 15th there is much scope for advancement and putting interesting ideas to the test – probably no one can beat you for sheer creativity now. If you can bring these to a head by the 21st–22nd, the subsequent period can be a fulfilling time of consolidation when finances are also in better shape. However, the 27th–29th are days on which not to expect too much (especially from colleagues and loved ones).

June: A period that ought to bring out your best side, not merely on account of monetary reassurance! The other factor seems to be family life around the 5th–7th (an excellent period for reliving old times). The lunar high of the 10th–11th should increase your sense that anything is now possible, while the New Moon of the 13th centres on finance again and there is scope for successful investments or purchases. From the 21st–22nd life should get not only quite interesting, with much new input, but busy too. Just make sure you don't take on more responsibility than you can really handle from the 23rd to the 25th.

July: A time when what you hear from others may put you on just the right track, though on the 5th–7th your love life may put you to the test in some way. However, by the 12th–13th romantic issues look set to become far more enjoyable, with improved communication on the New Moon of the 13th. The 21st–22nd may be heavy-going workwise with outside pressures threatening to mount up. There are compensations, however, as this is the beginning of a rewarding time in the home, with the Full Moon of the 28th showing that intimate pleasures and family contentment are now but a step away!

August: The month begins with a taste of possible good fortune on the 4th–5th. So long as you're ready to act boldly on new opportunities, this could be a lucky time. Highlights surrounding domestic life continue, and on the 6th–7th a partner may have welcome news. A matter on the home front on the 11th may be heart-warming too. By the 23rd–24th romance has far more going for it, and winning the affection of others is none too difficult. This is a time when your ego is likely to soar skywards!

September: Though you're not about to shy away from the crowds during this period, don't expect everything to work out perfectly in social encounters on the 2nd–4th (though everything should work out fine on the 1st). The middle part of the month has mixed influences. The 13th–15th ought to be a respite from thinking about important matters, while on the 16th–17th you can capitalise on any new and ingenious ideas in personal or professional developments. By the 23rd–24th goings on at work should show you have been moving in exactly the right direction – just don't let the 25th's Full Moon undermine your confidence here.

October: Your powerful personality is to the fore for much of the month, something you can put to good use on the 5th–7th when your tongue is extremely persuasive. The 7th also sees an upswing to fortunes in the romantic sphere, while the New Moon on the 9th indicates a go-ahead for a practical project. Get as much done as possible during this period, for by the 11th–12th planetary influences may well be against you somehow. From the 23rd–24th personal relationships are boosted enormously and social life may find you in huge demand. On the 25th–26th a word in the right ear may improve prospects for current aims.

November: Positive highlights surround relationships around the 1st–2nd with much in the way of support – through others you gain strength. However, it may be best to let others be out in front around the lunar low of the 7th–8th. The 21st–22nd ought to see good results in the practical sphere, but it's also favourable for new initiatives. Perhaps one of these ought to be to rid yourself of any outworn situations owing to a new planetary trend on the 23rd–25th. This coincides with the Full Moon on the 23rd, making it doubly important to assess your current position – don't get bogged down with material obligations.

December: This month you may feel somewhat insecure at times (especially on the lunar low of the 4th–6th), though reassurance arrives through relationships on the 7th–8th. Mid-month brings emotional issues to the fore and a partner may be feeling uncertain – your words now count a great deal. By the lunar high on the 19th and the Full Moon on the 22nd you should be far surer of your next move. There are bonuses now via extended travel and social or cultural pursuits. Perhaps being a 'stay at home' this Christmas is simply not for you!

GEMINI

The Twins: a mutable, air sign
May 22nd–June 21st

Your ruling planet: Mercury
Special day: Wednesday
Gems: beryl, aquamarine
Colour: yellow
Mental expression: curiosity, versatility
Celtic tree affiliations: hawthorn, oak
Nature: versatile, quick-witted, charming

KEYNOTE for 1999: A favourable time for social matters, though soul-searching is the real key to happiness.

FAVOURABLE AND CHALLENGING DATES

	Social	Business	Travel	Challenging
Jan.	4th–5th, 17th–18th	6th–7th, 27th–28th	10th–11th, 20th–21st	13th–15th
Feb.	1st–2nd, 9th–10th	4th–5th, 20th–21st, 24th–26th	7th–8th, 15th–16th	9th–11th
Mar.	5th–6th, 19th–20th	10th–12th, 21st–23rd	2nd–3rd, 25th–26th	7th–8th
Apr.	1st–2nd, 12th–13th	8th–9th, 18th–19th	21st–22nd, 27th–28th	5th–7th
May	2nd–3rd, 27th–28th, 30th–31st	5th–6th, 16th–17th, 21st–23rd	10th–11th, 25th–26th	2nd–4th
Jun.	3rd–5th, 9th–10th	6th–8th, 12th–13th, 21st–22nd	19th–20th, 28th–29th	26th–27th
Jul.	1st–2nd, 22nd–23rd, 25th–26th	5th–7th, 10th–11th	8th–9th, 19th–20th	23rd–24th
Aug.	11th–12th, 12th–13th	6th–7th, 18th–20th	2nd–3rd, 10th–11th	19th–21st
Sep.	4th–5th, 16th–17th	2nd–3rd, 29th–30th	10th–12th, 13th–15th	16th–17th
Oct.	5th–6th, 17th–18th	1st, 23rd–24th, 27th–29th	8th–9th, 25th–26th	13th–15th
Nov.	5th–7th, 16th–17th, 23rd–24th	9th–10th, 25th–26th	3rd–4th, 16th–18th	9th–11th
Dec.	1st–2nd, 11th–13th	5th–6th, 21st–22nd	15th–17th, 29th–31st	7th–8th

MONTHLY FORECASTS

January: The start to the year sees you riding the crest of a wave socially. On the 4th–5th you should get along with others famously (they all seem to want to be in your good books). However, by the 7th–8th there may be contentious matters arising through dealings in love. This may cause some second thoughts, with mid-month trends when there is a dispiriting lunar low. The 11th and 13th–15th are days when practical issues may put you to the test – handle these carefully. However, by the 20th you should see a major lift in your confidence and spirits, and the 27th–28th is a definite morale raiser!

February: This period gets off to an optimistic start, fulfilling your usual need to be 'on the go' (especially around the 2nd–3rd). The 9th–10th may coincide with flagging energy and hold-ups, though the New Moon of the 11th may indicate new ways of broadening your horizons. Trends around the 12th–13th may help put you in an advantageous position in career matters. From the 20th onwards, these favourable trends should reach a positive climax with much to feel pleased about, and it's likely you'll be able to double your luck in major objectives on the 23rd–24th.

March: Press ahead with major ambitions – here is where you seem to have the 'green light' at present, certainly around the 2nd–4th. The 8th–9th may be a sluggish period, when getting your own way seems almost impossible. Not so for the 17th–19th (the first date of which is the New Moon), when calling the shots in the spheres of ambition leads to the right kind of results. Take the initiative and you may get a pleasant surprise, though on the 22nd–23rd you should have little trouble getting others to see things your way, whether they're business or romantic partners. By the Full Moon of the 30th issues in your love life may need discussing.

April: Though personal/emotional matters are emphasised now, the 1st–2nd sees positive highlights in group activities. However, the 5th–7th are days for keeping a low profile while you recharge the old batteries. But by the 12th–13th you really seem to be at the centre of social activity again. From the 20th–21st, the low profile returns, but this is a period for self-assessment when you should entertain new ideas for the long-term future.

May: The month may get off to a rather unfulfilling start. The lunar low of the 2nd–4th is hardly designed for much 'get up and go', and around the 5th–7th pleasing others may seem well nigh impossible. The 8th–10th may have a rather slack feel too, though the New Moon of the 15th should help you put a tiresome situation well behind you. This paves the way for progressive trends on the 16th–17th when you ought to have the go-ahead for a new idea. An increase of confidence from the 21st–22nd gives you an edge in decision making and getting along with others – now you can really turn things to your advantage.

June: A period that ought to show favourable trends in both private and career concerns, though you should resist sitting on the fence over an important move on the 5th–6th. The New Moon on the 13th may well see luck breaking out all over the place, but remember 'nothing ventured, nothing gained'. This is also the time of the lunar high, creating a sense of new possibility. From the 21st to the 22nd a new trend appears, giving your finances a boost and the chance to capitalise on new beginnings. There is, however, a lull patch on the 26th–27th when unexpected setbacks could occur.

July: Pursuing practical matters ought to bring you some success in the first half of the month, and the 5th–6th are key days in this respect. Getting others to see things your way on the 10th–11th is something you're rather good at, and the New Moon of the 13th may also allow you to make financial gain wherever chances are taken. A new planetary shift around this time also helps you to enjoy some nostalgia. By the 21st–22nd you are wise to keep abreast of all news and views (you can never be sure when such information is going to prove useful). But keep a low profile on the 24th.

August: The month commences with high spirits, and the lunar high of the 6th–7th may result in a personal triumph without your having to try too hard. Social matters on the New Moon of the 11th are boosted as you bring your entertaining personality to the proceedings and can handle several different interests with some success now. Not so for the 19th–21st, when there's a lunar low (attend to unfinished business and keep your sights low). From the 23rd to the 24th the real rewards are through domestic and family involvements.

September: While domestic life continues to be fulfilling, so do professional involvements on the 2nd–3rd (your best days for going after what you want from life). However, a relationship issue on the 4th–5th may force you to take a closer look at a partner's needs as it's plain that some self-denial is now the best way forward. By the 16th–17th, the focus may be on outside pressures that you must meet half way or see them simply pile up. From the 23rd to the 24th you should find yourself far more at the centre of things when it comes to love, leisure and romance – a time of ego-fulfilment, for sure!

October: You should be able to make a good personal impression on others during the first half of the month. Don't let your need for enjoyment lead to sloppiness where practical issues are concerned on the 5th–6th. The New Moon on the 9th should be a peak romantically, though mid-month trends (such as the lunar low on the 13th–15th) may result in unfulfilled expectations regarding colleagues and partners – play it safe and take nothing for granted. Satisfying results should be on the horizon by the 23rd when you're much better organised, especially after the rather sluggish Full Moon of the 24th.

November: There may be more than one way of making the desired progress early this month, and by the 9th–10th a brand new project should be well underway and on target. There is a brief planetary lull patch on the 11th, however, when you should avoid pitfalls and keep to the tried and tested path. Progressive trends continue in the workplace up until the 21st – 22nd when the emphasis turns to partnership and your love life – now is the time to think in pairs if you really want to be happy! The lunar high of the 23rd–24th should enhance your ability to get others on your side, especially those in positions of authority.

December: Favourable highlights continue through relationships, especially in co-operative ventures at work on the 5th–6th. While the lunar low of the 7th–8th may be a 'treading water' period, communication matters may unearth something vital mid-month (especially around the 11th–13th). The 21st–22nd ought to be lucky for you in some way, especially regarding personal aims and objectives, but expect a little disorganisation in your private life from the 23rd onwards when perhaps you may feel more concerned over money than is necessary.

CANCER

The Crab: a cardinal, water sign
June 21st–July 22nd

Your ruling planet: the Moon
Special day: Monday
Gems: moss agate, pearl
Colours: violet, silver
Mental expression: imagination
Celtic tree affiliations: oak, holly
Nature: sensitive, maternal, romantic

KEYNOTE for 1999: A go-ahead, 'step-up' time career-wise, though friendships may cause you to revise expectations.

FAVOURABLE AND CHALLENGING DATES

	Social	Business	Travel	Challenging
Jan.	4th–5th, 7th–8th	1st–2nd, 29th–30th	10th–12th, 15th–16th	16th–17th
Feb.	5th–6th, 17th–18th	1st, 23rd–24th, 27th–29th	4th–5th, 25th–26th	13th–15th
Mar.	1st–3rd, 16th–17th	5th–7th, 25th–26th	9th–10th, 16th–18th	11th–13th
Apr.	4th–5th, 17th–18th, 20th–21st	6th–7th, 20th–22nd	10th–11th, 13th–14th	13th–15th
May	7th–8th, 9th–11th, 15th–16th	10th–11th, 18th–19th	20th–21st, 29th–30th	5th–6th
Jun.	5th–6th, 7th–8th, 25th–26th	10th–12th, 14th–15th	6th–7th, 19th–20th	1st–3rd, 28th–30th
Jul.	5th–7th, 12th–13th	13th–15th, 23rd–24th	2nd–4th, 18th–19th	26th–27th
Aug.	3rd–4th, 24th–25th	8th–9th, 16th–17th	2nd–4th, 25th–26th	22nd–23rd
Sep.	4th–5th, 9th–10th, 26th–27th	2nd–3rd, 12th–13th, 21st–22nd	6th–8th, 28th–29th	18th–20th
Oct.	7th–9th, 11th–13th, 21st–22nd	2nd–3rd, 29th–30th	7th–8th, 23rd–24th	16th–17th
Nov.	9th–11th, 16th–17th	4th–5th, 25th–26th	2nd–3rd, 18th–19th	12th–13th
Dec.	5th–6th, 21st–22nd	1st–2nd, 23rd–24th	13th–15th, 25th–26th	9th–11th

MONTHLY FORECASTS

January: Progress should be fairly stable as the year begins, and there's even a lucky boost on the 1st–2nd when chancing your arm may be the way to make a huge difference to the present. By the 7th–8th a brand new influence should put you in the social limelight and a private discussion may put you in the picture regarding current ambitions. There may be pitfalls to avoid on the 16th–17th, especially in dealings with others. Progressive social trends continue, however, up until the 20th–21st when the emphasis shifts to sorting out the wheat from the chaff in your personal life (get rid of whatever may be holding you back).

February: Favourable highlights continue through emotional matters, though your sense of adventure and need for the 'new' is stimulated on the 4th–5th. The lunar low of the 12th–13th may see progress slacken. By the 17th–18th communication issues at work may unearth something of major importance, leaving you with a big decision to make. From the 19th, the subsequent period is highly favourable with opportunities for broadening your horizons – don't get stuck in a rut now! The 25th–26th ought to see a winning streak both personally and professionally – these are days on which to act on powerful hunches.

March: Much of the month ought to help you improve culturally (travel and mental pursuits are favoured), though gains of another kind – professional ones – should be the order of the day around the 5th–6th. Refusing to take chances on the lunar low of the 11th–13th should prove to be a wise thing. You can, however, plan ahead to the 21st–22nd when career developments are positively highlighted – you should now have more power when it comes to changing your short-term future path. This trend ought to peak on the 25th–26th, though on the Full Moon of the 31st family issues come more to the fore.

April: The month may get off to a somewhat unpromising start. The lunar low on the 8th–9th may bring hold-ups and the feeling that others are getting ahead much quicker, while relationships on the 12th–13th may require difficult compromises. However, things should move on to the plus side by the 17th–18th with your social life lifting your spirits. From the 21st onwards you should find yourself a happy team player. The 22nd is a lucky day for you.

May: Friendships continue to be your most rewarding area, though at home things may seem rather different as dissenting voices are heard around the 7th–8th. The previous two days may see you hanging back with a major initiative, but this is no bad thing. The planetary atmosphere changes round the 9th–11th with benefits accruing in romance and your love life. By the 18th–19th you should tempt fate and see what Lady Luck has in store. Moves made now should prove decisive, and by the 22nd you ought to be indulging yourself in matters related to the past. Ambitions may tail off somewhat though.

June: This month probably sees uninspiring beginnings with the lunar low of the 1st–3rd, though at least on the 5th–6th you can take pleasure in life's simpler comforts. Important good news seems to be on the horizon around the 7th–8th – perhaps by letter or telephone call. Even so, you may be dithering over something with the 13th New Moon – let it pass before fully making up your mind. The 14th–15th is an excellent time to put a new idea into operation, while the 21st and onwards sees your power and influence return to full throttle. By the 28th's Full Moon your sway over others should get you just what you want.

July: Self-confidence makes a world of difference in the first half of the month, and the go-ahead for certain projects can only increase it. The 5th–7th and 12th–13th (the latter of which is a New Moon) are favourable in this regard and you should enjoy most challenges and competitive situations. Mid-month trends may help put you in an advantageous social position when charm and flattery will get you everywhere. By the 23rd–24th though, your mind should be on far more practical issues for here is where you can benefit from work and financial developments (but there could be some hiccups on the 26th–27th).

August: Your efforts towards progress should pay off in the early part of the month. The lunar high of the 8th–9th shows potential rewards via speculation, and by the 11th–12th material affairs seem much more settled. The 15th–17th focuses on quite a relaxed and happy atmosphere at home – all the contentment you need seems to be right there on your doorstep! On the 22nd–23rd don't agree to new proposals before checking the facts (this is an 'unlucky' lunar low). However, the period after the 24th blows away the mental cobwebs!

September: Present influences now favour meetings and appointments, but these will only work in your favour if you play down argumentative tendencies (especially on the 2nd–3rd). The lunar high on the 4th–5th will smooth down life's rough edges and aid progress. By the New Moon of the 9th a critical issue may hang in the balance – it's up to your better judgement now to put things right. There may be further stumbling-blocks on the 18th–20th, though a partner comes to the rescue. From the 21st–22nd a new domestic influence appears, which should at least give you something to celebrate at home (though not on the 25th!).

October: Both career and domestic life bring out the best in you with the lunar high of the 2nd–3rd (certainly days for getting your own way). Tricky decisions may be the order of the day on the 7th–9th, and there's now a chance to turn an important matter completely around. By the 18th–19th you may be better off getting on with things alone – somehow others seem unresponsive or 'difficult'. Things should certainly lighten up by the Full Moon of the 24th, however, after which your personality seems stronger and you can bring a little joy to almost every situation you encounter.

November: For most of the month you should find yourself the centre of attention, gaining good notice from friends, colleagues and loved ones. This is especially so on the 9th–11th, though the following two days (lunar lows) may coincide with a drop in energy and enthusiasm – it's best to keep expectations to a minimum. By the 21st–22nd you need to get organised in preparation for increased responsibility, though being busy is nonetheless enjoyable now. Though the 23rd's Full Moon is a warning against hasty decisions, the 25th–26th are days when you can press ahead confidently with your career aims and ambitions.

December: The month begins with positive spirits and a tonic in the romantic department – love may well now seek out certain Cancerians around the 5th–7th. Present trends continue to favour pet projects and practical issues, though the 9th–11th are days when you should keep things as simple and undemanding as possible. From the Full Moon of the 22nd bonuses are possible, both in terms of personal fortune and fulfilling social encounters. But don't let yourself be the silent partner in co-operative endeavours!

87

LEO

The Lion: a fixed, fire sign
July 23rd–August 23rd

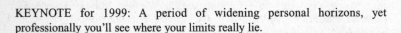

Your ruling planet: the Sun
Special day: Sunday
Gem: sapphire
Colour: orange
Mental expression: comprehension
Celtic tree affiliations: holly, hazel
Nature: proud, creative, devoted

KEYNOTE for 1999: A period of widening personal horizons, yet professionally you'll see where your limits really lie.

FAVOURABLE AND CHALLENGING DATES

	Social	Business	Travel	Challenging
Jan.	5th–6th, 19th–20th, 25th–26th	3rd–5th, 28th–31st	1st–3rd, 9th–11th	18th–19th
Feb.	4th–5th, 17th–18th	6th–7th, 27th–28th	10th–11th, 13th	14th–15th
Mar.	7th–8th, 9th–11th	10th–11th, 27th–28th	2nd–4th, 29th–30th	14th–15th
Apr.	12th–13th, 17th–18th	4th, 20th–21st, 23rd–24th	6th–7th, 18th–19th	10th–11th
May	3rd–4th, 22nd–23rd	9th–10th, 20th–21st	4th–5th, 28th–29th	7th–8th
Jun.	5th–7th, 27th–28th	1st–2nd, 16th–18th	17th–19th, 25th–26th	4th–5th
Jul,	7th–9th, 11th–13th	12th–13th, 14th–15th	16th–17th, 23rd–24th	1st, 28th–29th
Aug.	11th–12th, 16th–17th, 27th–28th	2nd–3rd, 10th–11th, 22nd–23rd	12th–13th, 18th–19th	24th–26th
Sep.	6th–7th, 16th–17th	10th–11th, 14th–15th, 23rd–24th	13th–15th, 19th–20th	21st–22nd
Oct.	3rd–5th, 24th–25th	6th–7th, 16th–17th,	2nd–4th, 31st	18th–20th, 25th–26th
Nov.	9th–10th, 21st–22nd	1st, 4th–5th, 27th–28th	6th–7th, 12th	14th–16th
Dec	5th–7th, 10th–11th, 25th–26th	2nd–3rd, 21st–22nd	7th–8th, 10th	12th–13th

MONTHLY FORECASTS

January: The month should get off to an optimistic start with the lunar high on the 3rd–5th – an excellent time for putting new ideas into operation. While there is a favourable focus on the practical side of life, there are good things happening too of a romantic nature round the 6th–7th with a carefree feeling all round. Mid-month influences around the 18th–19th may see slackened progress, though by the 20th you should have all the help you need when relationship issues improve. Late month trends around the 26th–27th may see domestic pressures when a supposed minor matter turns out to be not so small after all!

February: After the energetic start of the 1st's lunar high, the early part of the month may fail to enlarge your optimism. There may be serious questions to ask regarding your future course on the 12th–13th, and the 14th–15th may see hold-ups to plans and schemes. The second half may be a turning-point, and by the 20th–21st you can put stumbling-blocks behind you. You gain much from the advice of partners and loved ones as support never seems very far away. The Moon returns to your sign on the 27th–28th, signifying a boost in the luck department and the chance to create brand new opportunities on the personal level.

March: The month ought to see favourable happenings via the communication sphere. On the 2nd–4th there may be important news on the horizon, and the more you get out and about the better. Mid-month trends show the lunar low on the 14th–15th and the New Moon on the 17th. These are times at which to proceed with caution where important matters are concerned, especially close relationships. By the 18th–19th, however, the 'green light' may be on in professional developments and by the 21st–22nd you should have the best of both worlds, making progress in your career and seeing a good deal more of the world than usual!

April: Long journeys and intellectual exchange may have a vital role to play in your life early this month, and days from the 10th–13th are peaks in this respect when social newcomers may be around. Go-ahead trends may tail off by the 17th–18th, when you may have to seriously change tack. However, you have the 20th–21st to look forward to, when plans and ambitions get properly back on course. The 23rd–24th are days when your luck is in too.

May: Long-term ambitions ought to get the go-ahead for much of the month. While confidence is on the up, so is your tendency to argue where unnecessary on the 5th–6th. Choose your words carefully, or there may be some explaining to do by the lunar low of the 7th–8th. However, the 9th–10th brings new input that lights the path ahead and the New Moon of the 15th may help turn a few things around career-wise and give you a new break. From the 21st onwards you should be in a more advantageous social position, and teamwork comes to the fore. The 30th's Full Moon should help you stand out in the crowd!

June: Though life may fail to inspire around the 4th's lunar low, charm and coercion get you everywhere on the 5th–7th when you should find yourself in the best of company. Much of the month is geared towards positive group encounters, though you may have to think carefully of your effect on others during the 8th–9th. Mid-month provides a further boost to social life. Be on the lookout for new faces on the New Moon of the 13th and expect to be the focus of some attention on the 16th–18th. However, by the 21st–22nd you may prefer to keep a low profile. This is likely to be a low-key phase with more emphasis on life's little things.

July: Keep most major decisions on ice during the early month if possible. You may find things turning out the reverse of what's expected, especially on the 1st. Family issues may be unsettling on the 5th–6th, though there is a minor tonic for monetary issues around the 12th–13th. The wheels of progress turn faster from the 14th–15th and by the 23rd making a fresh start seems easier now you have more personal influence at your fingertips. Confidence soars now, and not even the Full Moon of the 28th can hold back your optimism and enthusiasm. But perhaps you should keep expectations moderate all the same!

August: There should be much in the way of personal satisfaction early this month, with impact on others strong on the 1st–2nd. There should be a few obstacles to progress on the 10th–11th. In fact you should put your luck to the test, since mid-month is a favourable period for new initiatives. By the 22nd–23rd you can capitalise on new ventures as the going is good for practical and financial issues. The testing points really arrive around the 24th–26th when you should stop thinking the world revolves around you!

September: By focusing on material issues you may find much scope for advancement in the first half of the month. But getting along with others may prove difficult on the 2nd–3rd (perhaps you're being a little too assertive). However, the 6th–8th ought to see you on a winning streak when it comes to getting important tasks done – these are days on which to act on your intuitions. During mid-month, getting down to brass tacks and avoiding unnecessary distractions proves wise (there may be too much at stake). Keep sights low on the 21st–22nd, while thereafter you can afford to think ahead far more expansively.

October: You may have some ingenious ideas up your sleeve in the first half of the month – it's time to set about convincing others of their value. This trend peaks early on the 4th–5th, so get busy! By the 6th–7th there may well be benefits accruing in the financial department, particularly through close partners. There may be much to feel good about in this respect on the New Moon of the 9th. Mid-month may find you correcting mistakes, if you proceed without caution on the 18th–20th's lunar low. However, from the 23rd there's much personal reassurance and fulfilment to be found through all family-related matters.

November: Being surrounded by familiar faces is what makes life really rewarding for much of the month, and a chance to relive the past around the 8th–10th is especially heart-warming. The 14th–16th is not a time to press for your own way as the Moon falls in your opposite sign (this may be a time of professional stresses and strains too). From the 22nd your sunny personality is to the fore and others find you hugely entertaining company. This influence brings out all that's best in you, and tempting fate in the romantic stakes on the 27th–28th may lead to your getting far more than you bargained for.

December: Favourable influences continue to surround domestic and love life, especially with the 8th's New Moon – a time when new romance may begin. Mid-month finds you in a freewheeling mood socially, though high spirits must be measured against possible disappointments at work on the 12th–13th. The Full Moon of the 22nd may coincide with moody behaviour as something turns you in upon yourself. But the subsequent days (like the 25th's lunar high) shows that you can't keep a good Leo down – a high-octane period!

VIRGO

The Virgin: a mutable, earthy sign
August 24th–September 23rd

Your ruling planet: Mercury
Special day: Wednesday
Gem: sardonyx
Colour: pale green
Mental expression: discrimination
Celtic tree affiliations: hazel, the vine
Nature: helpful, practical, clever

KEYNOTE for 1999: A year to rid yourself of life's dead wood and clear the decks, probably not without some struggle!

FAVOURABLE AND CHALLENGING DATES

	Social	Business	Travel	Challenging
Jan.	4th–5th, 8th–9th	6th–7th, 22nd–23rd	10th–11th, 13th–14th	20th–21st
Feb.	10th–11th, 19th–20th	2nd–4th, 27th–28th	14th–15th, 25th–26th	16th–18th
Mar.	7th–9th, 14th–15th	1st–2nd, 4th, 29th–30th	18th–10th, 27th–28th	16th–17th
Apr.	2nd–3rd, 16th–17th, 27th–28th	10th–11th, 22nd–23rd, 25th–26th	4th–6th, 18th–19th, 20th–21st	12th–13th
May	5th–6th, 8th–9th	3rd–5th, 22nd–24th	1st–3rd, 6th–7th	10th–11th
Jun.	4th, 20th–21st, 26th–27th	15th–17th, 23rd–24th	10th–11th, 18th–19th	6th–7th
Jul.	5th–6th, 12th–14th	9th–10th, 16th–17th	7th–8th, 28th–29th	3rd–4th, 30th–31st
Aug.	9th–10th, 21st–22nd	12th–14th, 22nd–23rd	6th–7th, 12th	1st, 27th, 28th
Sep.	2nd–3rd, 10th–11th, 25th–26th	1st, 16th–17th, 21st–22nd	12th–13th, 18th	23rd–24th
Oct.	7th–9th, 27th–28th	6th–7th, 16th–18th	4th–5th, 25th–26th	21st–22nd
Nov.	6th–7th, 16th–17th	2nd, 9th–11th, 14th–15th, 29th–30th	13th–15th, 19th–20th	14th–16th
Dec.	5th–7th, 22nd–23rd	1st–2nd, 16th–17th	18th–20th, 27th–28th	14th–16th

MONTHLY FORECASTS

January: This month gets off to a smooth start where work progress is concerned – there's now all the help you need to make a success of things. The lunar high on the 6th–7th is a mental/physical peak when positive action leads to good results. Mid-month sees favourable trends in romantic matters, and by the New Moon of the 17th a matter of the heart should turn out just as expected. The 20th–21st is a 'lay off' period between major activities – keep life as simple as possible now. Practical matters help you get the best from life by the 22nd–23rd, and the more ambitious your objectives the better.

February: For much of the month you should see opportunities to further your aims. A boost to ambitions could come as early as the 2nd–3rd with the lunar high. The 11th–12th may see useful information coming your way through practical discussion and by the New Moon of the 16th you should be more than ready to take decisive action. The following two days however may see things slowing down and results not quite so easy to come by. The 19th–20th is likely to see relationships having a little more sparkle – certainly things go better in twos! Your emotional life should get even better from the 21st–22nd onwards.

March: Personal relationships are your most fulfilling area for the major part of the month. Most major decisions, especially regarding problem solving, go well on the 2nd–4th while social life round the 14th brings out the best in you. However, on the New Moon of the 17th your personal influence seems to be on a downslide, and from the 21st to the 22nd you may find that life doesn't run too smoothly at all. But this is a transitionary phase when you should take an 'off with the old, on with the new' approach. Financially, you may need to pay closer attention to budgeting on the 31st's Full Moon.

April: Strong emotions underlie close relationships much of the month. Perhaps a change of scenery will lighten the mood around the 1st–2nd. However, changes seem to be on the horizon regarding a personal matter (something you may be forced to make by the 12th–13th). The 20th–21st is a time for broadening your mental and physical horizons, and the 25th–26th should prove a peak for personal freedom and contentment.

May: A time when you're not short of new ideas to further the cause of progress, especially where monetary gain is involved (the 4th–6th are significant days here). On the 8th–9th the input you receive from others may well light the path ahead, though caution is advised when taking the next step on the lunar low of the 10th–11th. A New Moon on the 15th is excellent for taking long journeys to broaden the mind. By the 22nd–23rd your ambitions are really driving you forward and you should now have the power to determine exactly what happens in the short term (with the 24th bringing a little luck!).

June: For the major part of the month career issues are on the up and up. While impressing higher-ups on the 4th–5th seems easy enough, you may have your work cut out to please loved ones at this time. The lunar low on the 6th–7th is a time to stay out of the limelight and get on with something simpler. The 13th's New Moon is a time to forge ahead professionally and leave petty details to others. Influences on the 19th–20th are likewise geared to help circumstances go as expected. From the 21st onwards your social life improves enormously, and you benefit from communications among large groups of folk.

July: Though friendship matters have much going on for them now, you run the risk of spoiling things by over-zealous ideas. The lunar low on the 3rd–4th may lead to some misguided notions on your part, and around the 5th–6th you mustn't let your critical nature get the better of you! Mid-month trends, however, may help point you in a better direction. Socially and romantically your powers of attraction increase, and you show good judgement in a major decision around the lunar high of the 16th–17th. You should be wary of being led up the garden path, however, on the 24th – things may not be quite as they seem at this time!

August: You may prefer indulging in more rest and relaxation much of the month. It's a low key period when 'treading water' seems the best option. The 11th–12th and 15th–16th, for example, are times when effectiveness may suffer and relationship issues may be somewhat insecure. There are high spots however, such as the 'lucky' lunar high on the 12th–14th, when getting your own way proves easier than usual. But by the 21st–22nd it seems to be full steam ahead with all major aims – your personal influence has probably never been as strong.

September: Now you should project yourself into the world with much more gusto and will-power (though on the 2nd–3rd a domestic issue may remind you of your limitations). The New Moon on the 9th may lead to fortunate encounters with others, when you're advised to keep your eyes and ears open! Mid-month influences on the 16th–17th may coincide with success in financial speculation, especially for those in business. The 23rd–24th shows mixed influences. Financial consolidation seems to be on the horizon, when you can build on past successes, though deferment to partners will also prove crucial at this time.

October: The continued emphasis is on property and possessions. If your everyday schedule is properly organised on the 4th–5th, new input may help you gain on the material level. By the 6th–7th you should be preparing to put new initiatives into action – don't be talked out of doing what you know is right at this time. The 9th may even see your luckiest time of the month with the New Moon – materially and emotionally good things look set to come your way. By the 21st–22nd, you should keep to the tried and trusted path, though from the 23rd onwards the world gets a little bigger, and much more interesting!

November: Social interactions tend to be quite stimulating much of the month – it's also a good time to travel. The 2nd–3rd and 9th–10th should see you happily on the go, with the New Moon of the 8th indicating a necessary change of tack, helping keep personal aims on target. Mid-month, with the lunar influences of the 14th–16th, may be less inspiring as work may entail some frustrations. Domestic and family affairs from the 21st to the 22nd provide the planetary highlights (an excellent period for entertaining at home). On the 29th–30th a new professional or personal objective suggests you should strike while the iron is hot.

December: Matters from the past still seem to be a source of joy for much of the month, though career developments may seem slack. Even so, your powers seem at a premium on the 1st, and on the 5th–7th when your persuasive tongue is put to work. The 11th–12th may see much social activity on the home front, possibly with unexpected visitors. Mid-month once more seems to present challenges to progress and tests to your patience, though by the 22nd you're much more in party mood with romantic issues almost tailor made for you!

LIBRA

The Scales: a cardinal, air sign
September 24th–October 23rd

Your ruling planet: Venus
Special day: Friday
Gem: opal
Colour: indigo blue
Mental expression: impartiality
Celtic tree affiliations: the vine, ivy
Nature: adaptable, gracious, judicial

KEYNOTE for 1999: Relationships may well see new beginnings, though you should also dig deeper to your inmost emotions.

FAVOURABLE AND CHALLENGING DATES

	Social	*Business*	*Travel*	*Challenging*
Jan.	4th–5th, 24th–25th	8th–9th, 18th–19th	10th–11th, 29th–30th	22nd–23rd
Feb.	10th–12th, 22nd–23rd, 27th–28th	4th, 7th–8th, 10th–11th, 22nd–23rd	3rd–4th, 21st–23rd	19th–20th
Mar.	6th–7th, 16th–17th, 21st–22nd	2nd–4th, 11th, 14th–15th, 29th–30th	13th–15th, 19th–20th	18th–19th
Apr.	5th–7th, 22nd–23rd	1st–2nd, 27th–29th	12th–13th, 10th–11th	14th–15th
May	3rd–5th, 19th–20th	14th–15th, 25th–26th	16th–18th, 26th	12th–13th
Jun.	4th, 18th–20th, 27th–28th	1st, 7th, 21st–22nd	14th–15th, 25th–26th	8th–9th
Jul.	4th–6th, 27th–28th	12th–13th, 18th–20th	16th–17th, 21st,	5th–7th
Aug.	11th–12th	3rd–5th, 15th–16th	1st–3rd, 20th–21st	2nd–3rd, 29th–30th
Sep.	1st–2nd, 23rd–24th, 29th–30th	4th–5th, 16th–18th	8th–9th, 25th–26th	25th–26th
Oct.	2nd–3rd, 16th–17th, 20th–21st	8th–10th, 18th–19th	12th–13th, 22nd–23rd	23rd–24th
Nov.	9th–10th, 11th–12th	4th–6th, 29th–30th	10th–11th, 16th–17th	19th–20th
Dec.	4th–5th, 22nd–23rd	2nd–3rd, 9th–10th	12th–14th, 29th–30th	17th–18th

MONTHLY FORECASTS

January: Domestic matters predominate this month – there may be some good news with the Full Moon on the 2nd. Romantically, the 4th–5th sees favourable trends and there's much you can take for granted in your social and professional life on the 8th–9th. However, the Full Moon on the 17th may coincide with a tricky decision at home. From the 21st onwards your love life receives a fresh new boost, though the 22nd–23rd may pose stumbling-blocks when it comes to winning over others. On the 31st (a Full Moon) you may have to compromise much more than you thought in group situations.

February: Favourable influences dominate your love life and pleasure pursuits – this is a time to take life much more in your stride. Your personal charisma is strong on the 4th–6th and 11th–12th. The New Moon on the 16th may lead to your stealing the spotlight from others, though by the 19th–20th you may not be able to get away with much! Good things happen in practical matters from the 22nd onwards as current influences show benefits here, but only so long as you're properly organised. Your critical eye is unlikely to miss much now, and you will be good at problem solving with your quick mind at work.

March: Work continues as the most positively highlighted area for much of the month, and input from others on the 2nd–4th may prove extremely valuable. The 2nd's Full Moon may set this trend in motion – be ready to take swift action! Later on, the New Moon of the 17th may plunge you deeply into an emotional matter that could be a possible cause of distraction elsewhere. Meanwhile decision making may be best put off until after the lunar low of the 18th–19th. From the 21st–22nd onwards you should find much in the way of help and assistance where it is required, especially on the 29th–30th – a lucky period for new beginnings.

April: It seems there's success to be had now through co-operative matters – business or pleasure – though by the 12th–13th striking out on your own may bring benefits via travel and intellectual interests. However, mid-month (especially the 14th–18th) may force a rethink about present endeavours. It's best not to avoid the issue, for by the 20th–21st you may find there are situations holding you back somehow – and it's likely something has to go!

May: The time seems ripe for a personal spring-clean – clear out the dead wood from your life and clear the ground for new changes. Early in the month, around the 3rd–5th, should see you in a far more assertive mood, ready to go after what you want, though caution is advised on the path of progress on the 12th–13th. The New Moon of the 15th is a time when stability and security is not guaranteed, and financially you may have to get by with few resources. From the 21st onwards your personal horizons should broaden, however. Now there's the chance to get far more out of life (the 25th–26th is good for risk-taking too).

June: Look for a change of scenery now if you want to stay happy. This applies socially, too, and the 4th and 5th are dates when you should discover the extent of your popularity. The 8th and 9th are hardly your luckiest days, so avoid risky business. The New Moon of the 13th may satisfy your curiosity over a recent matter, and even open your eyes to much wider issues. By the 21st–22nd your ambitions ought to be fired up, with career prospects looking rosier than ever. This present planetary influence has all the makings of success, and by the Full Moon of the 28th a decision you have made should turn into a personal triumph!

July: A time indicating better professional headway, even though a minor setback may irritate around the 5th–7th. Just don't overreact! The New Moon on the 10th makes career involvements all the more rewarding, with higher-ups looking favourably on you. However, on the 12th–14th your love life could be giving you a lot of trouble – you'll need to discuss serious issues with a partner. Another peak on the 18th–20th gives you the green light for personal aims, while from the 23rd onwards group encounters provide you with fulfilling moments. The 28th's Full Moon emphasises your sparkling and amiable personality.

August: There's much to be said for being part of a team now. Social life should take off around the 12th–13th, but don't expect too much co-operation as the month begins (there is a lunar low on the 2nd–3rd). On the New Moon of the 11th, someone may cause you to change your mind over a personal matter as you realise the truth about things. Mid-month ought to see professional aims on target and a far more self-willed, optimistic Libran. From the 2nd to 23rd keep your objectives much simpler, especially on the 29th–30th's lunar low.

September: Your influence over others may wane for much of the month. In fact you seem to be quite susceptible to their opinions and expectations – such may be obvious by the 9th's New Moon. The lunar high on the 11th–12th may represent your most favourable period when it comes to making important decisions and generally getting your own way (act while the going is good!). After the 16th you should find you've amassed much useful information and soon it will be a time to make use of it. From the 22nd to the 23rd you should be on a winning streak, making a powerful impact on those who can further your ambitions.

October: Mostly this is a month when you can call the shots wherever the major action is going on, and a brand new plan seems to have much going for it. Though the 4th–5th may seem somewhat of a chore, you're not short of creative ideas for making life happier. Around the time of the New Moon on the 9th (also a lunar high) you can easily get others on your side, and your objectives are likely to work out as expected. This progressive trend lasts through mid-month, though the lunar low of the 23rd–24th may signal its end. Thereafter, though, you consolidate in areas of work, property and finance.

November: This month, focus on making life as secure and settled as possible from the monetary point of view. No such advice is needed in love around the 9th–10th when romantic benefits may be on their way (possibly triggered by the lunar high, earlier on the 4th–6th). Don't get waylaid by trivial distractions mid-month – this is a time to be busy and productive, though results may fall off by the 19th–20th. The Full Moon of the 23rd may bring on some wanderlust, though this is easily satisfied by the planetary shift occurring around now. All travel and communication matters are set to work largely in your favour.

December: Positive trends now work through discussions and appointments, and your persuasiveness is strong. Financially, minor gains look possible around the 5th–7th, in fact up to the 8th New Moon. Mid-month, there's much to keep you happily on the go and stimulate your curiosity, but don't believe everything you hear from others without checking facts. Avoid pessimism on the 17th–18th (a lunar low), as things may look worse than they are. From the 22nd–23rd home life and family bring all the contentment you've ever needed!

SCORPIO

The Scorpion: a fixed water sign
October 24th–November 22nd

Your ruling planets: Mars and Pluto
Special day: Tuesday
Gems: topaz, malachite
Colours: dark green, aquamarine
Mental expression: determination
Celtic tree affiliation: the reed
Nature: powerful, reserved, penetrating mind

KEYNOTE for 1999: Opportunity may come knocking at work, though partnerships entail heavier responsibilities.

FAVOURABLE AND CHALLENGING DATES

	Social	Business	Travel	Challenging
Jan.	4th–6th, 20th–21st	7th–9th, 11th–12th	14th–15th, 25th–26th	24th–26th
Feb.	11th–13th, 19th–20th	7th–8th, 27th–28th	2nd–3rd, 9th–10th	21st–22nd
Mar.	2nd–3rd, 16th–17th	6th–8th, 18th–19th, 21st–22nd	12th–13th, 22nd–23rd	20th–21st
Apr.	12th–14th, 20th–21st	3rd–4th, 23rd–24th	8th–9th, 25th–26th	16th–17th
May	4th–5th, 24th–25th	1st, 6th–7th, 18th–19th	8th–9th, 29th–30th	14th–15th
Jun.	3rd–4th, 10th–11th, 23rd–25th	5th–7th, 15th–16th	1st–3rd, 21st–22nd	10th–11th
Jul.	10th–12th, 22nd–23rd	5th–7th, 23rd–24th	3rd–4th, 28th–29th	8th–9th
Aug.	10th–11th, 29th–30th	15th–16th, 17th–18th	1st–2nd, 25th	4th–5th, 31st
Sep.	2nd–3rd, 22nd–23rd	13th–15th, 28th–29th	17th–18th, 29th–30th	1st, 27th
Oct.	6th–8th, 15th–15th, 29th–30th	11th–12th, 19th–20th	13th–15th, 21st–22nd	25th–26th
Nov.	7th–8th, 14th–15th	1st–2nd, 22nd–23rd	12th–13th, 27th–29th	21st–22nd
Dec.	5th–6th, 19th–20th	11th–12th, 15th, 16th	16th–18th, 22nd–23rd, 25th–26th	19th–20th

MONTHLY FORECAST

January: Keeping abreast of major news and views this month is a good idea, though the year may get off to a sluggish start (something rather obvious by the 4th–6th) and your need for freedom (on the 2nd's Full Moon) may go unfulfilled. However, by the 7th–9th social happenings give you much in the way of inspiration – things start to look brighter. This is especially so on the lunar high of the 11th–12th when luck may easily come your way. Mid-month trends show new projects properly up and running, though the pace of life will probably slow down again from the 21st, especially with the lunar low on the 24th–26th.

February: Domestic involvements seem to be the main preoccupation for most of the month, though on the 11th–13th, issues keeping you in the social spotlight are very rewarding. This period may well see some new beginnings in friendship. Professional advantages may arise on the earlier lunar high of the 7th–8th, leading to favourable results against competitors. Thereafter, mid-month may pose minor drawbacks here (be prepared to act on impulse on these days). The latter part of the month sees a happier love life for you, when you should find yourself the prominent partner of the ship. But beware of the 'negative' lunar low on the 21st–22nd.

March: A stronger social theme is now under way and as early as the 6th–8th your charm is well received by all concerned. This may extend to the workplace where an encounter with a newcomer puts a smile on your face. The going is good here right up to the 17th's New Moon in fact, though by the 20th–21st you may feel somewhat deflated through minor setbacks (and possibly being left to your own devices too). The period around the 21st–22nd sees a more co-operative air in partnerships and this is just as well, since your workload may increase at this time. However, it seems there are few challenges you cannot handle.

April: Now is the time to join forces with partners if you're to get the most from life – you could even get more than you bargained for with the lunar high of the 3rd–4th. The 12th–14th should see you getting your own way in romantic attachments, though there may be less satisfaction in the workplace around the 16th's New Moon (a period when unexpected obligations may arise). From the 20th, however, practical matters go far more successfully.

May: Go-ahead trends are not too prominent early in the month – barring the 1st. Will-power and enthusiasm may soon sag, especially around the 3rd–5th, and though the 8th–9th shows pleasant social encounters, there may be little dynamic progress made elsewhere. Suspend major decision making around the 14th–15th – your judgement may be less than keen. From the 21st–22nd, however, you seem to thrive on change. This is a time when you need to uproot any unworkable situations and streamline your life. By the 27th–29th you may find the way ahead is clear for new personal initiatives and success in getting them off the ground.

June: Though your personal life may be rather unsettled, you seem prepared to rise to any challenge now. Career involvements are favoured on the 5th–7th, signifying both a boost in confidence and the chance to impress, though you may have to realise certain limitations around the 8th–9th – just get busy with priorities. The New Moon on the 13th may denote a crisis point in the need to renew and transform your life (much depends on actions you take now). From the 21st–22nd you should enjoy a more light-hearted, freewheeling phase, with some important news at last on its way with the Full Moon of the 28th.

July: 'Variety is the spice of life' seems to be your motto for much of the month, and around the 5th–7th you should have bags of energy for personal pursuits. Do avoid haste and impatience at work though, especially on the 8th–9th's lunar low when expectations should be kept at a minimum. Mid-month influences keep you involved socially and you may prefer freedom from a loved one now. By the 21st–22nd you can outdo much of the competition, especially in professional spheres, and from the 23rd–24th plans and schemes should be well under way with your powers and effectiveness at a peak.

August: Long-term ambitions and professional aims are likely to be within easier reach this month, and a word in the right ear on the 11th–12th should really make things happen (though the 4th–5th's lunar low is a caution to keep your sights realistic). Mid-month you should turn on the charm when it comes to getting what you want, especially on the 15th. A planetary 'lucky' boost on the 17th–18th may pave the way for an exciting social life around the 22nd–23rd, when teamwork issues tend to be your most rewarding area.

September: Success now comes mostly through group matters, whether business or pleasure. But trends on the 2nd–3rd show that money (and its acquisition) seems to be your main concern. Just don't let possessiveness extend to friends and partners. During mid-month (around the 16th–17th) you may be forced to reassess the effect you have on others. You may simply not have been 'getting through' to them, though the lunar high of the 13th–15th may have had you thinking everything was rosy! By the 23rd–24th it may be plain that a change of attitude towards others is necessary, though keeping a low profile may also be a good idea.

October: Your powers of persuasion and personal efficiency may now be on a downturn and this is not the best time for taking bold leaps. The quickened pace around the 4th–5th will either keep you on your toes or result in frustrations, though the 11th–12th's lunar high should put plans back on course and lead to some satisfying results. With careful planning for the short term, by the 23rd you should find new avenues will open for personal dreams and schemes. This is when you'll have a winning streak, and forge ahead with full confidence in your powers. You should get just what you want, except on the 25th–26th's lunar low!

November: A month when you should be at the forefront of important goings on, and Lady Luck seems to be on your side around the 7th–8th. However, your love life may be in the doldrums around the 9th–10th, reminding you you're not infallible! Mid-month influences continue to reveal your powerful impact on others. Your energy levels seem higher than usual, though burning the candle at both ends on the 20th–21st is unwise! The period following the unsettling Full Moon of the 23rd should see consolidation and security with rosier financial prospects – good for all kinds of monetary speculation or investment.

December: Property and financial interests are positively highlighted for much of the month, and you may want to splash out on something special where partners are concerned as the 5th–6th shows a boost to love life. Material trends continue smoothly mid-month, though the Full Moon of the 22nd may end this cycle. During the late month, from the 23rd, a hectic cycle begins – mental stimulus comes your way via travel and social discussions. However, your desire to get out and about may clash with a partner's needs during this period.

SAGITTARIUS

The Archer: a mutable fire sign
November 23rd–December 21st

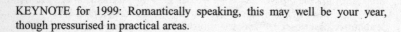

Your ruling planet: Jupiter
Special day: Thursday
Gem: turquoise
Colour: blue
Mental expression: creative vision
Celtic tree affiliation: elder
Nature: outspoken, optimistic, generous

KEYNOTE for 1999: Romantically speaking, this may well be your year, though pressurised in practical areas.

FAVOURABLE AND CHALLENGING DATES

	Social	Business	Travel	Challenging
Jan.	4th–5th, 24th–25th	13th–15th, 29th–30th	6th–7th, 15th–16th	27th–28th
Feb.	2nd–4th, 19th–20th	5th–7th, 10th–11th	1st–3rd, 15th–16th	23rd–24th
Mar.	2nd–4th, 20th–21st	9th–10th, 28th–29th	17th–18th, 29th–30th	22nd–23rd
Apr.	12th–15th, 16th–17th	5th–6th, 20th–22nd	14th–15th, 29th–30th	18th–19th
May	4th–6th, 20th–21st, 25th–27th	7th–9th, 11th–12th, 14th–15th	4th–5th, 25th–26th	16th–17th
Jun.	5th–7th, 8th, 14th–15th, 19th–20th	1st–2nd, 26th–27th	8th–9th, 21st–22nd	12th–13th
Jul.	12th–13th, 16th–17th	3rd–4th, 18th–19th, 23rd–24th	5th–6th, 22nd–23rd, 25th–26th	10th–11th
Aug.	12th–14th, 20th–21st	3rd–4th, 19th–21st, 23rd–24th	16th–17th, 30th–31st	6th–7th
Sep.	4th–5th, 22nd–23rd	13th–14th, 16th–17th	8th–9th, 23rd–24th	2nd–3rd, 29th–30th
Oct.	10th–11th, 14th–15th	7th–8th, 29th–30th	2nd–3rd, 13th–15th	1st, 27th, 28th
Nov.	9th–10th, 26th–27th	9th–11th, 22nd–23rd	5th–6th, 27th–29th	23rd–24th
Dec.	5th–6th, 19th–20th	7th–8th, 16th–18th	11th–12th, 22nd–23rd	21st–22nd

100

MONTHLY FORECASTS

January: Present trends favour matters connected with finance and the practical world for much of the month. This is a time for strengthening securities and building on any recent beginnings. Key dates in this respect are the Full Moon of the 2nd, and the 4th–6th. Mid-month, around the 13th–15th, should see a little luck coming your way – at least you shouldn't have to try too hard to make a success of things. And two days later, on the New Moon, there is potential for monetary gain. A planetary shift on the 20th–21st gives you the advantage where major decisions are at stake, but put things on the back burner for the 27th–28th.

February: For the major part of the month you should keep in touch with news and views coming your way. You never know what you might learn, especially on the 2nd–3rd, which is also a favourable period for vital discussion with superiors. From the lunar high of the 9th–11th to the 16th's New Moon any new ideas up your sleeve should be set in motion. You may find you're more successful than at other times, though it's also during this phase that a partner may require kid glove treatment over a personal issue. By the 19th–20th current demands slacken and your real focus should be domestic and family priorities.

March: Domestic matters continue to be the main focus of attention this month, though on the 2nd–4th romantic and social affairs help put a smile on your face. Don't be talked out of doing something you've set your mind on around the 9th–10th – this is a lunar high when superior judgement is yours. Trends in mid-month favour short journeys, if you can get away from duties in the home (where there are important things to decide on the New Moon of the 17th). Romantic and leisure pursuits put you happily in the limelight from the 20th to the 21st, though perhaps it's best not to push your luck on the 23rd–24th (a lunar low).

April: Good times through love and leisure seem to continue for Sagittarius for much of the month. The 5th–7th and 12th–14th are all key dates, the latter of which finds you with oodles of personal charm. As mid-month continues, get as much done on the practical level as you can, as the lunar low of the 18th–19th may see obstacles to progress. However, the influences of the 20th–21st assist whatever you're working towards, especially practical matters.

May: Material affairs and pet projects are, on the whole, favourably highlighted this month, though you may not want to meet others half way in group ventures on the 5th–6th. Striking out on your own would be the best way forward, especially on the 8th–9th – just make sure you're not being unrealistic with plans. The New Moon on the 15th shows success with tasks both old and new, but hang back with vital decisions on the 16th–17th's lunar low. From the 21st–22nd you seem to have the secret of popularity well worked out – you should get along with others famously now and partnerships should reach a peak.

June: One-to-one relationships are where you find fulfilment for much of the month, wherever you happen to be. There may be new faces on the horizon around the 5th–7th. However, far more serious concerns may arise round the 8th–9th, perhaps requiring some soul-searching on your part. You may be left in the dark over an important issue on the 12th–13th when the Moon is 'low' on your solar chart (wait until this brief period is over, then make your move). From the 21st–22nd you should make whatever changes are needed in personal affairs, and actions taken on the 26th–27th will prove vital.

July: Personal initiatives may be difficult to get going properly for much of the month, something you may discover too plainly on the 5th–7th. However, the 12th–14th (following possible setbacks on the two previous days) shows a minor boost to career prospects and much depends now on your diplomatic and tactical skills. The mid-month New Moon challenges you to get rid of some of life's dead wood, and if this is done successfully by the 23rd–24th there should be far more scope for individual freedom and the fulfilling of wishes. During the late month you'll be happy to have your eyes opened to the wider world beyond.

August: Your personal life ought to be far more settled, making getting out and about even more pleasurable. While on the 6th–7th you may be lacking in enthusiasm, this is a temporary lull which soon passes. By the 11th–12th it seems that social encounters help bring out the best in you – your sense of humour, for one. The 19th–21st are important dates when you'll see how strong your luck is, and the period following indicates planetary support for all matters professional – don't be surprised to find yourself with several advantages.

September: Long-term aims and career involvements are most satisfactory now and despite whatever challenges the lunar low of the 2nd–3rd may bring you should still come out on top. The 4th–5th, 13th–14th and 16th–17th are all 'go-ahead' days, so put your best foot forward to garner successful results. A romantic attachment during this mid-month period may ensure that you don't take everything in life for granted! From the 23rd onwards teamwork and co-operative matters have a more important role to play, and it's not the best time to be wrapped up in your ego – and the same goes for the 29th–30th.

October: The month may get off to an uninspiring start. On the 1st you may have to make heavy compromises to get anywhere near having your own way. The 5th–6th may lead to misunderstandings caused by poor communication. Try to make yourself clear to others now, as a crisis point may be reached on the 9th's New Moon. Trends look set to improve around the 13th–15th (a lunar high) when you seem to be getting things right again! But this may be short lived. The planetary picture from the 23rd–24th indicates a tailing off of personal success, and then you may have to be content with small things.

November: You may be more motivated by what you can do for others (as opposed to personal gain) for much of the time. It seems that group involvements do have a lot going for them, especially on the 9th–10th, while the following day looks good for taking minor risks. Mid-month influences may allow little chance for personal advancement, though that is set to change on the 21st–22nd when your star is on the rise again! Favourable new trends make initiatives go with a swing and your confidence should soar. Around the 23rd–24th, however, a Full Moon advises taking careful thought about major aims.

December: On the whole this is a month when you ought to have more personal kudos than at other times (a peak time being the lunar high on the 7th–8th). The only area that seems to be less than exciting is close relationships (a situation may require attention on the 5th–6th). If you can keep pace with others on the 11th–12th, life ought to be fairly rewarding. From the 23rd favourable developments arise in financial and property spheres – you may find unexpected bonuses coming your way over the festive season!

CAPRICORN

The Goat: a cardinal earth sign
December 22nd–January 20th

Your ruling planet: Saturn
Special day: Saturday
Gems: white onyx, moonstone, garnet
Colour: indigo
Mental expression: concentration
Celtic tree affiliation: birch
Nature: self-controlled, aspiring, serious, responsible

KEYNOTE for 1999: Domestically a fulfilling period, yet your love life may not be without challenges in some way.

FAVOURABLE AND CHALLENGING DATES

	Social	Business	Travel	Challenging
Jan.	5th–7th, 14th–15th	3rd–4th, 16th–17th	12th–13th, 19th–20th	1st–2nd, 29th–30th
Feb.	12th–13th, 16th–17th	2nd–3rd, 18th–20th, 23rd–24th	5th–6th, 22nd–23rd	25th–26th
Mar.	12th–14th, 18th–19th	3rd–4th, 11th–13th, 23rd–24th	16th–17th, 30th–31st	25th–26th
Apr.	12th–14th, 25th–26th	8th–9th, 25th–27th	14th–15th, 16th–17th	20th–22nd
May	1st–2nd, 14th–15th	8th–9th, 1st–2nd	12th–13th, 27th–28th	5th–6th
Jun.	4th–6th, 7th–9th, 21st–22nd	1st–3rd, 15th–16th, 28th–30th	2nd–3rd, 24th–25th	12th–13th
Jul.	2nd–4th, 19th–20th	5th–7th, 10th–11th	14th–15th, 16th–17th	12th–13th
Aug.	2nd–4th, 15th–16th	10th–12th, 22nd–23rd	2nd–3rd, 24th–25th	8th–9th
Sep.	9th–10th, 26th–27th	4th–5th, 23rd–25th	16th–17th	18th–20th
Oct	5th–6th, 23rd–24th	16th–17th, 19th–20th	7th–8th, 16th–18th	2nd–3rd, 29th–30th
Nov.	5th–6th, 16th–17th, 19th–20th, 23rd–24th	12th–13th, 14th–15th, 23rd–24th, 27th–28th	2nd–4th, 18th–19th	25th–26th
Dec.	5th–6th, 22nd–23rd	2nd–3rd, 9th–11th	11th–13th, 28th–30th	23rd–24th

MONTHLY FORECASTS

January: A period when your powers seem to be at a peak. Though the lunar low of the 1st–2nd is unrewarding, the 3rd–4th seems tailor-made for professional advancement and you should find authority figures looking upon you with some favour. On the 7th–8th your quick thinking may well save the day! The mid-month New Moon on the 17th is an energy peak when you can accomplish a great deal – very successfully too. The 20th–21st is a favourable period for getting settled financially. Where other projects are concerned, channelling energies into one main priority is a wise move. The 29th–30th however, may be a low point.

February: Financial matters and 'me and mine' are the priorities now. By the 2nd–3rd you should have more control over budgetary issues, which will help planning for the short term. On the 12th–13th you may have to dig in your heels over a recent decision you've made, while the mid-month New Moon on the 17th may see a money matter showing potential for increase. From the 19th–20th improved communication is crucial as life gets busier (though far more interesting, too). However, the 25th and 26th are lunar low days when important decisions are best left to a trusted colleague or adviser.

March: This is a good time to put your persuasive tongue to work in any negotiations or discussions, and it could help put your current objectives on target around the 2nd–4th (even though there may be little peace and quiet at home). From the lunar high on the 11th–13th up to the New Moon of the 17th, personal objectives should see success with half the usual effort. Thereafter the productive phase may slacken off. Family involvements from the 20th–21st are especially enjoyable, as are trips down memory lane. There may, however, be professional let downs around the 25th–26th: keep a lid on all ambitions at this time.

April: Involvements through familiar faces and places bring out the best in you now, and the 8th–9th may see an unexpected encounter with a figure from your past. Mid-month, a helping hand may be required in a current endeavour. Seek out those in the know, especially where vital decisions are to be made on the 17th. After the dispiriting lunar low on the 20th–22nd, your love life looks set to be more eventful and enjoyable.

May: Your ego is in the ascendant now, and you make entertaining company for most folks, though not all will warm to you on the 1st–2nd! The 5th–8th is a period when you ought to steam ahead with ambitions since early triumph may result from efforts made now. The only caution here is not to take yourself too much for granted when dealing with higher ups. The mid-month lunar low (on the 12th–13th) may show little scope for personal gain. In fact you might be inclined to put yourself at others' disposal, assisting with their plans and schemes. From the 21st onwards you should return to efficient work and career matters.

June: Favourable influences fall on the workplace now, and round the 5th–6th there seems to be plenty of reassurance and support from loved ones, emotionally and moneywise. Certain long-term objectives are best left on the shelf on the 12th–13th, though this seems an excellent time to simply rest and relax. One-to-one relationships may be the source of personal happiness from the 21st to the 22nd when things go far better in pairs, though late month trends look good for ambitious Capricorns. The New Moon in your sign on the 28th shows strong potential for a successful fresh start, maybe in your career.

July: Partnerships of all kinds receive the most beneficial planetary highlights this month, though going solo around the 5th–7th may be preferable in light of the compromise you'd have to make. The New Moon on the 13th, while indicating that your strength of will may be dwindling, seems excellent for travel pursuits. Get away from the routine if you can at this time, or at least find ways of broadening your horizons. By the 23rd, it may be obvious that certain situations in your life have run their course – the challenge now is to be rid of what's no longer of value. Look forward to the 'lucky' 26th and 27th too.

August: Support systems may be put to the test early in the month and the message is still 'off with the old, on with the new', something you ought to have set about by the 11th–12th – try to make life less complex. The New Moon on the 11th may be critical in this respect, but thereafter your personal life ought to feel more settled. There is a romantic bonus mid-month too, reducing much recent pressure, and by the 22nd onwards you seem to do far better with personal dreams and schemes. But freedom is really the key to happiness at this time.

September: Opt for a change of scenery and get as much variety into your life as possible now (the 4th–5th should see most of your wishes fulfilled). Getting along with others may have its drawbacks on the 6th–7th. A cautious approach is advised in personal encounters, or you may find someone taking the wind out of your sails! Mid-month looks to be favourable for collecting useful information with regard to present ambitions. Get ready to act, so long as it's not on the lunar low of the 18th–20th! Beneficial influences affect your career life from the 23rd – it looks like it's the time to take a step up the ladder somehow.

October: Though professional developments continue to give you a firm footing, you should play things safe on the lunar low of the 2nd–3rd when potential pitfalls are around. Socially, around the 5th–6th it seems that most folk want to be on your good side, and by the 9th's New Moon personal favours may be coming your way in your professional life. Mid-month continues to see you in an enterprising mood, especially on the 16th–17th. Long-range hopes and aspirations may preoccupy you in late month – now is the time to make plans. Socially, while this is mostly a beneficial phase, you may be let down on the 29th–30th.

November: A period that catches you more in the social mainstream, to the point where your personality really shines on the 9th–10th – others' eyebrows may well be raised! The New Moon on the 8th should see teamwork matters succeeding, while there is room for improvement in personal objectives with the lunar high of the 12th–13th. Thereafter, the pace of life may slow down somewhat (certainly by the 21st, when you may be steeped in the past's emotional issues). But your love life seems to be quite rewarding now. Also, a new trend from the 26th stirs you into life, turning you into something of the go-getter of old!

December: The month mainly centres on matters of private concern. Your need for seclusion may be strong (though the 5th–6th may shower you with social invitations!). Your 'luckiest' moments probably come on the 9th–11th when taking chances with life seems reasonably safe. The desire to withdraw may be apparent mid-month too (on the 12th–13th), but what's really vital now is clear communication, especially with loved ones. After the mood-making 23rd, your sunny personality is evident to all concerned!

AQUARIUS

The Water-bearer: a fixed, airy sign
January 21st–February 19th

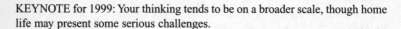

Your ruling planets: Saturn and Uranus
Special day: Saturday
Gems: amethyst
Colour: violet
Mental expression: experimental
Celtic tree affiliation: rowan
Nature: truthful, independent, humanitarian

KEYNOTE for 1999: Your thinking tends to be on a broader scale, though home life may present some serious challenges.

FAVOURABLE AND CHALLENGING DATES

	Social	Business	Travel	Challenging
Jan.	5th–6th, 23rd–24th	2nd–4th, 19th–21st	7th–8th, 16th–18th	3rd–5th, 31st
Feb.	5th–6th, 14th–16th, 23rd–24th	2nd–3rd, 12th–13th	15th–16th, 22nd–24th	1st, 27th–28th
Mar.	2nd–3rd, 22nd–23rd	14th–15th, 17th–18th	3rd–4th, 29th–30th	27th–28th
Apr.	12th–14th, 25th–26th	10th–11th, 14th–15th	15th–17th, 20th–21st	23rd–24th
May	1st–2nd, 9th–10th	7th–9th, 23rd–24th	5th–6th, 22nd	20th–21st
Jun.	6th–7th, 14th–15th	4th–5th, 8th–9th, 21st–22nd	1st–2nd, 22nd–23rd	16th–17th
Jul.	5th–7th, 23rd–24th	1st, 3rd–4th, 16th–17th, 28th–29th	12th–13th, 29th–30th	14th–15th
Aug.	12th–13th, 16th–17th	2nd–3rd, 24th–26th	5th–6th, 23rd–24th	10th–11th
Sep.	3rd–4th, 18th–19th	16th–17th, 21st–22nd	9th–10th, 28th–30th	6th–8th
Oct.	2nd–4th, 19th–20th	18th–20th, 23rd–24th	14th–15th, 18th–20th	4th–5th
Nov.	9th–10th, 21st, 26th	9th–11th, 14th–16th	18th–19th, 28th–30th	1st, 27th
Dec.	12th–14th, 27th–28th	5th–6th, 12th–13th	16th–17th	25th–26th

MONTHLY FORECASTS

January: You may find much of the month pretty low key when it comes to getting ahead, and the early lunar low of the 3rd–5th is hardly very inspiring. On the 7th–8th you may be left in the dark regarding the outcome of a personal decision (patience is best now). It may not be until mid-month that the wheels of progress really turn, after the New Moon of the 17th when there is a two-day peak in your fortunes. This should set the ball rolling for short-term future success and by the 20th–21st you ought to feel much more like your old self. Even challenges during late month (26th–27th and 31st) leave you largely unmoved!

February: Peak powers in both personal and professional life should make this largely a successful time. Keeping up a high profile on the 2nd–3rd can only work in your favour. Finances should be far less limited on the 12th–13th, and in fact there is every possibility for gain now. On the 14th–15th's lunar high you can do much to sway those who might do you favours. The New Moon on the 16th may point you in a rather different – and much better – direction. By the 19th–20th gain through monetary speculation seems to be on the agenda, though avoid risky gambles on the last two days of the month.

March: While you should focus on making plans and ideas more concrete during the early part of the month, a slower, more studied approach to life may be in order on the 2nd–4th. Keep to one or two simple priorities. Mid-month trends around the 14th–15th may result in favours from colleagues and partners that make a world of difference to your plans. The 17th's New Moon may bring some of the 'good things of life' your way, but it looks as if you've earned them! From the 20th–21st a much more expansive social atmosphere gets you out and about. This is a good time for day trips, bar the 'unlucky' lunar low of the 27th–28th.

April: Positive communication is the key to success this month. What you hear from others may prove vital, especially on the lunar high of the 10th–11th. The leisurely side to life should be prominent around the 12th–13th and you seem to be many folks' favourite now. The 16th may bring in a brief hectic phase, though by the 20th–21st home life and domesticity are the trends in operation and there may be an opportunity to relive the past.

May: Family life tends to bring out the best in you in early month, though mixed influences around the 5th–6th indicate a sense of wanderlust where you need to broaden both mental and physical horizons. The 7th–8th seems to have an underlying element of good fortune, when important moves should be made, while the New Moon of the 15th should see a matter close to your heart settled once and for all. The stamina you need to make life a success may be missing on the 20th–21st, but thereafter new planetary trends help you shine in social and romantic situations – the onset of a mostly enjoyable period.

June: You seem to be popular with everybody right now, and your love life should prove eventful and exciting around the 6th–7th. Any ambitious ideas you want to set in motion around the 8th–9th should now receive the 'green light' – move decisively. However, mid-month trends around the 16th–17th may see sluggish progress, so it's best to keep expectations modest. From the 20th–21st plans and schemes get a boost as efficiency improves, and at work things seem to be in far better focus.

July: You may be just a little too impatient for your own good around the 5th–7th, for although your ambitions are stronger the results you seek will require patient and methodical effort. Emotional support from loved ones will be a comfort on the 12th–14th, but its also nice to give! The New Moon of the 13th may kick start a new idea of yours. But don't neglect other responsibilities, especially on the 14th–15th's lunar low – no matter how demanding! By the 23rd–24th one-to-one relationships are your most favourable area, and there may be social newcomers on the horizon.

August: There seems to be much greater emphasis on social life this month and most encounters with others go smoothly. Though the New Moon of the 11th may disappoint where others are concerned, the 12th–13th and 15th–16th are dates when romance and friendships should work in your favour and without much effort on your part. Later in the month, trends around the 24th may force you to make serious changes to your personal routine (this will eventually be all for the best, though it may not seem so at the time). Around the 26th, however, some light will be seen at the end of the tunnel.

September: Renewal and revitalisation in your personal life are now the keys to success, and by the 4th–5th it may even be plain that something has to be abandoned if you are to move ahead. The lunar low of the 6th–8th may be particularly challenging in this respect, but don't expect miracles! The New Moon on the 9th keeps this theme going, though breaking with the past should now prove easier. Mid-month may find you at loggerheads with others and the safest method is to agree to disagree (especially on the 16th–17th). From the 24th onwards you will feel generally more secure and there are high spirits around this time too.

October: Individual freedom now becomes the overriding theme, at least if you want to stay happy. Try not to get stuck with too many mundane obligations, especially around the 2nd–5th, when you may find you're doing a little more than treading water. The New Moon of the 9th tends to bring you into contact with the new and unusual (it's also a favourable period to travel). Taking large steps with current projects is inadvisable around the 16th–17th – wait until the following two days. However, from the 23rd–24th you should see the beginning of new progress in your job or profession, and you're moving more in the frame for calling the shots.

November: Professional developments continue to bring rewards, and a step up the ladder shouldn't be impossible this month – though the 1st hardly delivers expectations here. The 9th–10th may find you in the right place at the right time. During mid-month, the lunar high on the 14th–16th may see both personal and professional favours coming your way – make the most of this influence. By the 21st–22nd, group activities seem to dominate and there may be fruitful encounters with influential folk. Around the 26th–27th you seem to have a far more competitive streak, but don't go tilting at windmills on the 28th!

December: A month that should find you happily in the social spotlight. Where important affairs are afoot teamwork is the way forward, though you won't be able to please all the people all the time on the 10th–11th. The mid-month lunar high on the 12th–13th may be the last real opportunity before the holiday season for reaping the benefit from important plans and schemes. From the 22nd–23rd you may be drawn back much more into issues arising from the past. Family life is especially rewarding now, though avoid moody behaviour on the 25th–26th.

PISCES

The Fishes: a mutable, water sign
February 20th–March 20th

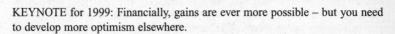

Your ruling planets: Jupiter and Neptune
Special day: Thursday
Gems: chrysolite, bloodstone
Colour: deep purple or bluish purple
Mental expression: insight
Celtic tree affiliation: ash
Nature: sympathetic, easy-going, imaginative

KEYNOTE for 1999: Financially, gains are ever more possible – but you need to develop more optimism elsewhere.

FAVOURABLE AND CHALLENGING DATES

	Social	*Business*	*Travel*	*Challenging*
Jan.	7th–8th, 16th–17th	3rd–4th, 20th–21st	14th–15th, 28th–29th	6th–7th
Feb.	12th–13th, 19th–20th	4th–5th, 16th–18th	5th–6th, 26th–27th	2nd–3rd
Mar.	5th–6th, 23rd–24th	2nd–4th, 16th–17th, 21st–23rd	7th–8th, 18th–19th	1st, 29th, 30th
Apr.	12th–13th, 23rd–24th	12th–13th, 16th–17th	2nd–4th, 9th–11th	25th–26th
May.	1st–3rd, 20th–21st	10th, 11th, 14th–16th	7th–8th, 29th–30th	22nd–24th
Jun.	8th–9th, 12th–13th, 21st–22nd	6th–7th, 14th–15th	4th–5th, 15th–16th	19th–20th
Jul.	1st–2nd, 12th–13th	3rd–4th, 23rd–24th, 30th–31st	5th–6th, 28th	14th–15th
Aug.	6th–7th, 14th–15th, 24th–25th	1st–3rd, 8th–9th, 27th–28th	1st–2nd, 22nd–23rd	12th–14th
Sep.	1st–2nd, 14th–15th	7th–9th, 23rd–24th	5th–6th, 29th–30th	9th–10th
Oct.	4th–6th, 16th–17th	9th–10th, 21st–22nd	11th–12th, 26th–27th	6th–7th
Nov.	2nd–4th, 9th–11th	9th–10th, 17th–18th, 21st–22nd	4th–5th, 23rd–24th	2nd–3rd, 29th–30th
Dec.	5th–6th, 22nd–23rd	10th–11th, 14th–16th	5th–7th, 26th	1st, 27th, 28th

109

MONTHLY FORECASTS

January: The focus is on group encounters and goings on in the social mainstream this month, with you tending to stand out from the crowd during the Full Moon of the 2nd. However, closer to home someone may prove rather irksome on the 4th–5th, requiring greater compromise than you'd expected. Social life continues to be fulfilling early on, especially on the 7th–8th – a positive trend continuing right up to the New Moon of the 17th. Around the 20th–21st you may be forced to look within to a private matter. As far as outer ambitions go this is likely to be a low key phase, though lifted briefly by the lunar high.

February: The pace of life may be rather slow for much of the month, and in the period around the 2nd–3rd you seem to keep in the background. Perhaps it's best this way with the Moon in your opposite sign! By the 12th–13th you can balance times of withdrawal with energetic social activity (you never know what you might learn too!). Mid-month sees your 'luckiest' time, but even here results may be no more than moderate. The New Moon on the 16th focuses on intimate issues and now is the time to reach a final agreement on an emotional matter with a partner. From the 20th onwards all your personal strengths make a reappearance!

March: This is the month to focus on what you really want. New initiatives get the go-ahead around the 2nd–4th (after a dull start on the 1st), and whatever is working well in your life should not be changed now. The 17th's New Moon offers the possibility of a break with past ties and the chance to do something completely new. It should also garner warm responses from friends and colleagues. A beneficial period regarding money and property begins on the 21st when getting what you want from life involves much less struggle. However, this may not be true for the 29th's lunar low – just cease striving for now!

April: Life on the whole may prove far more stable this month. This may have much to do with your improved financial prospects around the 12th–13th (a lunar high) and some of life's luxuries coming your way on the New Moon of the 16th. Mid-month, your love life seems quite rewarding and by the 20th–21st the pace of everyday life increases, bringing new input and inspiration. But avoid situations involving personal risk on the 25th–26th.

May: The month mainly centres on communication issues in the outer world, though your attention may be caught on the 5th–6th with certain upside down matters at home. Give others the benefit of the doubt if you feel you're being led up the garden path. The lunar high on the 10th–11th should set certain matters right and it's also a favourable period for important discussions and negotiation. The New Moon on the 15th should put you in the picture over a recent personal objective – the way ahead is now clear. Active trends tail off from the 20th–21st when family concerns become more of a priority.

June: Personal and domestic concerns now bring out the best in you, though there are social bonuses to be had on the 4th–5th when others find out how charming and entertaining you can be. Your 'luckiest' moments probably arrive round the 6th–7th when taking chances with life may lead to more than you'd expect. Mid-month influences around the 13th may find you as the 'stay at home', with the focus on your nearest and dearest. The lunar low of the 19th–20th may be somewhat wearisome, though from the 21st your sunny side is uppermost and life probably seems fulfilling and enjoyable – time for leisure!

July: Your love life and romance should be generally uplifting and eventful this month (certainly by the 12th), though first you may have to tackle others on a personal issue around the 5th–7th. The New Moon on the 13th ought to find you the centre of attention and your powers of attraction are now at a premium, though the following two days may see a slight decline in your personal charms! From the 23rd–24th positive new work trends are in operation, when getting plans up and running seems easier than usual. However, the 30th–31st should be viewed as a break from important activities and ambitious thinking.

August: Practical involvements may mean you really have your work cut out, so to speak, during the early part of the month, but your objectives now seem in reach. The 1st, 2nd and 3rd are all 'go-ahead' days, as is the progressive New Moon on the 11th. Mid-month may cause second thoughts about a partner – just keep expectations realistic here, especially on the 16th. From the 24th personal relationships are much more positively highlighted with possible new friendships in the offing – get out and about.

September: You can look forward to much busier social encounters this month, though not necessarily successful ones. As early as the 4th–5th you may have difficulty as a team player and relating to groups. However, encounters with close friends should go smoothly. The lunar low of the 9th–10th disappoints where practical achievements are concerned, though the 16th and 17th are rewarding days when intimate matters between yourself and a loved one work well. Late-month influences around the 23rd may augur changes to your personal life. It's best simply to go with the flow – this is a lunar high pointing you in the right direction.

October: This month, areas of your life that need revitalising should come to light. Though pressures may seem difficult to bear on the 2nd–3rd, changes made now should soon turn out to be all for the best. By the New Moon of the 9th you should be able to see ahead far more clearly. Mid-month, around the 16th–17th, should find you getting along famously with others and there may be pleasant new acquaintances to make now. The lunar high of the 21st should herald a far more uplifting period that helps widen your personal horizons and generally get far more out of life. This is an excellent time for extensive travel.

November: You may well find you have more freedom and time on your hands to pursue hobbies and personal aims this month, despite possible early setbacks with the lunar low on the 2nd–3rd. A partner may come up trumps financially wherever help is really needed around the 9th–10th. During mid-month, major aims are not only on target but you could score a bulls-eye with moves made now (watch out for the lunar high on the 17th–18th!). From the 21st onwards career developments really take off. Large steps taken now could prove very beneficial in the near future. This is a time when you can easily impress superiors, too.

December: Professional matters move ahead as planned this month – the bigger your thinking, the better! The early part of the month is favourable for social life too (look forward to something new and uplifting around the 5th–6th). The New Moon of the 8th may well be a lucky time to make an ambitious decision. Even if you want to change your mind later, you have the 10th or 11th on which to do it (mid-month also indicates good fortune!). From the 22nd onwards benefits will come from group activities – the more the merrier, in fact.

RACING WITH THE FLAT RACE AND STEEPLECHASE JOCKEYS 1999

The astrologically compiled dates below are presented to racegoers in the hope that they will point the way to some successful winning periods during the 1999 racing season.

The favourable periods of Flat Race Jockeys

F. DETTORI, born 15th December 1970, should be noted on short-priced 2-year-old and 3-year-old horses. His winning periods are: March 12th to 21st (17th to 19th specially recommended), 26th to 29th, April 1st to 8th (3rd to 5th s.r.), 10th to 12th, 16th to 30th (28th s.r.), May 3rd to 6th (4th s.r.), 8th to 13th (12th, 13th s.r.), 20th to 22nd, 27th to 29th, June 2nd to 7th (6th s.r.), 10th to 13th, 19th to 22nd (20th s.r.), 25th to 27th (27th s.r.), July 2nd to 4th, 6th, 7th, 13th to 15th, 19th to 24th (20th to 23rd s.r.), 29th to 31st, August 1st to 23rd (6th to 8th s.r.), 27th to 31st (31st s.r.), September 3rd to 8th (7th, 8th s.r.), 11th to 15th, 21st to 25th, 29th, 30th (both s.r.), October 4th to 10th, 13th to 16th (15th s.r.), 20th to 24th (22nd s.r.), 29th to 31st (all s.r.), November 6th to 15th (13th s.r.), 21st, 22nd.

K. FALLON, born 22nd February 1965, should be noted on low-weighted 2-year-old and 3-year-old horses. His winning periods are: March 17th to 30th (27th specially recommended), April 7th to 9th, 19th to 24th (all s.r.), 26th to 28th, May 1st, 7th to 13th (9th, 10th s.r.), 17th to 19th, 24th to 31st, June 1st, 7th to 9th (7th, 8th s.r.), 16th, 17th, 23rd to 29th (27th, 28th s.r.), July 3rd to 6th (all s.r.), 20th to 31st (20th to 22nd, 26th, 29th s.r.), August 9th to 16th, 19th to 27th (24th, 25th s.r.), 31st, September 1st to 4th, 9th to 11th (9th, 10th s.r.), 14th to 20th (17th to 20th s.r.), 25th to 28th (27th, 28th s.r.), October 9th to 12th, 17th to 19th, 25th to 31st (all s.r.), November 1st to 11th (9th s.r.), 14th to 17th.

K. DARLEY, born 5th August 1960, should be noted on low-weighted 2-year-old and 3-year-old horses in short-distance races. He should have a very good year. His winning periods are: March 15th, 16th, 20th, 27th to 29th, April 1st, 2nd, 5th, 6th, 16th to 18th, 20th to 24th, 29th, 30th, May 1st to 3rd (1st, 2nd specially recommended), 5th to 7th (6th s.r.), 16th to 24th (17th s.r.), 29th, June 5th to 8th (6th, 7th s.r.), 13th to 27th (16th to 22nd s.r.), July 1st to 7th (3rd, 4th s.r.), 18th to 20th, 22nd to 24th, 29th to 31st s.r., August 1st to 12th (3rd to 5th s.r.), 19th to 26th (19th to 22nd s.r.), September 1st to 7th, 14th to 24th (15th to 22nd s.r.), 29th, 30th, October 1st to 10th (4th to 9th s.r.), 19th to 31st (24th, 25th s.r.), November 1st to 15th (3rd to 5th, 7th, 9th s.r.).

N. WILLIAMSON, born 16th January 1969, should be noted on low-weighted 4-year-old horses and short-priced mares. His fortunate periods are: January 1st to 6th, 14th to 18th, 25th to 31st (28th to 31st specially recommended). February 1st, 2nd, 12th to 20th (14th to 19th s.r.), March 2nd to 4th (all s.r.), 14th to 18th (16th to 18th s.r.), 27th to 31st, April 1st to 13th (8th to 10th s.r.), 16th to 23rd (18th s.r.), 21st to 23rd, 29th, May 1st to 7th (4th to 7th s.r.), 10th to 15th, 17th to 20th (18th, 19th, s.r.), August 3rd to 5th, 18th to 23rd (19th to 23rd s.r.), 28th to 31st (29th to 31st s.r.), September 1st to 10th (6th, 7th s.r.), 14th to 24th (16th to 23rd s.r.), 27th to 30th, October 1st, to 7th, 10th to 25th (13th to 22nd s.r.), 31st. November and December: he will have an exceptionally good period and should be considered every time he rides.

A. McCOY, born 4th May 1974, should be noted on high-weighted and short-priced 3-year-old horses. His winning periods are: January 1st, 2nd, 7th to 15th (12th to 15th specially recommended), 23rd, 27th to 29th, February 3rd, 4th, 11th to 14th (12th, 13th s.r.), 26th to 28th, March 1st, 12th to 30th (10th to 14th s.r.), April 6th to 21st (10th to 15th s.r.), 27th to 29th, May 1st to 31st (3rd, 4th, 10th, 11th, 13th to 17th, 20th to 23rd s.r.), August 1st, 15th to 19th (18th s.r.), 24th to 31st (27th s.r.), September 1st to 5th, 12th to 30th (30th s.r.), October 1st, 2nd (both s.r.), 10th, 11th, 15th to 19th (16th to 18th s.r.), 22nd to 24th, 30th, 31st, November 1st, 14th to 17th (14th to 16th s.r.), 29th, 30th (both s.r.), December 1st, 4th to 7th, 12th to 17th (15th to 17th s.r.), 24th to 30th.

A. MAGUIRE, born 29th April 1971, should be noted on 3-year-old and 4-year-old horses racing on soft ground. His winning periods are: January 1st to 11th, 15th to 31st (15th to 18th specially recommended), February 1st to 12th (1st to 3rd s.r.), 17th to 21st (18th to 20th s.r.), 26th to 28th, March 1st to 5th, 16th to 31st (18th to 25th s.r.), April 1st to 3rd, 8th to 10th, 15th to 30th (21st to 24th s.r.), May 4th to 7th, 14th to 23rd, 27th to 31st, August 1st to 31st (5th, 6th, 20th to 22nd s.r.), September 1st to 4th, 12th to 15th, 24th to 29th (20th to 22nd s.r.), October 3rd to 6th, 13th to 28th (18th to 20th s.r.), November 2nd to 26th (5th, 13th to 20th s.r.), December 6th to 20th (7th to 17th s.r.), 27th to 30th (28th, 29th s.r.).

PLANETARY AND COSMIC PHENOMENA IN 1999

ECLIPSES DURING THE YEAR

When the Moon interposes itself between the Earth and the light of the Sun an eclipse of the Sun occurs. For this to happen, the Sun and the Moon must be in conjunction. When the Earth interposes itself between the light of the Sun and the Moon a lunar eclipse occurs. In this case, the Sun and Moon are in opposition.

During 1999 there will be three eclipses, two of the Sun, and one of the Moon.

I – An annular eclipse of the Sun on 16th February is visible as a partial eclipse from southern Africa, Madagascar, the Indian Ocean, Malaysia, the Philippines, the Southern Ocean, Australia and Antarctica. It begins at 03h. 52m. and ends at 09h. 15m. The track of the annular phase crosses the Southern Ocean and the Indian Ocean before crossing Australia and ending in the Coral Sea. The annular phase begins at 04h. 57m. and ends at 08h. 11m. The maximum duration is 1m. 18s.

II – A partial eclipse of the Moon occurs on 28th July and is visible from the Americas, the Pacific Ocean, Australasia, eastern Asia, the Indian Ocean and Antarctica. The eclipse begins at 10h. 22m. and ends at 12h. 45m. At maximum 40 per cent of the Moon's diameter is obscured.

III – A total eclipse of the Sun on 11th August is visible as a partial eclipse from eastern North America, Greenland, Iceland, the Atlantic Ocean, Europe, Asia, northern Africa, Asia and the Indian Ocean. It starts at 08h. 26m. and ends at 13h. 40m. The path of totality starts in the Atlantic Ocean just south of Newfoundland, and crosses extreme south-west England, northern France, Germany, Austria, Hungary, Romania, northern Bulgaria, Turkey, northern Iraq, Iran, Pakistan, and ends in the Indian Ocean just east of India.

All times are in GMT.

The Planets and the Solar System

Times when the planets will be most favourably situated for observation in northern latitudes during 1999

The Sun

Diameter	865,300 miles (1,392,500 km)
Period of rotation on its axis (at equator)	25 days

By galactic standards, the Sun is a fairly ordinary star. From its colour (luminosity) and temperature (about 10,000°C) it is classed as a yellow dwarf. About 98 per cent of the mass of the solar system is contained in the Sun.

Observations of sunspots have helped astronomers to calculate the axial rotation of the Sun. Because it is not a solid body, rotation at the equator is shorter than at higher latitudes (at the poles it is thought to be about 35 days)

The Earth

Diameter	7,927 miles (12,757 km)
Mean distance from the Sun	93,000,000 miles (150,000,000 km)
Time taken to revolve round the Sun	365 days 6 hours
Period of rotation on its axis	24 hours

Like all the planets, the Earth moves eastwards round the Sun in an elliptical orbit. When its distance to the Sun is closest (about the beginning of January), the Earth is in its perihelion; at its longest (about the beginning of July), it is in its aphelion.

The Moon

Diameter	2,163 miles (3,481 km)
Mean distance from the Earth	238,857 miles (384,403 km)
Time of revolution round the Earth	27 days 7 hrs 43 mins 11secs

The Moon is about a quarter of the size of the Earth, which is relatively large for a satellite. It does not actually revolve round the centre of the Earth – both revolve round a common centre of gravity.

Mercury

Diameter	3,100 miles (5,000 km)
Mean distance from the Sun	36,000,000 miles (58,000,000 km)
Time taken to revolve round the Sun	88 days
Period of rotation on its axis	59 days

Mercury is the innermost and smallest planet of the solar system. There is a virtual lack of atmosphere, resulting in a wide range of temperatures at different parts of its surface and according to whether it is day or night (up to 425ºC and as low as −180ºC). The surface is similar to that of the Moon, rocky and covered with craters and mountains.

Being so close to the Sun (never more than 28º away), Mercury can only be seen under exceptional circumstances just after sunset or just before sunrise. When favourably placed for observation, Mercury presents a bright and sparkling appearance. When viewed through a telescope it shows phases similar to those of the Moon.

Mercury is only visible for a few days in the west after sunset around 3rd March, 28th June, and 24th October, and for a few days low in the east before sunrise around 16th April, 14th August and 3rd December.

Venus

Diameter	7,700 miles (12,400 km)
Mean distance from the Sun	67,000,000 miles (108,000,000 km)
Time taken to revolve round the Sun	225 days
Period of rotation on its axis	243 days

The second in distance from the Sun, the planet Venus is the brightest object in the sky apart from the Sun and the Moon. Its brilliance is due to dense clouds, mainly of carbon dioxide, which completely hide the surface. The greenhouse effect produced by this atmosphere has resulted in searing surface temperatures (about 450ºC). Atmospheric pressures are about 90 times those on the Earth's surface. Radar mapping from spacecraft has revealed rolling planes and some continent-sized mountainous regions.

Venus is a brilliant object in the west in the evenings after sunset until mid-August. From late August until the end of the year it is visible in the east in the morningss before sunrise.

Mars

Diameter	4,200 miles (6,800 km)
Mean distance from the Sun	142,000,000 miles (229,000,000 km)
Time taken to revolve round the Sun	687 days
Period of rotation on its axis	24 hrs 37 mins 23 secs
Moons	2

The planet Mars lies outside the orbit of the Earth. Much information about the planet has been obtained by *Mariner* space probes and the *Viking I* and *II* spacecraft landings. The reddish colour of Mars arises from large amounts of red dust, which can be carried high up in the thin atmosphere by winds. The atmosphere consists mainly of carbon dioxide and its pressure is less than 1 per cent of that at the Earth's surface. Like the Moon, the surface of Mars is pitted with craters. The tiny, irregularly shaped moons, Phobos and Deimos, are also cratered.

Mars is a morning object until opposition in April whereafter it is an evening object for the rest of the year..

Jupiter

Diameter	89,000 miles (143,000 km)
Mean distance from the Sun	484,000,000 miles (779,000,000 km)
Time taken to revolve round the Sun	12 years
Period of rotation on its axis	9 hrs 55 mins
Moons	16

Jupiter is the largest planet of the solar system. Its volume exceeds that of the Earth by more than 1,300 times, and the planet contains about 70 per cent of the planetary mass of the solar system.

Its rocky core is surrounded by fluid hydrogen. The atmosphere, over 12,000 miles (20,000 km) deep, contains hydrogen and helium, with an outer cloud layer of ammonia crystals at very low temperatures (–120°C). Coloured bands cross the Jovian orb; the light ones are gases from the interior rising to the surface of the atmosphere, and the darker ones are where material is descending again. The Great Red Spot is thought to be a perpetual whirling storm, the red colour perhaps caused by the presence of red phosphorus.

In 1979, an extremely faint ring system was detected around the planet by *Voyager I* cameras. The four largest of Jupiter's moons were discovered in 1610 by Galileo – Io, Europa, Ganymede and Callisto. Ganymede is the largest satellite in the solar system, with a diameter greater than that of Mercury.

Jupiter is an evening object until March. It becomes a morning object in April until opposition in October. For the rest of the year it is an evening object.

Saturn

Diameter	75,000 miles (121,000 km)
Mean distance from the Sun	887,000,000 miles (1,427,000,000 km)
Time taken to revolve round the sun	29.5 years
Period of rotation on its axis	10 hrs 38 mins
Moons	17

Saturn is a fascinating object on account of its ring system, which may be seen even with small telescopes. The rings are composed of myriads of particles of varying size and composition. The planet is of very low density and has, like Jupiter, an outer layer of hydrogen with some helium. As with Jupiter, the atmosphere is crossed by coloured bands, though they are not so conspicuous. Saturn's largest moon, Titan, has a diameter of over 3,200 miles (5,100 km) and is visible with a small telescope. Seven other major satellites, known before the arrival of space probes, are: Rhea, Iapetus, Tethys, Dione, Enceladus, Mimas and Phoebe.

Saturn is an evening object until April. From June until opposition in November it is a morning object. For the rest of the year it is an evening object.

Uranus

Diameter	31,600 miles (50,900 km)
Mean distance from the Sun	1,780,000,000 miles (2,870,000 km)
Time taken to revolve round the Sun	84 years
Period of rotation on its axis	17 hrs 15 mins
Moons	15

The planet Uranus was discovered by Sir William Herschel in 1781. It is occasionally just visible to the naked eye, in clear dark skies. However, a telescope is usually required to locate it (look for a greenish disc). The planet is of very low density. It is thought to consist of a rocky core about 9,300 miles (15,000 km) in diameter above which is a mantle containing frozen methane, ammonia and water some 6,200 miles (10,000 km) thick. The atmosphere above is mainly hydrogen and helium.

Uranus has a very faint ring system. Until the planet was explored by *Voyager 2* in 1986, only five of its moons were known: Titania (the largest), Oberon, Miranda, Ariel and Umbriel. The first and largest of the 10 new discoveries was named Puck.

Using a telescope or binoculars, Uranus is visible as a morning object from March until opposition in August. It is then visible in the evenings until December. Uranus is in the constellation of Capricornus.

Neptune

Diameter	30,800 miles (49,600 km)
Mean distance from the Sun	2,794,000,000 miles (4,497,000,000 km)
Time taken to revolve round the Sun	165 years
Period of rotation on its axis	19 hours
Moons	8

Before Neptune had ever been seen by an observer its position was calculated mathematically from the deviations from the predicted positions to the actually observed positions of Uranus. It was first seen at Berlin Observatory in 1846. The planet is slightly smaller than Uranus and has similar density. The cameras of the *Voyager 2* space probe showed bands of different shades of blue with streaks of cirrus cloud parallel with the equator. A dark hole in the clouds has been named the Great Dark Spot. The upper clouds consist of frozen methane; below them is a cloud-layer of hydrogen sulphide.

Only two moons, Triton and Nereid, were known before *Voyager 2* discovered six more – and a faint ring system too.

Neptune is only visible through a telescope. It is situated in the constellation of Capricornus.

Pluto

Diameter	3,600 miles (5,800 km)
Mean distance from the Sun	3,666,000,000 miles (5,900,000,000 km)
Time taken to revolve round the Sun	248 years
Period of rotation on its axis	6 days
Moons	1

The position of this planet was predicted by Percival Lowell in 1915. After a systematic search it was eventually located on a photographic plate by Clyde Tombaugh, in 1930. Pluto is slightly smaller than our Moon and has an extremely eccentric orbit – part of it is outside the zodiacal belt. For 20 years, Pluto comes inside the orbit of Neptune (this last happened in 1979, and until 1999 Neptune is the outermost planet). Pluto's mass and density are low; the planet may consist of rock and ice.

In 1978 a moon was discovered. This is half the size of Pluto itself and has been named Charon.

Pluto's present position is in the constellation of Ophiuchus.

STATIONARY POSITIONS OF THE PLANETS IN 1999

	d	h	m		d	h	m
Mercury				**Saturn**			
March	10	9	11	August	30	1	24
April	2	9	20				
July	12	23	32	**Uranus**			
August	6	3	27	May	21	22	27
November	5	2	59	October	23	6	14
December	25	3	55				
				Neptune			
Venus				May	7	0	48
July	30	1	43	October	14	1	26
September	11	0	24				
				Pluto			
Mars				March	13	21	34
March	18	13	40	August	19	1	41
June	4	6	12				
Jupiter							
August	25	2	38				
December	20	14	50				

The mean obliquity of the ecliptic is 23° 26' 22"

Raphael's Sun and Moon Tables 1999

JANUARY

Moon's Phases and Apsides

	d.	h.	m.	
Full Moon	2	02	50	(11♋15)
Last Quarter	9	14	22	(18♎52)
New Moon	17	15	46	(27♑05)
First Quarter	24	19	15	(4♉21)
Full Moon	31	16	07	(11♌20)
Apogee	11	11	44	
Perigee	26	21	34	

Moon's Positions

	d.	h.	m.	
Max. Dec.	1	22	47	19N34
On Equator	8	18	02	
Max. Dec.	16	05	48	19S33
On Equator	22	23	46	
Max. Dec.	29	08	27	19N32

FEBRUARY

Moon's Phases and Apsides

	d.	h.	m.	
Last Quarter	8	11	58	(19♏16)
New Moon	16	06	39	(27♒08)
First Quarter	23	02	43	(4♊02)
Apogee	8	08	51	
Perigee	20	14	25	

Moon's Positions

	d.	h.	m.	
On Equator	5	03	19	
Max. Dec.	12	14	54	19S31
On Equator	19	06	10	
Max. Dec.	25	15	04	19S32

JANUARY

Day of M	W	Sun rise h. m.	Sun set h. m.	Moon rise h. m.	Moon transit h. m.	Moon set h. m.	age d.
1	F	8 06	16 01	15 52	23 56	6 58	14
2	Sa	8 06	16 03	16 53	—	7 59	15
3	Su	8 06	16 04	18 01	0 54	8 50	16
4	M	8 06	16 05	19 11	1 51	9 31	17
5	Tu	8 05	16 06	20 21	2 44	10 05	18
6	W	8 05	16 07	21 30	3 33	10 33	19
7	Th	8 05	16 09	22 37	4 20	10 57	20
8	F	8 04	16 10	23 42	5 04	11 20	21
9	Sa	8 04	16 11	—	5 47	11 41	22
10	Su	8 03	16 13	0 45	6 29	12 03	23
11	M	8 03	16 14	1 49	7 12	12 27	24
12	Tu	8 02	16 16	2 51	7 56	12 53	25
13	W	8 01	16 17	3 54	8 41	13 23	26
14	Th	8 00	16 18	4 54	9 28	13 58	27
15	F	8 00	16 20	5 53	10 18	14 41	28
16	Sa	7 59	16 22	6 46	11 08	15 31	29
17	Su	7 58	16 23	7 34	12 00	16 29	30
18	M	7 57	16 25	8 16	12 52	17 34	1
19	Tu	7 56	16 26	8 52	13 44	18 44	2
20	W	7 55	16 28	9 24	14 35	19 57	3
21	Th	7 54	16 30	9 52	15 26	21 11	4
22	F	7 53	16 31	10 18	16 16	22 26	5
23	Sa	7 52	16 33	10 44	17 06	23 42	6
24	Su	7 50	16 35	11 10	17 58	—	7
25	M	7 49	16 36	11 39	18 51	0 59	8
26	Tu	7 48	16 38	12 13	19 46	2 15	9
27	W	7 46	16 40	12 52	20 43	3 30	10
28	Th	7 45	16 42	13 40	21 41	4 41	11
29	F	7 44	16 43	14 36	22 39	5 45	12
30	Sa	7 42	16 45	15 40	23 36	6 39	13
31	Su	7 41	16 47	16 48	—	7 24	14

FEBRUARY

Day of M	W	Sun rise h. m.	Sun set h. m.	Moon rise h. m.	Moon transit h. m.	Moon set h. m.	age d.
1	M	7 39	16 49	17 59	0 30	8 01	15
2	Tu	7 38	16 51	19 09	1 22	8 32	16
3	W	7 36	16 52	20 18	2 10	8 59	17
4	Th	7 34	16 54	21 25	2 56	9 22	18
5	F	7 33	16 56	22 30	3 40	9 45	19
6	Sa	7 31	16 58	23 34	4 23	10 07	20
7	Su	7 29	17 00	—	5 06	10 29	21
8	M	7 28	17 01	0 37	5 50	10 54	22
9	Tu	7 26	17 03	1 40	6 34	11 22	23
10	W	7 24	17 05	2 41	7 20	11 55	24
11	Th	7 22	17 07	3 40	8 08	12 34	25
12	F	7 20	17 09	4 35	8 58	13 20	26
13	Sa	7 19	17 11	5 26	9 49	14 15	27
14	Su	7 17	17 12	6 11	10 42	15 17	28
15	M	7 15	17 14	6 50	11 34	16 26	29
16	Tu	7 13	17 16	7 24	12 27	17 39	0
17	W	7 11	17 18	7 54	13 19	18 55	1
18	Th	7 09	17 20	8 21	14 11	20 12	2
19	F	7 07	17 21	8 48	15 02	21 30	3
20	Sa	7 05	17 23	9 14	15 54	22 48	4
21	Su	7 03	17 25	9 43	16 47	—	5
22	M	7 01	17 27	10 15	17 42	0 05	6
23	Tu	6 59	17 29	10 52	18 38	1 21	7
24	W	6 57	17 30	11 36	19 34	2 32	8
25	Th	6 55	17 32	12 28	20 31	3 37	9
26	F	6 52	17 34	13 28	21 27	4 33	10
27	Sa	6 50	17 36	14 33	22 21	5 20	11
28	Su	6 48	17 37	15 41	23 13	5 59	12

All times on this page are GMT

Raphael's Sun and Moon Tables 1999

MARCH	APRIL

Moon's Phases and Apsides (MARCH)

	d.	h.	m.	
Full Moon	2	06	58	(11♍15)
Last Quarter	10	08	40	(19♐19)
New Moon	17	18	48	(26♓44)
First Quarter	24	10	18	(3♋20)
Full Moon	31	22	49	(10♎46)
Apogee	8	05	05	
Perigee	20	00	07	

Moon's Phases and Apsides (APRIL)

	d.	h.	m.	
Last Quarter	9	02	51	(18♑49)
New Moon	16	04	22	(25♈45)
First Quarter	22	19	02	(2♌12)
Full Moon	30	14	55	(9♏49)
Apogee	4	21	22	
Perigee	17	05	18	

Moon's Positions (MARCH)

	d.	h.	m.	
On Equator	4	11	44	
Max. Dec.	11	23	47	19S35
On Equator	18	14	41	
Max. Dec.	24	20	18	19N39
On Equator	31	18	53	

Moon's Positions (APRIL)

	d.	h.	m.	
Max. Dec.	8	07	48	19S46
On Equator	15	01	13	
Max. Dec.	21	02	54	19N52
On Equator	28	01	18	

Day of M	W	Sun rise h. m.	Sun set h. m.	Moon rise h. m.	Moon transit h. m.	Moon set h. m.	age d.	Day of M	W	Sun rise h. m.	Sun set h. m.	Moon rise h. m.	Moon transit h. m.	Moon set h. m.	age d.
1	M	6 46	17 39	16 51	—	6 32	13	1	Th	5 36	18 32	19 07	0 13	6 13	15
2	Tu	6 44	17 41	18 00	0 02	7 00	14	2	F	5 34	18 34	20 12	0 56	6 35	16
3	W	6 42	17 43	19 08	0 48	7 24	15	3	Sa	5 32	18 35	21 15	1 39	6 58	17
4	Th	6 40	17 44	20 14	1 33	7 47	16	4	Su	5 30	18 37	22 18	2 23	7 23	18
5	F	6 37	17 46	21 20	2 17	8 09	17	5	M	5 27	18 39	23 18	3 08	7 52	19
6	Sa	6 35	17 48	22 24	3 00	8 32	18	6	Tu	5 25	18 41	—	3 54	8 25	20
7	Su	6 33	17 50	23 26	3 44	8 56	19	7	W	5 23	18 42	0 16	4 41	9 04	21
8	M	6 31	17 51	—	4 28	9 22	20	8	Th	5 21	18 44	1 09	5 30	9 50	22
9	Tu	6 29	17 53	0 28	5 13	9 52	21	9	F	5 18	18 46	1 57	6 19	10 44	23
10	W	6 26	17 55	1 28	6 00	10 28	22	10	Sa	5 16	18 47	2 39	7 10	11 44	24
11	Th	6 24	17 57	2 24	6 48	11 10	23	11	Su	5 14	18 49	3 16	8 01	12 52	25
12	F	6 22	17 58	3 16	7 38	12 00	24	12	M	5 12	18 51	3 49	8 52	14 04	26
13	Sa	6 20	18 00	4 03	8 29	12 59	25	13	Tu	5 10	18 52	4 18	9 44	15 20	27
14	Su	6 17	18 02	4 44	9 21	14 04	26	14	W	5 07	18 54	4 46	10 36	16 39	28
15	M	6 15	18 03	5 20	10 13	15 15	27	15	Th	5 05	18 56	5 13	11 30	18 00	29
16	Tu	6 13	18 05	5 52	11 06	16 30	28	16	F	5 03	18 57	5 41	12 25	19 23	0
17	W	6 10	18 07	6 20	11 59	17 49	29	17	Sa	5 01	18 59	6 11	13 21	20 46	1
18	Th	6 08	18 09	6 48	12 52	19 09	1	18	Su	4 59	19 01	6 46	14 20	22 06	2
19	F	6 06	18 10	7 15	13 45	20 29	2	19	M	4 57	19 02	7 27	15 20	23 20	3
20	Sa	6 04	18 12	7 44	14 40	21 50	3	20	Tu	4 55	19 04	8 16	16 19	—	4
21	Su	6 01	18 14	8 15	15 35	23 09	4	21	W	4 53	19 06	9 12	17 17	0 25	5
22	M	5 59	18 15	8 51	16 32	—	5	22	Th	4 51	19 07	10 15	18 13	1 19	6
23	Tu	5 57	18 17	9 34	17 30	0 23	6	23	F	4 48	19 09	11 22	19 06	2 03	7
24	W	5 55	18 19	10 24	18 27	1 31	7	24	Sa	4 46	19 11	12 30	19 56	2 39	8
25	Th	5 52	18 20	11 21	19 23	2 31	8	25	Su	4 44	19 12	13 39	20 43	3 09	9
26	F	5 50	18 22	12 24	20 17	3 20	9	26	M	4 42	19 14	14 46	21 28	3 34	10
27	Sa	5 48	18 24	13 31	21 08	4 01	10	27	Tu	4 40	19 16	15 52	22 11	3 57	11
28	Su	5 45	18 25	14 39	21 57	4 35	11	28	W	4 39	19 17	16 58	22 54	4 18	12
29	M	5 43	18 27	15 48	22 44	5 03	12	29	Th	4 37	19 19	18 02	23 37	4 40	13
30	Tu	5 41	18 29	16 55	23 29	5 28	13	30	F	4 35	19 21	19 06	—	5 02	14
31	W	5 39	18 30	18 02	—	5 51	14								

All times on this page are GMT

Raphael's Sun and Moon Tables 1999

MAY		JUNE	

MAY

Moon's Phases and Apsides

	d.	h.	m.	
Last Quarter	8	17	29	(17≈41)
New Moon	15	12	05	(24♉14)
First Quarter	22	05	34	(0♍43)
Full Moon	30	06	40	(8♐26)
Apogee	2	05	59	
Perigee	15	15	01	
Apogee	29	08	00	

JUNE

Moon's Phases and Apsides

	d.	h.	m.	
Last Quarter	7	04	20	(16♓00)
New Moon	13	19	03	(22♊20)
First Quarter	20	18	13	(28♍59)
Full Moon	28	21	37	(6♑45)
Perigee	13	00	31	
Apogee	25	15	21	

Moon's Positions (MAY)

	d.	h.	m.	
Max. Dec.	5	14	58	20S00
On Equator	12	12	12	
Max. Dec.	18	12	12	20N05
On Equator	25	07	56	

Moon's Positions (JUNE)

	d.	h.	m.	
Max. Dec.	1	21	44	20S10
On Equator	8	21	53	
Max. Dec.	14	23	21	20N12
On Equator	21	15	28	
Max. Dec.	29	04	38	20S13

MAY

M	W	Sun rise h. m.	Sun set h. m.	Moon rise h. m.	Moon transit h. m.	Moon set h. m.	age d.
1	Sa	4 33	19 22	20 09	0 20	5 26	15
2	Su	4 31	19 24	21 11	1 05	5 53	16
3	M	4 29	19 26	22 10	1 50	6 24	17
4	Tu	4 27	19 27	23 05	2 37	7 01	18
5	W	4 25	19 29	23 55	3 25	7 44	19
6	Th	4 24	19 30	—	4 14	8 34	20
7	F	4 22	19 32	0 38	5 03	9 32	21
8	Sa	4 20	19 34	1 17	5 53	10 35	22
9	Su	4 19	19 35	1 50	6 43	11 43	23
10	M	4 17	19 37	2 19	7 33	12 56	24
11	Tu	4 15	19 38	2 46	8 23	14 11	25
12	W	4 14	19 40	3 12	9 14	15 30	26
13	Th	4 12	19 42	3 38	10 08	16 51	27
14	F	4 11	19 43	4 07	11 03	18 15	28
15	Sa	4 09	19 45	4 39	12 01	19 38	29
16	Su	4 08	19 46	5 17	13 02	20 58	1
17	M	4 06	19 48	6 02	14 03	22 10	2
18	Tu	4 05	19 49	6 57	15 05	23 12	3
19	W	4 03	19 51	8 00	16 04	—	4
20	Th	4 02	19 52	9 08	17 00	0 01	5
21	F	4 01	19 53	10 18	17 52	0 41	6
22	Sa	3 59	19 55	11 28	18 41	1 13	7
23	Su	3 58	19 56	12 37	19 27	1 40	8
24	M	3 57	19 58	13 44	20 10	2 04	9
25	Tu	3 56	19 59	14 49	20 53	2 26	10
26	W	3 55	20 00	15 54	21 36	2 46	11
27	Th	3 54	20 01	16 58	22 19	3 08	12
28	F	3 53	20 03	18 02	23 03	3 31	13
29	Sa	3 52	20 04	19 04	23 48	3 56	14
30	Su	3 51	20 05	20 04	—	4 26	15
31	M	3 50	20 06	21 01	0 34	5 00	16

JUNE

M	W	Sun rise h. m.	Sun set h. m.	Moon rise h. m.	Moon transit h. m.	Moon set h. m.	age d.
1	Tu	3 49	20 07	21 53	1 22	5 41	17
2	W	3 48	20 08	22 39	2 11	6 29	18
3	Th	3 48	20 09	23 19	3 00	7 24	19
4	F	3 47	20 10	23 53	3 49	8 25	20
5	Sa	3 46	20 11	—	4 39	9 31	21
6	Su	3 46	20 12	0 23	5 27	10 40	22
7	M	3 45	20 13	0 50	6 16	11 53	23
8	Tu	3 45	20 14	1 15	7 05	13 07	24
9	W	3 44	20 15	1 40	7 56	14 25	25
10	Th	3 44	20 16	2 06	8 48	15 45	26
11	F	3 43	20 16	2 34	9 43	17 07	27
12	Sa	3 43	20 17	3 08	10 42	18 28	28
13	Su	3 43	20 18	3 49	11 43	19 46	29
14	M	3 43	20 18	4 39	12 45	20 54	1
15	Tu	3 43	20 19	5 39	13 47	21 52	2
16	W	3 42	20 19	6 46	14 46	22 38	3
17	Th	3 42	20 20	7 58	15 42	23 14	4
18	F	3 42	20 20	9 11	16 34	23 44	5
19	Sa	3 42	20 21	10 22	17 22	—	6
20	Su	3 43	20 21	11 32	18 08	0 09	7
21	M	3 43	20 21	12 39	18 52	0 32	8
22	Tu	3 43	20 21	13 44	19 34	0 53	9
23	W	3 43	20 21	14 49	20 17	1 14	10
24	Th	3 43	20 22	15 53	21 00	1 36	11
25	F	3 44	20 22	16 55	21 45	2 01	12
26	Sa	3 44	20 22	17 57	22 31	2 28	13
27	Su	3 45	20 21	18 55	23 19	3 01	14
28	M	3 45	20 21	19 50	—	3 39	15
29	Tu	3 46	20 21	20 38	0 08	4 25	16
30	W	3 46	20 21	21 20	0 57	5 18	17

All times on this page are GMT

Raphael's Sun and Moon Tables 1999

JULY

Moon's Phases and Apsides

	d. h. m.	
Last Quarter	6 11 57	(13♈59)
New Moon	13 02 24	(20♋17)
First Quarter	20 09 50	(27♎14)
Full Moon	28 11 25	(4≈≈58)
Perigee	11 06 01	
Apogee	23 05 39	

Moon's Positions

	d. h. m.	
On Equator	6 05 19	
Max. Dec.	12 10 22	20N13
On Equator	18 23 56	
Max. Dec.	26 12 02	20S12

AUGUST

Moon's Phases and Apsides

	d. h. m.	
Last Quarter	4 17 27	(11♉54)
New Moon	11 11 08	(18♌21)
First Quarter	19 01 47	(25♍40)
Full Moon	26 23 48	(3♓17)
Perigee	7 23 26	
Apogee	19 23 25	

Moon's Positions

	d. h. m.	
On Equator	2 11 04	
Max. Dec.	8 19 26	20N11
On Equator	15 08 46	
Max. Dec.	22 19 56	20S12
On Equator	29 16 55	

Day of M	W	Sun rise h. m.	Sun set h. m.	Moon rise h. m.	Moon transit h. m.	Moon set h. m.	age d.	Day of M	W	Sun rise h. m.	Sun set h. m.	Moon rise h. m.	Moon transit h. m.	Moon set h. m.	age d.
1	Th	3 47	20 21	21 57	1 47	6 18	18	1	Su	4 23	19 49	21 50	3 00	8 44	19
2	F	3 48	20 20	22 28	2 36	7 22	19	2	M	4 24	19 47	22 15	3 48	9 58	20
3	Sa	3 48	20 20	22 55	3 25	8 31	20	3	Tu	4 26	19 45	22 40	4 37	11 14	21
4	Su	3 49	20 19	23 21	4 13	9 41	21	4	W	4 27	19 44	23 08	5 28	12 30	22
5	M	3 50	20 19	23 45	5 02	10 54	22	5	Th	4 29	19 42	23 40	6 21	13 47	23
6	Tu	3 51	20 18	—	5 50	12 09	23	6	F	4 30	19 40	—	7 16	15 04	24
7	W	3 52	20 18	0 09	6 40	13 25	24	7	Sa	4 32	19 38	0 19	8 13	16 16	25
8	Th	3 53	20 17	0 35	7 32	14 44	25	8	Su	4 33	19 37	1 07	9 13	17 22	26
9	F	3 53	20 17	1 05	8 27	16 03	26	9	M	4 36	19 35	2 05	10 13	18 17	27
10	Sa	3 54	20 16	1 41	9 25	17 21	27	10	Tu	4 37	19 33	3 11	11 12	19 03	28
11	Su	3 55	20 15	2 25	10 26	18 33	28	11	W	4 38	19 31	4 24	12 08	19 40	0
12	M	3 57	20 14	3 19	11 28	19 36	29	12	Th	4 40	19 29	5 38	13 01	20 11	1
13	Tu	3 58	20 13	4 23	12 29	20 28	0	13	F	4 41	19 27	6 52	13 51	20 37	2
14	W	3 59	20 12	5 33	13 27	21 10	1	14	Sa	4 43	19 25	8 04	14 38	21 00	3
15	Th	4 00	20 11	6 48	14 22	21 44	2	15	Su	4 44	19 23	9 14	15 24	21 22	4
16	F	4 01	20 10	8 02	15 13	22 11	3	16	M	4 46	19 21	10 21	16 08	21 44	5
17	Sa	4 02	20 09	9 14	16 01	22 36	4	17	Tu	4 48	19 19	11 27	16 52	22 07	6
18	Su	4 03	20 08	10 23	16 47	22 58	5	18	W	4 49	19 17	12 32	17 36	22 32	7
19	M	4 05	20 07	11 31	17 30	23 19	6	19	Th	4 51	19 15	13 35	18 21	23 01	8
20	Tu	4 06	20 06	12 37	18 14	23 41	7	20	F	4 52	19 13	14 35	19 07	23 34	9
21	W	4 07	20 05	13 41	18 57	—	8	21	Sa	4 54	19 11	15 33	19 55	—	10
22	Th	4 09	20 03	14 45	19 41	0 04	9	22	Su	4 55	19 09	16 26	20 44	0 14	11
23	F	4 10	20 02	15 47	20 27	0 31	10	23	M	4 57	19 07	17 14	21 34	1 02	12
24	Sa	4 11	20 01	16 46	21 14	1 01	11	24	Tu	4 59	19 05	17 55	22 24	1 57	13
25	Su	4 13	19 59	17 43	22 02	1 37	12	25	W	5 00	19 02	18 31	23 15	2 58	14
26	M	4 14	19 58	18 34	22 52	2 20	13	26	Th	5 02	19 00	19 02	—	4 06	15
27	Tu	4 16	19 57	19 19	23 42	3 11	14	27	F	5 03	18 58	19 29	0 05	5 17	16
28	W	4 17	19 55	19 58	—	4 09	15	28	Sa	5 05	18 56	19 55	0 55	6 31	17
29	Th	4 18	19 53	20 31	0 32	5 12	16	29	Su	5 07	18 54	20 19	1 44	7 46	18
30	F	4 20	19 52	21 00	1 22	6 21	17	30	M	5 08	18 52	20 44	2 34	9 03	19
31	Sa	4 21	19 50	21 26	2 11	7 32	18	31	Tu	5 10	18 49	21 11	3 25	10 20	20

All times on this page are GMT

Raphael's Sun and Moon Tables 1999

SEPTEMBER	OCTOBER

SEPTEMBER

Moon's Phases and Apsides

	d.	h.	m.	
Last Quarter	2	22	17	(10♊00)
New Moon	9	22	02	(16♍47)
First Quarter	17	20	06	(24♐29)
Full Moon	25	10	51	(1♈56)
Perigee	2	18	04	
Apogee	16	18	42	
Perigee	28	16	50	

Moon's Positions

	d.	h.	m.	
Max. Dec.	5	01	59	20N14
On Equator	11	17	13	
Max. Dec.	19	04	07	20S19
On Equator	26	00	40	

OCTOBER

Moon's Phases and Apsides

	d.	h.	m.	
Last Quarter	2	04	02	(8♋31)
New Moon	9	11	34	(15♎44)
First Quarter	17	15	00	(23♑48)
Full Moon	24	21	02	(1♉00)
Last Quarter	31	12	04	(7♌37)
Apogee	14	13	54	
Perigee	26	13	05	

Moon's Positions

	d.	h.	m.	
Max. Dec.	2	07	11	20N25
On Equator	9	00	49	
Max. Dec.	16	12	10	20S33
On Equator	23	10	51	
Max. Dec.	29	13	34	20N39

September

M	W	Sun rise h. m.	Sun set h. m.	Moon rise h. m.	Moon transit h. m.	Moon set h. m.	age d.
1	W	5 11	18 47	21 42	4 17	11 37	21
2	Th	5 13	18 45	22 18	5 11	12 54	22
3	F	5 15	18 43	23 03	6 08	14 06	23
4	Sa	5 16	18 40	23 56	7 05	15 13	24
5	Su	5 18	18 38	—	8 04	16 11	25
6	M	5 19	18 36	0 57	9 02	16 59	26
7	Tu	5 21	18 34	2 06	9 58	17 38	27
8	W	5 22	18 31	3 19	10 51	18 10	28
9	Th	5 24	18 29	4 32	11 41	18 38	29
10	F	5 26	18 27	5 44	12 30	19 02	1
11	Sa	5 27	18 25	6 55	13 16	19 24	2
12	Su	5 29	18 22	8 04	14 01	19 46	3
13	M	5 30	18 20	9 12	14 45	20 09	4
14	Tu	5 32	18 18	10 17	15 29	20 33	5
15	W	5 34	18 15	11 22	16 14	21 00	6
16	Th	5 35	18 13	12 24	17 00	21 31	7
17	F	5 37	18 11	13 23	17 47	22 08	8
18	Sa	5 38	18 08	14 17	18 35	22 52	9
19	Su	5 40	18 06	15 07	19 24	23 43	10
20	M	5 42	18 04	15 50	20 14	—	11
21	Tu	5 43	18 02	16 28	21 04	0 42	12
22	W	5 45	17 59	17 01	21 55	1 47	13
23	Th	5 46	17 57	17 29	22 45	2 57	14
24	F	5 48	17 55	17 56	23 35	4 10	15
25	Sa	5 50	17 52	18 21	—	5 26	16
26	Su	5 51	17 50	18 46	0 26	6 44	17
27	M	5 53	17 48	19 13	1 18	8 03	18
28	Tu	5 55	17 45	19 43	2 11	9 23	19
29	W	5 56	17 43	20 18	3 06	10 42	20
30	Th	5 58	17 41	21 00	4 03	11 58	21

October

M	W	Sun rise h. m.	Sun set h. m.	Moon rise h. m.	Moon transit h. m.	Moon set h. m.	age d.
1	F	5 59	17 39	21 50	5 01	13 08	22
2	Sa	6 01	17 36	22 49	5 59	14 08	23
3	Su	6 03	17 34	23 56	6 57	14 58	24
4	M	6 04	17 32	—	7 52	15 39	25
5	Tu	6 06	17 30	1 06	8 45	16 13	26
6	W	6 08	17 27	2 18	9 36	16 41	27
7	Th	6 09	17 25	3 29	10 24	17 05	28
8	F	6 11	17 23	4 40	11 10	17 28	29
9	Sa	6 13	17 21	5 49	11 55	17 49	0
10	Su	6 14	17 18	6 57	12 39	18 11	1
11	M	6 16	17 16	8 04	13 24	18 34	2
12	Tu	6 18	17 14	9 09	14 08	19 00	3
13	W	6 19	17 12	10 13	14 54	19 29	4
14	Th	6 21	17 10	11 13	15 40	20 04	5
15	F	6 23	17 08	12 10	16 28	20 44	6
16	Sa	6 25	17 06	13 01	17 16	21 32	7
17	Su	6 26	17 03	13 46	18 05	22 27	8
18	M	6 28	17 01	14 26	18 54	23 28	9
19	Tu	6 30	16 59	14 59	19 43	—	10
20	W	6 31	16 57	15 29	20 33	0 34	11
21	Th	6 33	16 55	15 56	21 22	1 45	12
22	F	6 35	16 53	16 21	22 13	3 00	13
23	Sa	6 37	16 51	16 46	23 04	4 17	14
24	Su	6 38	16 49	17 11	23 57	5 37	15
25	M	6 40	16 47	17 40	—	6 59	16
26	Tu	6 42	16 45	18 14	0 53	8 21	17
27	W	6 44	16 43	18 54	1 51	9 42	18
28	Th	6 45	16 41	19 43	2 51	10 57	19
29	F	6 47	16 39	20 40	3 52	12 03	20
30	Sa	6 49	16 38	21 46	4 51	12 58	21
31	Su	6 51	16 36	22 56	5 49	13 42	22

All times on this page are GMT

Raphael's Sun and Moon Tables 1999

NOVEMBER

Moon's Phases and Apsides

	d.	h.	m.	
New Moon	8	03	53	(15♏17)
First Quarter	16	09	03	(23≈33)
Full Moon	23	07	04	(0Ⅱ32)
Last Quarter	29	23	19	(7♍17)
Apogee	11	05	41	
Perigee	23	22	01	

Moon's Positions

	d.	h.	m.	
On Equator	5	07	33	
Max. Dec.	12	19	46	20S48
On Equator	19	22	09	
Max. Dec.	25	22	55	20N52

DECEMBER

Moon's Phases and Apsides

	d.	h.	m.	
New Moon	7	22	32	(15♐22)
First Quarter	16	00	50	(23♓36)
Full Moon	22	17	31	(06♋25)
Last Quarter	29	14	04	(7♎24)
Apogee	8	11	20	
Perigee	22	11	01	

Moon's Positions

	d.	h.	m.	
On Equator	2	14	05	
Max. Dec.	10	02	51	20S56
On Equator	17	08	16	
Max. Dec.	23	10	44	20N57
On Equator	29	21	21	

NOVEMBER

Day of M	W	Sun rise h. m.	Sun set h. m.	Moon rise h. m.	Moon transit h. m.	Moon set h. m.	Moon age d.
1	M	6 53	16 34	—	6 43	14 18	23
2	Tu	6 54	16 32	0 08	7 34	14 47	24
3	W	6 56	16 30	1 19	8 22	15 11	25
4	Th	6 58	16 29	2 30	9 08	15 34	26
5	F	7 00	16 27	3 38	9 52	15 55	27
6	Sa	7 01	16 25	4 46	10 36	16 16	28
7	Su	7 03	16 24	5 53	11 20	16 38	29
8	M	7 05	16 22	6 58	12 04	17 02	0
9	Tu	7 07	16 20	8 03	12 49	17 30	1
10	W	7 09	16 19	9 05	13 36	18 02	2
11	Th	7 10	16 17	10 04	14 23	18 40	3
12	F	7 12	16 16	10 57	15 11	19 24	4
13	Sa	7 14	16 14	11 44	15 59	20 16	5
14	Su	7 16	16 13	12 25	16 47	21 14	6
15	M	7 17	16 12	13 00	17 36	22 17	7
16	Tu	7 19	16 10	13 31	18 24	23 25	8
17	W	7 21	16 09	13 57	19 11	—	9
18	Th	7 22	16 08	14 22	20 00	0 35	10
19	F	7 24	16 06	14 46	20 49	1 49	11
20	Sa	7 26	16 05	15 10	21 41	3 06	12
21	Su	7 27	16 04	15 36	22 35	4 26	13
22	M	7 29	16 03	16 07	23 32	5 49	14
23	Tu	7 31	16 02	16 44	—	7 13	15
24	W	7 32	16 01	17 29	0 33	8 34	16
25	Th	7 34	16 00	18 25	1 35	9 48	17
26	F	7 36	15 59	19 30	2 38	10 50	18
27	Sa	7 37	15 58	20 41	3 39	11 41	19
28	Su	7 39	15 57	21 55	4 37	12 20	20
29	M	7 40	15 57	23 08	5 30	12 52	21
30	Tu	7 42	15 56	—	6 20	13 18	22

DECEMBER

Day of M	W	Sun rise h. m.	Sun set h. m.	Moon rise h. m.	Moon transit h. m.	Moon set h. m.	Moon age d.
1	W	7 43	15 55	0 20	7 07	13 41	23
2	Th	7 44	15 55	1 29	7 52	14 02	24
3	F	7 46	15 54	2 37	8 35	14 23	25
4	Sa	7 47	15 54	3 44	9 19	14 44	26
5	Su	7 48	15 53	4 49	10 02	15 07	27
6	M	7 50	15 53	5 54	10 47	15 33	28
7	Tu	7 51	15 52	6 57	11 33	16 03	29
8	W	7 52	15 52	7 57	12 19	16 38	1
9	Th	7 53	15 52	8 53	13 07	17 20	2
10	F	7 54	15 52	9 43	13 56	18 10	3
11	Sa	7 55	15 51	10 26	14 44	19 05	4
12	Su	7 56	15 51	11 03	15 32	20 06	5
13	M	7 57	15 51	11 34	16 19	21 12	6
14	Tu	7 58	15 51	12 02	17 06	22 20	7
15	W	7 59	15 52	12 26	17 53	23 30	8
16	Th	8 00	15 52	12 49	18 40	—	9
17	F	8 01	15 52	13 12	19 28	0 43	10
18	Sa	8 02	15 52	13 36	20 19	1 58	11
19	Su	8 02	15 52	14 03	21 13	3 17	12
20	M	8 03	15 53	14 35	22 11	4 39	13
21	Tu	8 04	15 53	15 14	23 12	6 01	14
22	W	8 04	15 54	16 04	—	7 20	15
23	Th	8 04	15 54	17 05	0 16	8 31	16
24	F	8 05	15 55	18 16	1 19	9 29	17
25	Sa	8 05	15 56	19 32	2 21	10 16	18
26	Su	8 06	15 56	20 49	3 19	10 52	19
27	M	8 06	15 57	22 04	4 13	11 22	20
28	Tu	8 06	15 58	23 17	5 02	11 47	21
29	W	8 06	15 59	—	5 49	12 09	22
30	Th	8 06	16 00	0 26	6 34	12 29	23
31	F	8 06	16 01	1 34	7 17	12 50	24

All times on this page are GMT

Rising and Setting of the Planets 1999

Date	☿ Mercury Rises or Sets	☿ Mercury Transit	♀ Venus Rises or Sets	♀ Venus Transit	♂ Mars Rises or Sets	♂ Mars Transit	♃ Jupiter Rises or Sets	♃ Jupiter Transit	♄ Saturn Rises or Sets	♄ Saturn Transit	♅ Uranus Rises or Sets	♅ Uranus Transit	♆ Neptune Rises or Sets	♆ Neptune Transit
	Rise		Set		Rise		Set		Set		Set		Set	
Jan 1	6 44	10 42	17 12	13 10	0 54	6 29	22 30	16 49	1 46	18 59	18 38	14 11	17 47	13 30
11	7 17	11 06	17 42	13 23	0 41	6 08	22 00	16 16	1 08	18 20	18 02	13 34	17 10	12 52
21	7 40	11 35	18 15	13 34	0 27	5 46	21 31	15 43	0 30	17 42	17 26	12 57	16 32	12 14
	Set												Rise	
31	16 21	12 05	18 48	13 43	0 11	5 22	21 03	15 11	23 50	17 05	16 50	12 20	7 18	11 37
											Rise			
Feb 10	17 25	12 36	19 20	13 50	23 49	4 56	20 36	14 39	23 15	16 28	7 13	11 43	6 40	10 59
20	18 34	13 03	19 52	13 56	23 26	4 28	20 09	14 08	22 40	15 51	6 35	11 06	6 01	10 21
Mar 2	19 27	13 17	20 23	14 01	22 59	3 58	19 43	13 37	22 06	15 16	5 57	10 29	5 23	9 43
12	19 15	12 49	20 55	14 06	22 26	3 23	19 17	13 06	21 33	14 40	5 19	9 52	4 44	9 05
	Rise													
22	5 35	11 44	21 27	14 12	21 47	2 45	18 51	12 35	21 00	14 05	4 40	9 14	4 06	8 27
Apr 1	5 01	10 48	21 59	14 19	21 02	2 01	18 25	12 05	20 28	13 30	4 02	8 37	3 27	7 48
							Rise							
11	4 40	10 25	22 30	14 28	20 10	1 13	5 10	11 35	19 55	12 56	3 24	7 59	2 48	7 10
21	4 24	10 22	22 59	14 38	19 13	0 20	4 35	11 04	19 23	12 21	2 45	7 21	2 09	6 31
					Set				Rise					
May 1	4 08	10 34	23 21	14 48	4 32	23 21	4 00	10 33	4 43	11 47	2 06	6 42	1 30	5 52
11	3 55	10 57	23 35	14 59	3 43	22 28	3 24	10 03	4 06	11 12	1 27	6 03	0 51	5 12
21	3 50	11 35	23 39	15 08	2 56	21 39	2 49	9 32	3 29	10 38	0 48	5 24	0 11	4 33
	Set													
31	20 52	12 27	23 33	15 14	2 12	20 55	2 14	9 00	2 53	10 03	0 09	4 45	23 28	3 53
June 10	21 48	13 16	23 18	15 16	1 31	20 16	1 38	8 28	2 16	9 28	23 25	4 05	22 48	3 13
20	21 59	13 45	22 56	15 14	0 52	19 41	1 03	7 56	1 39	8 53	22 45	3 25	22 08	2 33
30	21 39	13 52	22 27	15 06	0 16	19 11	0 27	7 23	1 02	8 18	22 06	2 45	21 28	1 53
July 10	20 57	13 32	21 52	14 51	23 38	18 44	23 47	6 49	0 25	7 42	21 26	2 04	20 48	1 12
20	19 58	12 43	21 11	14 27	23 06	18 21	23 10	6 14	23 44	7 05	20 46	1 23	20 08	0 32
	Rise												Set	
30	4 14	11 37	20 21	13 50	22 35	18 00	22 33	5 39	23 06	6 29	20 05	0 43	4 11	23 48
Aug 9	3 15	10 53	19 24	13 00	22 07	17 41	21 55	5 02	22 28	5 51	19 25	0 02	3 30	23 07
			Rise								Set			
19	3 11	10 54	5 33	11 59	21 40	17 24	21 16	4 24	21 50	5 13	3 52	23 17	2 50	22 27
29	4 04	11 25	4 23	10 58	21 16	17 09	20 37	3 45	21 11	4 34	3 11	22 36	2 09	21 47
Sept 8	5 17	12 00	3 24	10 08	20 54	16 56	19 58	3 05	20 32	3 54	2 30	21 55	1 29	21 07
	Set													
18	18 27	12 26	2 43	9 34	20 35	16 45	19 17	2 23	19 52	3 14	1 49	21 15	0 48	20 27
28	18 08	12 46	2 20	9 13	20 19	16 35	18 36	1 40	19 12	2 33	1 08	20 34	0 08	19 47
Oct 8	17 49	13 01	2 11	9 01	20 07	16 26	17 55	0 57	18 31	1 52	0 28	19 54	23 25	19 07
18	17 31	13 13	2 13	8 54	19 58	16 18	17 13	0 12	17 51	1 10	23 44	19 15	22 45	18 28
							Set							
28	17 13	13 16	2 23	8 51	19 53	16 11	6 21	23 23	17 10	0 28	23 05	18 36	22 06	17 49
									Set					
Nov 7	16 48	12 50	2 38	8 50	19 52	16 04	5 34	22 39	6 58	23 41	22 26	17 57	21 28	17 10
	Rise													
17	7 01	11 31	2 58	8 51	19 53	15 57	4 48	21 56	6 14	22 58	21 48	17 18	20 49	16 31
27	5 45	10 34	3 20	8 54	19 57	15 50	4 04	21 13	5 31	22 16	21 10	16 40	20 11	15 53
Dec 7	5 57	10 30	3 45	8 58	20 02	15 42	3 21	20 31	4 48	21 34	20 33	16 02	19 33	15 15
17	6 38	10 47	4 11	9 05	20 07	15 34	2 40	19 51	4 06	20 53	19 56	15 24	18 56	14 37
27	7 21	11 12	4 38	9 13	20 13	15 25	2 02	19 12	3 24	20 12	19 19	14 46	18 18	13 59
31	7 37	11 24	4 49	9 17	20 15	15 21	1 47	18 56	3 08	19 56	19 04	14 31	18 03	13 43

Geocentric Longitudes of the Planets in 1999

Date 12h GMT	☉ Sun	☿ Mer.	♀ Venus	♂ Mars	♃ Jupiter	♄ Saturn	♅ Uranus	♆ Nept.	♇ Pluto
	° ′	° ′	° ′	° ′	° ′	° ′	° ′	° ′	° ′
Jan. 1	10 ♑ 37	21 ♐ 58	26 ♑ 01	18 ♎ 38	22 ♓ 01	26 ♈ 47	10 ♒ 59	1 ♒ 05	9 ♐ 08
9	18 46	3 ♑ 34	6 ♒ 02	22 30	23 16	26 53	11 25	1 22	9 24
17	26 55	15 46	16 03	26 10	24 39	27 06	11 52	1 40	9 39
25	5 ♒ 04	28 32	26 02	29 35	26 09	27 26	12 19	1 59	9 52
Feb. 2	13 11	11 ♒ 57	6 ♓ 00	2 ♏ 45	27 45	27 52	12 47	2 17	10 03
10	21 17	26 06	15 56	5 34	29 27	28 24	13 15	2 34	10 13
18	29 23	10 ♓ 43	25 51	8 00	1 ♈ 12	29 02	13 43	2 51	10 20
26	7 ♓ 26	24 16	5 ♈ 42	9 57	3 02	29 45	14 09	3 08	10 26
Mar. 6	15 28	2 ♈ 55	15 30	11 21	4 53	0 ♉ 33	14 35	3 23	10 29
14	23 27	2 52	25 15	12 06	6 47	1 24	14 59	3 37	10 30
22	1 ♈ 25	26 ♓ 16	4 ♉ 56	12 06	8 43	2 18	15 22	3 49	10 28
30	9 20	21 16	14 32	11 19	10 39	3 15	15 42	3 59	10 25
Apr. 7	17 13	22 01	24 03	9 42	12 35	4 13	16 00	4 08	10 20
15	25 05	27 36	3 ♊ 27	7 23	14 31	5 14	16 15	4 15	10 12
23	2 ♉ 54	6 ♈ 29	12 45	4 34	16 25	6 15	16 28	4 19	10 04
May 1	10 41	17 45	21 55	1 34	18 18	7 16	16 37	4 22	9 53
9	18 26	1 ♉ 05	0 ♋ 54	28 ♎ 48	20 08	8 17	16 44	4 22	9 42
17	26 09	16 27	9 43	26 33	21 55	9 17	16 47	4 20	9 30
25	3 ♊ 51	3 ♊ 31	18 18	25 05	23 39	10 16	16 47	4 17	9 17
June 2	11 31	20 52	26 35	24 28	25 18	11 13	16 44	4 11	9 04
10	19 11	6 ♋ 32	4 ♌ 31	24 42	26 52	12 08	16 38	4 04	8 51
18	26 50	19 37	12 00	25 43	28 20	13 00	16 30	3 55	8 38
26	4 ♋ 27	29 50	18 52	27 27	29 42	13 48	16 18	3 44	8 26
July 4	12 05	6 ♌ 45	24 56	29 47	0 ♉ 56	14 32	16 05	3 33	8 16
12	19 43	9 29	29 56	2 ♏ 38	2 02	15 12	15 49	3 21	8 06
20	27 21	7 19	3 ♍ 28	5 57	2 59	15 46	15 32	3 08	7 58
28	4 ♌ 59	1 57	5 05	9 38	3 46	16 16	15 13	2 55	7 52
Aug. 5	12 38	28 ♋ 36	4 19	13 39	4 22	16 39	14 54	2 42	7 47
13	20 18	1 ♌ 37	1 09	17 58	4 46	16 56	14 35	2 30	7 45
21	28 00	11 27	26 ♌ 25	22 33	4 58	17 07	14 17	2 18	7 44
29	5 ♍ 43	25 50	21 52	27 20	4 57	17 11	13 59	2 07	7 46
Sept. 6	13 27	11 ♍ 27	19 12	2 ♐ 19	4 44	17 08	13 42	1 57	7 50
14	21 14	26 23	19 01	7 30	4 18	16 58	13 27	1 49	7 56
22	29 02	10 11	21 10	12 49	3 40	16 42	13 15	1 43	8 04
30	6 ♎ 53	22 56	25 10	18 17	2 53	16 20	13 04	1 38	8 14
Oct. 8	14 46	4 ♏ 44	0 ♍ 36	23 53	1 56	15 52	12 57	1 36	8 25
16	22 41	15 30	7 03	29 36	0 54	15 20	12 53	1 35	8 39
24	0 ♏ 38	24 44	14 18	5 ♑ 24	29 ♈ 50	14 44	12 52	1 37	8 53
Nov. 1	8 37	0 ♐ 53	22 08	11 18	28 45	14 07	12 54	1 41	9 10
9	16 38	0 15	0 ♎ 26	17 16	27 45	13 28	12 59	1 47	9 27
17	24 41	21 ♏ 00	9 05	23 18	26 50	12 50	13 08	1 55	9 45
25	2 ♐ 46	15 38	18 00	29 24	26 05	12 13	13 20	2 05	10 03
Dec. 3	10 52	20 37	27 10	5 ♒ 32	25 31	11 40	13 34	2 17	10 22
11	18 59	0 ♐ 34	6 ♏ 30	11 42	25 09	11 11	13 52	2 30	10 40
19	27 08	12 06	15 58	17 53	25 01	10 48	14 12	2 45	10 59
27	5 ♑ 16	24 10	25 32	24 05	25 06	10 31	14 34	3 01	11 17
31	9 ♑ 21	0 ♑ 20	0 ♐ 21	27 ♒ 11	25 ♈ 13	10 ♉ 25	14 ♒ 46	3 ♒ 09	11 ♐ 25

Time (GMT) when the Sun, Moon and Planets enter the Zodiacal Signs in 1999

JANUARY

Day		h. m.
1	☽♋	8 15
3	☽♌	10 31
4	♀♒	16 25
5	☽♍	15 50
7	☿♑	2 03
8	☽♎	0 53
10	☽♏	12 49
13	☽♐	1 23
15	☽♑	12 28
17	☽♒	21 11
20	☽♓	3 39
20	☉♒	12 37
22	☽♈	8 24
24	☽♉	11 52
26	☿♒	9 32
26	♂♏	11 59
26	☽♊	14 29
28	♀♓	16 17
28	☽♋	16 57
30	☽♌	20 16

FEBRUARY

Day		h. m.
2	☽♍	1 38
4	☽♎	9 56
6	☽♏	21 06
9	☽♐	9 38
11	☽♑	21 09
12	☿♓	15 27
13	♃♈	1 22
14	☽♒	5 56
16	☽♓	11 40
18	☽♈	15 06
19	☉♓	2 47
20	☽♉	17 29
21	♀♈	20 49
22	☽♊	19 54
24	☽♋	23 09
27	☽♌	3 45

MARCH

Day		h. m.
1	♄♉	1 25
1	☽♍	10 05
2	☿♈	22 52
3	☽♎	18 35
6	☽♏	5 23
8	☽♐	17 46
11	☽♑	5 53
13	☽♒	15 31
15	☽♓	21 29
18	☽♈	0 13
18	☿♓	9 21
18	♀♉	9 59
20	☽♉	1 09
21	☉♈	1 46
22	☽♊	2 05
24	☽♋	4 34
26	☽♌	9 23
28	☽♍	16 35
31	☽♎	1 50

APRIL

Day		h. m.
2	☽♏	12 49
5	☽♐	1 07
7	☽♑	13 39
10	☽♒	0 24
12	☽♓	7 33
12	♀♊	13 17
14	☽♈	10 45
16	☽♉	11 07
17	☿♈	22 08
18	☽♊	10 39
20	☽♋	11 27
20	☉♉	12 46
22	☽♌	15 07
24	☽♍	22 04
27	☽♎	7 47
29	☽♏	19 13

MAY

Day		h. m.
2	☽♐	7 36
4	☽♑	20 12
5	♂♎	21 33
7	☽♒	7 39
8	♀♋	16 29
8	☿♉	21 22
9	☽♓	16 15
11	☽♈	20 52
13	☽♉	21 56
15	☽♊	21 07
17	☽♋	20 40
19	☽♌	22 37
21	☉♊	11 52
22	☽♍	4 16
23	☿♊	21 22
24	☽♎	13 29
27	☽♏	1 05
29	☽♐	13 37

JUNE

Day		h. m.
1	☽♑	2 05
3	☽♒	13 36
5	♀♌	21 25
5	☽♓	23 00
7	☿♋	0 18
8	☽♈	5 06
10	☽♉	7 42
12	☽♊	7 48
14	☽♋	7 15
16	☽♌	8 08
18	☽♍	12 12
20	☽♎	20 11
21	☉♋	19 49
23	☽♏	7 18
25	☽♐	19 51
26	☿♌	15 41
28	☽♑	8 11
28	♃♉	9 29
30	☽♒	19 19

JULY

Day		h. m.
3	☽♓	4 34
5	♂♏	3 58
5	☽♈	11 21
7	☽♉	15 21
9	☽♊	16 59
11	☽♋	17 27
12	♀♍	15 19
13	☽♌	18 26
15	☽♍	21 39
18	☽♎	4 20
20	☽♏	14 30
23	☽♐	2 48
23	☉♌	6 44
25	☽♑	15 08
28	☽♒	1 54
30	☽♓	10 27
31	☿♋	18 50

AUGUST

Day		h. m.
1	☽♈	16 46
3	☽♉	21 08
5	☽♊	23 57
8	☽♋	1 53
10	☽♌	3 56
11	☿♌	4 16
12	☽♍	7 22
14	☽♎	13 24
15	♀♌	14 11
16	☽♏	22 40
19	☽♐	10 32
21	☽♑	22 59
23	☉♍	13 51
24	☽♒	9 48
26	☽♓	17 49
28	☽♈	23 09
31	☽♉	2 40
31	☿♍	15 15

Time (GMT) when the Sun, Moon and Planets enter the Zodiacal Signs in 1999

SEPTEMBER		h. m.	OCTOBER		h. m.	NOVEMBER		h. m.	DECEMBER		h. m.
2	☽♊	5 25	1	☽♋	13 32	2	☽♍	4 08	1	☽♎	17 30
2	♂♐	19 29	3	☽♌	17 14	4	☽♎	11 57	4	☽♏	3 36
4	☽♋	8 10	5	☿♏	5 13	6	☽♏	21 46	5	♀♏	22 41
6	☽♌	11 29	5	☽♍	22 40	9	♀♎	2 19	6	☽♐	15 28
8	☽♍	15 57	7	♀♍	16 50	9	☽♐	9 15	9	☽♑	4 14
10	☽♎	22 16	8	☽♎	5 52	9	☿♏	20 04	11	☿♐	2 09
13	☽♏	7 09	10	☽♏	15 02	11	☽♑	22 00	11	☽♒	16 58
15	☽♐	18 35	13	☽♐	2 19	14	☽♒	10 45	14	☽♓	4 17
16	☿♎	12 53	15	☽♑	15 03	16	☽♓	21 20	16	☽♈	12 30
18	☽♑	7 13	17	♂♑	1 35	19	☽♈	3 56	18	☽♉	16 44
20	☽♒	18 37	18	☽♒	3 16	21	☽♉	6 25	20	☽♊	17 38
23	☽♓	2 50	20	☽♓	12 33	22	☉♐	18 25	22	☉♑	7 44
23	☉♎	11 31	22	☽♈	17 40	23	☽♊	6 13	22	☽♋	16 52
25	☽♈	7 33	23	♃♈	5 49	25	☽♋	5 30	24	☽♌	16 33
27	☽♉	9 50	23	☉♏	20 52	26	♂♒	6 56	26	☽♍	18 36
29	☽♊	11 21	24	☽♉	19 24	27	☽♌	6 20	29	☽♎	0 14
			26	☽♊	19 33	29	☽♍	10 12	31	♀♐	4 54
			28	☽♋	20 10				31	☿♑	6 48
			30	☿♐	20 14				31	☽♏	9 37
			30	☽♌	22 47						

Star Tips for Farmers and Gardeners

Castration should not be performed when the Moon is in ♍, ♋, or ♏, or the animal will not thrive, and may die.

The tables on pages 128–29 will be found very useful for gardeners and farmers, for they will now be able to see at a glance when the Moon is in a good sign for their operations. Suppose I wish to put some peas in on 20th April. I find the Moon is in ♋ (Cancer), which I find from page 154 to be a fruitful sign. Hence I sow my seeds on 20th April. And if I wish the seed to grow very quickly, I should sow as the Moon is rising. Also, I find on page 154 that ♋ (Cancer) is a *movable* (cardinal) sign and hence it will accelerate the germination and growth of the seed. This is also a good time for cabbages, lettuces, beans and all sorts of pulse.

In June I think of sowing some beet, and it is necessary that this should germinate *very quickly*. So I must have the Moon increasing in light in a movable sign, and a movable sign rising. I find on page 122 that there is a New Moon on 28th June, so from that date the Moon will be increasing in light. And by looking down the column of June on page 128 I find ♑ (Capricorn), a *movable* sign, and that the Moon is in that sign until 19.19 GMT on 30th June. As the Moon is in that sign, it follows that when the Moon is rising that sign is rising too. Hence the best time to sow my beet is during those hours on 28th to 30th June.

GARDENING

Moon Guide to Planting

It is common knowledge that the moon affects the tides.
What is not so well known is the fact that the moon influences growth of plants. The table below will enable gardeners to gain maximum benefit for their plants from the moon.

Type of plant	*Best planting period*	*Moon positions*
Vegetables maturing *above* the ground and all trees and fruits.	Two days before New Moon until three days before Full Moon.	Moon in Cancer, Scorpio or Pisces. Earthy signs of Taurus, Virgo and Capricorn.
Root crops and all plants maturing *below* the ground.	Two days before Full Moon until three days before New Moon.	Moon in earthy signs or watery signs.
Flowering bulbs.	Between New Moon and Full Moon. Pruning should be done between Full Moon and New Moon when sap running down.	

Gardening Calendar

If you sow, plant or re-pot at the times set out below, it is reasonably certain you will have really fine results. (All times GMT.)

JANUARY

1, 2, 3	9.05 to 10.20 a.m. 12.35 to 3.10 p.m.
17, 18	8.55 to 10.25 a.m. 12.30 to 3.20 p.m.
31	8.45 to 10.30 a.m. 12.45 to 3.40 p.m.

Work in the Garden

Indoors. Sow carrots, leeks, cauliflowers, lettuce, mustard and cress, onions, radish and tomatoes. Plant lettuce in the greenhouse border, and chives and mint for forcing.

Sow sweet peas, begonia, carnations, petunia, salvia, verbena and pelargoniums. Plant hippeastrum and hyacinths.

Prune grape vines before the buds swell. Plant or transplant vines, peaches and nectarines.

Outdoors. Under cloches, sow broad beans, carrots, onions, peas (round-seeded) and spinach, and transplant lettuce.

Plant St Brigid anemones in mild areas. Prune roses (otherwise leave till March).

Plant fruit trees, bushes and canes of all kinds, provided the ground is not frozen or wet and sticky. Prune apples, pears, gooseberries, and red and white currants.

FEBRUARY

1	8.40 to 10.35 a.m. 12.10 to 3.15 p.m. 4.05 to 4.50 p.m.
15, 16, 17	8.35 to 10.15 a.m. 11.55 to 3.00 p.m. 4.10 to 4.50 p.m.

Work in the Garden

Indoors. Sow broccoli, Brussels sprouts, capsicum, cucumbers, lettuce, leeks, mustard and cress, onion, radishes, spinach, tomatoes.

Sow summer-flowering greenhouse plants such as gloxinia, streptocarpus and 'Charm' chrysanthemums; sweet peas and summer bedding plants that need a long growing season.

Outdoors. Sow broad beans and peas (round-seeded). Plant asparagus, garlic, Jerusalem artichokes, shallots; lettuces under cloches.

Prune winter-flowering shrubs when they finish flowering, and summer-flowering deciduous shrubs that flower on the current season's growth.

Plant fruit trees/bushes, if the ground is not frozen or very wet. Prune gooseberries. Cut down autumn raspberries to within 2–3 inches of the ground.

MARCH

1, 2, 3	8.20 to 10.10 a.m. 11.35 to 2.40 p.m. 3.40 to 5.10 p.m.
17, 18	8.05 to 10.25 a.m. 11.15 to 2.45 p.m. 3.50 to 5.50 p.m.
31	7.55 to 9.00 a.m. 10.55 to 2.30 p.m. 4.10 to 6.00 p.m.

Work in the Garden

Indoors. Sow aubergines, capsicums, cucumbers, celery, celeriac. For planting in frames or under cloches in late April or early May, sow cucumbers, courgettes and marrows. For growing in an unheated greenhouse for transplanting into the garden in April and May, sow tomatoes, summer cabbage, cauliflowers, spinach, leeks, lettuce, onions. Plant tomatoes in a heated greenhouse.

Sow half-hardy summer bedding plants.

Outdoors. Sow in warm, sheltered places or under cloches: beetroot, broad beans, onions, parsley, early peas, parsnips, spinach, early turnips. Plant Jerusalem artichokes, cabbage and cauliflowers raised in the greenhouse, lettuce, garlic, onion sets, autumn-sown Japanese onions, early potatoes (at end of month), shallots.

Plant roses, herbaceous perennials and summer-flowering bulbs. Prune summer-flowering shrubs.

Plant fruit trees/bushes, raspberries and strawberries. Prune gooseberries and cane fruits if not already done.

APRIL

1, 2	7.45 to 9.05 a.m. 11.20 to 2.15 p.m. 3.55 to 6.10 p.m.
16, 17	7.40 to 9.10 a.m. 11.05 to 3.00 p.m. 4.30 to 6.50 p.m.
30	7.50 to 9.25 a.m. 11.15 to 3.10 p.m. 5.00 to 7.10 p.m.

Work in the Garden

Indoors. Sow, to grow on outside, French beans, runner beans, broccoli, Brussels sprouts, cabbage, cauliflower, capsicum, courgettes, cucumbers, sweet corn (in pots), tomatoes.

Sow annual bedding plants (early in the month unless quick-maturing). Plant up hanging baskets ready to go out when the threat of frost is over.

Outdoors. Sow beetroot, broad beans (quick-maturing varieties), Brussels sprouts, kohl rabi, lettuce, summer spinach, carrots, peas, mange-tout and turnips. Plant onion sets and maincrop potatoes; brassicas in milder regions.

Sow hardy annuals direct where they are to flower. Transplant hardy biennials, such as wallflowers, stocks and hollyhocks, if not done in the autumn. Plant sweet peas, hardy perennials, evergreen shrubs and conifers. Prune roses. Cut back last year's growth on hardy fuchsias. To encourage new growth, cut out one stem in three from established berberis, eleagnus, forsythia and winter jasmine.

MAY

1	7.35 to 9.15 a.m. 12.10 to 4.05 p.m. 5.00 to 7.50 p.m.
15, 16	7.20 to 9.25 a.m. 12.25 to 4.40 p.m. 6.10 to 8.00 p.m.
29, 30	7.25 to 9.40 a.m. 1.05 to 5.20 p.m. 7.10 to 8.40 p.m.

Work in the Garden

Indoors. Sow courgettes, runner beans, dwarf French beans and sweet corn, for planting out; aubergine, capsicum and cucumbers for the greenhouse. Plant cucumbers, tomatoes.

Sow Brompton stocks, and pot plants for winter colour, such as calceolaria, cineraria.

Outdoors. Sow salad crops (chicory, endive, lettuce, etc.), calabrese, autumn and winter cauliflower, summer spinach, peas, carrots, parsnips, swedes, turnips. In mild areas, sow runner and dwarf French beans, ridge cucumbers. Plant Brussels sprouts, cabbages, cauliflowers, celeriac, chicory, leeks, marrows, onions. In mild areas, plant out French beans.

Sow cosmos and ten-week stocks, where they are to flower; in nursery beds, primrose, polyanthus and biennials such as Canterbury bells, double daisies, forget-me-nots, foxgloves, sweet Williams, wallflowers, and most herbaceous perennials. Plant out hardy annuals, dahlias, chrysanthemums and fuchsias. Pinch out centre-tips of chrysanthemums.

JUNE

13, 14	7.10 to 10.05 a.m. 1.40 to 5.25 p.m. 7.30 to 9.05 p.m.
28, 29	6.55 to 9.50 a.m. 1.25 to 5.35 p.m. 7.50 to 9.20 p.m.

Work in the Garden

Indoors. Plant tomatoes and late cucumbers. Stop cucumber laterals and remove male flowers.

Outdoors. Sow French beans, beetroot, calabrese, carrots, lettuce, and (not later than first half of the month) runner beans, cabbage, cauliflower, chicory, kale, ridge cucumbers, courgettes, marrows, sweet corn. Plant winter cabbage, cauliflower, kale, broccoli, leeks, courgettes, marrows and (not later than first half of the month) Brussels sprouts, celeriac, cucumbers, sweet corn, tomatoes. Keep side-shoots removed from tomatoes (unless bush varieties).

Sow hardy annuals such as calendulas, clarkias, cornflowers. And sow biennials, such as foxglove, for flowering next year. Plant out the last of the half-hardy annuals sown under glass in March and April.

Divide and replant hardy primulas and flag irises. Prune early flowering shrubs such as choisya, flowering currant, lilac and mahonia (cut one stem in three from established plants).

JULY

12, 13	6.45 to 8.50 a.m.
	11.55 to 4.45 p.m.
	6.10 to 8.40 p.m.
27, 28	6.30 to 9.10 a.m.
	12.20 to 3.55 p.m.
	5.40 to 8.10 p.m.

Work in the Garden

Indoors. Keep taking off tomato side-shoots. Remove male flowers from cucumbers.

Sow winter and spring-flowering pot plants, such as calceolarias, cinerarias, coleus. Pot old cyclamen corms.

Outdoors. Sow early in the month: beetroot, calabrese, carrots, chicory, endive, French beans, peas. Sow throughout: Chinese cabbage, spring cabbage, Florence fennel, kohl rabi, spinach beet, Swiss chard, spring onions, winter radish, turnips. Plant out leeks from March sowings, cabbage, cauliflower, celery, celeriac, endive.

Sow Brompton stocks, forget-me-nots, hollyhocks, pansies. Plant out biennials, such as Canterbury bells and wallflowers, in a nursery bed. Lift and divide spring-flowering bulbs. Prune shrubs that have just finished flowering, such as cytisus (brooms), deutzia, philadelphus, weigela and rambler roses. Cut out any suckers found on rose bushes as close to the ground as possible. Dead-head roses and summer bedding plants regularly.

AUGUST

11, 12	6.40 to 10.05 a.m.
	1.50 to 5.10 p.m.
	7.20 to 9.30 p.m.
25, 26	6.20 to 9.35 a.m.
	2.20 to 5.30 p.m.
	5.40 to 8.10 p.m.

Work in the Garden

Indoors. For over-wintering under glass and planting out in early spring, sow hardy annuals and biennials.

Outdoors. Early in the month, in mild areas, sow spring cabbage, winter radish and lettuce (this will need cloching later). Also early in the month, plant leeks, sprouting broccoli, kale and savoys. Where crops have been harvested, sow chicory, endive, Japanese onion, summer and winter radishes, spring onions, parsley and – except in the coldest regions – winter spinach, turnips. Take out growing tips of tomatoes (except bush varieties).

Sow Brompton stocks, pansies, herbaceous perennials. Plant evergreen shrubs, autumn-flowering crocus, colchicums, madonna lilies. Move biennial stocks to flowering quarters. If not already done, prune rambling and climbing roses after flowering. Prune early-flowering shrubs that flower on one-year-old wood.

Plant container-grown fruit trees and bushes. Cut out old fruited canes of raspberries, blackberries and loganberries.

SEPTEMBER

8, 9	7.50 to 10.30 a.m. 1.30 to 4.50 p.m. 6.20 to 8.35 p.m.
25, 26	7.40 to 9.50 a.m. 1.15 to 4.25 p.m. 5.40 to 7.00 p.m.

Work in the Garden

Indoors. Sow summer cauliflowers (for planting out next March), endive, lettuce, mustard and cress.

Sow salpiglossus and schizanthus, for a spring display. Move tender plants that have been used in summer bedding schemes to a frost-free greenhouse, such as Indian azalias, cannas, fuchsias, geraniums (pelargoniums).

Outdoors. Sow radishes, turnip (to harvest tops in spring), spinach for winter and spring (except in cold regions). Under cloches: summer cauliflowers and, in mild areas, hardy lettuces. Plant spring cabbages, Japanese onion sets, August-sown lettuces under cloches. 'Stop' growing point of tomatoes.

Sow hardy annuals and cover with cloches. Plant trees and shrubs, biennials and perennials sown earlier and spring bulbs, such as crocus, daffodil, scilla.

Plant strawberries, and strawberry runners. Complete summer pruning of apples, pears, and morello cherries. Cut out old canes of blackberries as fruiting finishes.

OCTOBER

9, 10	8.15 to 10.40 a.m. 12.40 to 3.55 p.m. 5.10 to 6.30 p.m.
23, 24	8.25 to 10.55 a.m. 12.50 to 3.10 p.m. 4.30 to 5.15 p.m.

Work in the Garden

Indoors. Sow winter lettuces, mustard and cress, radishes. Plant chicory for forcing.

Sow antirrhinums, stocks, sweet peas, alpines.

By the middle of the month, sow alpine strawberries in trays of moist compost.

Outdoors. Sow cornsalad. In the middle of the month, in a sheltered position, sow dwarf peas for overwintering. At the end of the month, sow broad beans. As soon as possible, plant spring cabbage; winter lettuces under cloches. Lift, divide and replant rhubarb for new clumps.

Sow sweet peas. Plant lilies, as soon as they are received, and tulip bulbs (at the end of the month). Plant container-grown trees and shrubs, conifer hedges, and hardy perennials and biennials. Prune rambler roses, deciduous climbing plants and summer-flowering shrubs. Clip privet and other evergreen hedges (except conifers). Lift and divide rampant rock plants.

Plant raspberries from suckers or canes, after leaf fall; apples, pears, plums.

NOVEMBER

8, 9	8.35 to 10.35 a.m. 12.40 to 2.55 p.m. 3.50 to 4.10 p.m.
23, 24	8.50 to 11.10 a.m. 1.20 to 3.15 p.m.

Work in the Garden

Indoors. Sow lettuce for over-wintering in greenhouse or frames before planting out, mustard and cress, cauliflower.

Prune grape vines, as soon as they are dormant.

Outdoors. Sow as soon as possible 'Aquadulce' broad bean in the milder parts of the country and where the soil is well drained. Plant in frames lettuces sown in October for harvesting in spring.

Plant roses and deciduous trees and shrubs, including bare-rooted plants. Plant tulip bulbs. Put in other spring-flowering bulbs without delay if not already done. Plant hardy perennials (lift and divide these if the weather is mild and the soil is not too wet – replant the younger growth, the outer part of the clump). Lift dahlia tubers, leaving about 6 inches of stem attached, for storage in a frost-free place.

Plant apples, pears, plums and soft fruits (excluding strawberries). Prune red and white currants, gooseberries, apple and pear trees (remove dead, diseased or crossing branches), black currants if not done after harvesting.

DECEMBER

6, 7	9.10 to 11.30 a.m. 1.45 to 2.55 p.m.
21, 22	9.05 to 11.40 a.m. 1.30 to 3.05 p.m.

Work in the Garden

Indoors. Sow mustard and cress. Where heating is adequate, sow a few tomatoes late in the month for a very early picking, and a few rows of forcing carrots in the greenhouse border. Hardy lettuce can be sown to plant out later under cloches. Onions for exhibition can be sown in late December. Plant out lettuces from October sowings.

Pot up lily of the valley crowns for forcing.

Outdoors. Broad beans can be sown early in the month, in light, well-drained soils (choose an extra-hardy variety such as 'Aquadulce'). If the soil is not wet and sticky, plant shallots and Jerusalem artichokes.

Plant trees and shrubs as soon as they arrive, unless the weather is very wet or the ground frozen (if it is, keep the plant in a shed and protect roots with damp peat or straw, or wrap them in polythene). December is a suitable time for planting a new hedge.

Plant tree, bush and cane fruits, when weather and soil conditions are favourable. Continue pruning shrubs.

Farmers' Tables

	January									February							
Day of month	Mare, 48 weeks	Cow, 40 weeks	Ewe and Goat, 21 weeks	Sow, 16 weeks	Bitch, 9 weeks	Goose, Rabbit, 30 days	Turkey, Duck, Peafowl, 28 days	Fowl, 21 days	Day of month	Mare, 48 weeks	Cow, 40 weeks	Ewe and Goat, 21 weeks	Sow, 16 weeks	Bitch, 9 weeks	Goose, Rabbit, 30 days	Turkey, Duck, Peafowl, 28 days	Fowl, 21 days
	dec	oct	may	apr	mar	jan	jan	jan		jan	nov	jun	may	apr	mar		feb
1	4	10	31	24	6	31	29	22	1	3	9	30	24	5	3	mar	22
2	5	11	jun	25	7	feb	30	23	2	4	10	july	25	6	4	2	23
3	6	12	2	26	8	2	31	24	3	5	11	2	26	7	5	3	24
4	7	13	3	27	9	3	feb	25	4	6	12	3	27	8	6	4	25
5	8	14	4	28	10	4	2	26	5	7	13	4	28	9	7	5	26
6	9	15	5	29	11	5	3	27	6	8	14	5	29	10	8	6	27
7	10	16	6	30	12	6	4	28	7	9	15	6	30	11	9	7	28
8	11	17	7	may	13	7	5	29	8	10	16	7	31	12	10	8	mar
9	12	18	8	2	14	8	6	30	9	11	17	8	jun	13	11	9	2
10	13	19	9	3	15	9	7	31	10	12	18	9	2	14	12	10	3
11	14	20	10	4	16	10	8	feb	11	13	19	10	3	15	13	11	4
12	15	21	11	5	17	11	9	2	12	14	20	11	4	16	14	12	5
13	16	22	12	6	18	12	10	3	13	15	21	12	5	17	15	13	6
14	17	23	13	7	19	13	11	4	14	16	22	13	6	18	16	14	7
15	18	24	14	8	20	14	12	5	15	17	23	14	7	19	17	15	8
16	19	25	15	9	21	15	13	6	16	18	24	15	8	20	18	16	9
17	20	26	16	10	22	16	14	7	17	19	25	16	9	21	19	17	10
18	21	27	17	11	23	17	15	8	18	20	26	17	10	22	20	18	11
19	22	28	18	12	24	18	16	9	19	21	27	18	11	23	21	19	12
20	23	29	19	13	25	19	17	10	20	22	28	19	12	24	22	20	13
21	24	30	20	14	26	20	18	11	21	23	29	20	13	25	23	21	14
22	25	31	21	15	27	21	19	12	22	24	30	21	14	26	24	22	15
23	26	nov	22	16	28	22	20	13	23	25	dec	22	15	27	25	23	16
24	27	2	23	17	29	23	21	14	24	26	2	23	16	28	26	24	17
25	28	3	24	18	30	24	22	15	25	27	3	24	17	29	27	25	18
26	29	4	25	19	31	25	23	16	26	28	4	25	18	30	28	26	19
27	30	5	26	20	apr	26	24	17	27	29	5	26	19	may	29	27	20
28	31	6	27	21	2	27	25	18	28	30	6	27	20	2	30	28	21
29	jan	7	28	22	3	28	26	19									
30	2	8	29	23	4	mar	27	20									
31	3	9	30	24	5	2	28	21									

These tables show when an animal served or an egg laid during the present month will give birth or hatch.

1999 United Kingdom Agricultural Shows

BAKEWELL Show: 4th–5th August

BINGLEY Show, Myrtle Park: 4th August

BLACK ISLE Show, Mannsfield, Muir–of–Ord, Ross–shire: 5th August

BORDER UNION Show, Kelso: 30th–31st July

BRITISH EQUINE Event, National Agricultural Centre, Stoneleigh:
7th November

BRITISH PIG AND POULTRY Fair, National Agricultural Centre,
Stoneleigh: 12th–13th May

BUCKS County Show, Weedon Park, nr. Aylesbury: 2nd September

CHESHIRE County Show, Tabley, Knutsford: 22nd–23rd June   ▶

Farmers' Tables

	March									April							
Day of month	Mare, 48 weeks	Cow, 40 weeks	Ewe and Goat, 21 weeks	Sow, 16 weeks	Bitch, 9 weeks	Goose, Rabbit, 30 days	Turkey, Duck, Peafowl, 28 days	Fowl, 21 days	Day of month	Mare, 48 weeks	Cow, 40 weeks	Ewe and Goat, 21 weeks	Sow, 16 weeks	Bitch, 9 weeks	Goose, Rabbit, 30 days	Turkey, Duck, Peafowl, 28 days	Fowl, 21 days
	feb	dec	july	jun	may	mar	mar	mar		mar	jan	aug	july	jun	may	apr	apr
1	1	8	29	22	4	31	29	22	1	4	8	29	23	4	1	29	22
2	2	9	30	23	5	apr	30	23	2	5	9	30	24	5	2	30	23
3	3	10	31	24	6	2	31	24	3	6	10	31	25	6	3	may	24
4	4	11	aug	25	7	3	apr	25	4	7	11	sep	26	7	4	2	25
5	5	12	2	26	8	4	2	26	5	8	12	2	27	8	5	3	26
6	6	13	3	27	9	5	3	27	6	9	13	3	28	9	6	4	27
7	7	14	4	28	10	6	4	28	7	10	14	4	29	10	7	5	28
8	8	15	5	29	11	7	5	29	8	11	15	5	30	11	8	6	29
9	9	16	6	30	12	8	6	30	9	12	16	6	31	12	9	7	30
10	10	17	7	july	13	9	7	31	10	13	17	7	aug	13	10	8	may
11	11	18	8	2	14	10	8	apr	11	14	18	8	2	14	11	9	2
12	12	19	9	3	15	11	9	2	12	15	19	9	3	15	12	10	3
13	13	20	10	4	16	12	10	3	13	16	20	10	4	16	13	11	4
14	14	21	11	5	17	13	11	4	14	17	21	11	5	17	14	12	5
15	15	22	12	6	18	14	12	5	15	18	22	12	6	18	15	13	6
16	16	23	13	7	19	15	13	6	16	19	23	13	7	19	16	14	7
17	17	24	14	8	20	16	14	7	17	20	24	14	8	20	17	15	8
18	18	25	15	9	21	17	15	8	18	21	25	15	9	21	18	16	9
19	19	26	16	10	22	18	16	9	19	22	26	16	10	22	19	17	10
20	20	27	17	11	23	19	17	10	20	23	27	17	11	23	20	18	11
21	21	28	18	12	24	20	18	11	21	24	28	18	12	24	21	19	12
22	22	29	19	13	25	21	19	12	22	25	29	19	13	25	22	20	13
23	23	30	20	14	26	22	20	13	23	26	30	20	14	26	23	21	14
24	24	31	21	15	27	23	21	14	24	27	31	21	15	27	24	22	15
25	25	jan	22	16	28	24	22	15	25	28	feb	22	16	28	25	23	16
26	26	2	23	17	29	25	23	16	26	29	2	23	17	29	26	24	17
27	27	3	24	18	30	26	24	17	27	30	3	24	18	30	27	25	18
28	28	4	25	19	31	27	25	18	28	31	4	25	19	july	28	26	19
29	mar	5	26	20	jun	28	26	19	29	apr	5	26	20	2	29	27	20
30	2	6	27	21	2	29	27	20	30	2	6	27	21	3	30	28	21
31	3	7	28	22	3	30	28	21									

These tables show when an animal served or an egg laid during the present month will give birth or hatch.

1999 UNITED KINGDOM AGRICULTURAL SHOWS cont'd

CUMBERLAND Show, Rickerby Park, Carlisle: 17th July

DENBIGHSHIRE & FLINTSHIRE Show, Denbigh: 19th August

DEVON County Show, Westpoint, Clyst St Mary, Exeter: 20th–22nd May

DORCHESTER Agricultural Show, Came Park: 4th September

DUMFRIES & LOCKERBIE Show, Park Farm, Dumfries: 7th August

EAST OF ENGLAND Show, Peterborough: 20th–22nd July

EGHAM & THORPE Royal Show, Runnymede: 28th–29th August

ESSEX County Show, Great Leighs, nr Chelmsford: 20th–22nd June (provisional)

GRAIN AND FARM IT, National Agricultural Centre, Stoneleigh: 24th–25th November

GREAT YORKSHIRE Show, Harrogate: 13th–15th July

Farmers' Tables

	May									June							
Day of month	Mare, 48 weeks	Cow, 40 weeks	Ewe and Goat, 21 weeks	Sow, 16 weeks	Bitch, 9 weeks	Goose, Rabbit, 30 days	Turkey, Duck, Peafowl, 28 days	Fowl, 21 days	Day of month	Mare, 48 weeks	Cow, 40 weeks	Ewe and Goat, 21 weeks	Sow, 16 weeks	Bitch, 9 weeks	Goose, Rabbit, 30 days	Turkey, Duck, Peafowl, 28 days	Fowl, 21 days
	apr	*feb*	*sep*	*aug*	*july*	*may*	*may*	*may*		*may*	*mar*	*oct*	*sep*	*aug*	*july*	*jun*	*jun*
1	3	7	28	22	4	31	29	22	1	4	10	29	22	4	1	29	22
2	4	8	29	23	5	*jun*	30	23	2	5	11	30	23	5	2	30	23
3	5	9	30	24	6	2	31	24	3	6	12	31	24	6	3	*july*	24
4	6	10	*oct*	25	7	3	*jun*	25	4	7	13	*nov*	25	7	4	2	25
5	7	11	2	26	8	4	2	26	5	8	14	2	26	8	5	3	26
6	8	12	3	27	9	5	3	27	6	9	15	3	27	9	6	4	27
7	9	13	4	28	10	6	4	28	7	10	16	4	28	10	7	5	28
8	10	14	5	29	11	7	5	29	8	11	17	5	29	11	8	6	29
9	11	15	6	30	12	8	6	30	9	12	18	6	30	12	9	7	30
10	12	16	7	31	13	9	7	31	10	13	19	7	*oct*	13	10	8	*july*
11	13	17	8	*sep*	14	10	8	*jun*	11	14	20	8	2	14	11	9	2
12	14	18	9	2	15	11	9	2	12	15	21	9	3	15	12	10	3
13	15	19	10	3	16	12	10	3	13	16	22	10	4	16	13	11	4
14	16	20	11	4	17	13	11	4	14	17	23	11	5	17	14	12	5
15	17	21	12	5	18	14	12	5	15	18	24	12	6	18	15	13	6
16	18	22	13	6	19	15	13	6	16	19	25	13	7	19	16	14	7
17	19	23	14	7	20	16	14	7	17	20	26	14	8	20	17	15	8
18	20	24	15	8	21	17	15	8	18	21	27	15	9	21	18	16	9
19	21	25	16	9	22	18	16	9	19	22	28	16	10	22	19	17	10
20	22	26	17	10	23	19	17	10	20	23	29	17	11	23	20	18	11
21	23	27	18	11	24	20	18	11	21	24	30	18	12	24	21	19	12
22	24	28	19	12	25	21	19	12	22	25	31	19	13	25	22	20	13
23	25	29	20	13	26	22	20	13	23	26	*apr*	20	14	26	23	21	14
24	26	*mar*	21	14	27	23	21	14	24	27	2	21	15	27	24	22	15
25	27	2	22	15	28	24	22	15	25	28	3	22	16	28	25	23	16
26	28	3	23	16	29	25	23	16	26	29	4	23	17	29	26	24	17
27	29	4	24	17	30	26	24	17	27	30	5	24	18	30	27	25	18
28	30	5	25	18	31	27	25	18	28	31	6	25	19	31	28	26	19
29	*may*	6	26	19	*aug*	28	26	19	29	*jun*	7	26	20	*sep*	29	27	20
30	2	7	27	20	2	29	27	20	30	2	8	27	21	2	30	28	21
31	3	8	28	21	3	30	28	21									

These tables show when an animal served or an egg laid during the present month will give birth or hatch.

1999 UNITED KINGDOM AGRICULTURAL SHOWS cont'd

HERTS County Show, Redbourn: 29th–30th May

KENT County Show, Detling, nr Maidstone: 15th–17th July

LEICESTERSHIRE County Show, Dishley Grange Farm, Loughborough: 2nd–3rd May

LINCOLNSHIRE Show, Grange–de–Lings, Lincoln: 23rd–24th June

MID–SOMERSET Show, Shepton Mallet: 15th August

MONMOUTHSHIRE Show, Vauxhall, Monmouth: 26th August

NATIONAL SHIRE HORSE SHOW, Peterborough: 13th–14th March (provisional)

NEW FOREST & HAMPSHIRE Show, Brockenhurst: 27th–29th July

NEWBURY & ROYAL COUNTY OF BERKSHIRE Show, Chievely, Newbury: 18th–19th September

▶

Farmers' Tables

July

Day of month	Mare, 48 weeks	Cow, 40 weeks	Ewe and Goat, 21 weeks	Sow, 16 weeks	Bitch, 9 weeks	Goose, Rabbit, 30 days	Turkey, Duck, Peafowl, 28 days	Fowl, 21 days
	jun	*apr*	*nov*	*oct*	*sep*	*july*	*july*	*july*
1	3	9	28	22	3	31	29	22
2	4	10	29	23	4	*aug*	30	23
3	5	11	30	24	5	2	31	24
4	6	12	*dec*	25	6	3	*aug*	25
5	7	13	2	26	7	4	2	26
6	8	14	3	27	8	5	3	27
7	9	15	4	28	9	6	4	28
8	10	16	5	29	10	7	5	29
9	11	17	6	30	11	8	6	30
10	12	18	7	31	12	9	7	31
11	13	19	8	*nov*	13	10	8	*aug*
12	14	20	9	2	14	11	9	2
13	15	21	10	3	15	12	10	3
14	16	22	11	4	16	13	11	4
15	17	23	12	5	17	14	12	5
16	18	24	13	6	18	15	13	6
17	19	25	14	7	19	16	14	7
18	20	26	15	8	20	17	15	8
19	21	27	16	9	21	18	16	9
20	22	28	17	10	22	19	17	10
21	23	29	18	11	23	20	18	11
22	24	30	19	12	24	21	19	12
23	25	*may*	20	13	25	22	20	13
24	26	2	21	14	26	23	21	14
25	27	3	22	15	27	24	22	15
26	28	4	23	16	28	25	23	16
27	29	5	24	17	29	26	24	17
28	30	6	25	18	30	27	25	18
29	*july*	7	26	19	*oct*	28	26	19
30	2	8	27	20	2	29	27	20
31	3	9	28	21	3	30	28	21

August

Day of month	Mare, 48 weeks	Cow, 40 weeks	Ewe and Goat, 21 weeks	Sow, 16 weeks	Bitch, 9 weeks	Goose, Rabbit, 30 days	Turkey, Duck, Peafowl, 28 days	Fowl, 21 days
	july	*may*	*dec*	*nov*	*oct*	*aug*	*aug*	*aug*
1	4	10	29	22	4	31	29	22
2	5	11	30	23	5	*sep*	30	23
3	6	12	31	24	6	2	31	24
4	7	13	*jan*	25	7	3	*sep*	25
5	8	14	2	26	8	4	2	26
6	9	15	3	27	9	5	3	27
7	10	16	4	28	10	6	4	28
8	11	17	5	29	11	7	5	29
9	12	18	6	30	12	8	6	30
10	13	19	7	*dec*	13	9	7	31
11	14	20	8	2	14	10	8	*sep*
12	15	21	9	3	15	11	9	2
13	16	22	10	4	16	12	10	3
14	17	23	11	5	17	13	11	4
15	18	24	12	6	18	14	12	5
16	19	25	13	7	19	15	13	6
17	20	26	14	8	20	16	14	7
18	21	27	15	9	21	17	15	8
19	22	28	16	10	22	18	16	9
20	23	29	17	11	23	19	17	10
21	24	30	18	12	24	20	18	11
22	25	31	19	13	25	21	19	12
23	26	*jun*	20	14	26	22	20	13
24	27	2	21	15	27	23	21	14
25	28	3	22	16	27	24	22	15
26	29	4	23	17	28	25	23	16
27	30	5	24	18	29	26	24	17
28	31	6	25	19	30	27	25	18
29	*aug*	7	26	20	*nov*	28	26	19
30	2	8	27	21	2	29	27	20
31	3	9	28	22	3	30	28	21

These tables show when an animal served or an egg laid during the present month will give birth or hatch.

1999 UNITED KINGDOM AGRICULTURAL SHOWS cont'd

NORTH SOMERSET Show, Ashton Court, Bristol: 3rd May

NOTTINGHAMSHIRE County Show, Winthorpe, Newark: 7th–8th May

PEMBROKESHIRE County Show, Withybush, Haverfordwest:
    17th–19th August

ROMSEY Show, Broadlands Park: 11th September

ROYAL BATH & WEST OF ENGLAND Show, Shepton Mallet:
    2nd–5th June

ROYAL CORNWALL Show, Wadebridge: 10th–12th June

ROYAL HIGHLAND Show, Ingliston, Edinburgh: 24th–27th June

ROYAL LANCASHIRE Show, Astley Park, Chorley: 23rd–25th July

ROYAL NORFOLK Show, Showground, Dereham Road, Norwich:
    30th June–1st July

Farmers' Tables

September

Day of month	Mare, 48 weeks	Cow, 40 weeks	Ewe and Goat, 21 weeks	Sow, 16 weeks	Bitch, 9 weeks	Goose, Rabbit, 30 days	Turkey, Duck, Peafowl, 28 days	Fowl, 21 days
	aug	*jun*	*jan*	*dec*	*nov*	*oct*	*sep*	*sep*
1	4	10	29	23	4	1	29	22
2	5	11	30	24	5	2	30	23
3	6	12	31	25	6	3	*oct*	24
4	7	13	*feb*	26	7	4	2	25
5	8	14	2	27	8	5	3	26
6	9	15	3	28	9	6	4	27
7	10	16	4	29	10	7	5	28
8	11	17	5	30	11	8	6	29
9	12	18	6	31	12	9	7	30
10	13	19	7	*jan*	13	10	8	*oct*
11	14	20	8	2	14	11	9	2
12	15	21	9	3	15	12	10	3
13	16	22	10	4	16	13	11	4
14	17	23	11	5	17	14	12	5
15	18	24	12	6	18	15	13	6
16	19	25	13	7	19	16	14	7
17	20	26	14	8	20	17	15	8
18	21	27	15	9	21	18	16	9
19	22	28	16	10	22	19	17	10
20	23	29	17	11	23	20	18	11
21	24	30	18	12	24	21	19	12
22	25	*july*	19	13	25	22	20	13
23	26	2	20	14	26	23	21	14
24	27	3	21	15	27	24	22	15
25	28	4	22	16	28	25	23	16
26	29	5	23	17	29	26	24	17
27	30	6	24	18	30	27	25	18
28	31	7	25	19	*dec*	28	26	19
29	*sep*	8	26	20	2	29	27	20
30	2	9	27	21	3	30	28	21

October

Day of month	Mare, 48 weeks	Cow, 40 weeks	Ewe and Goat, 21 weeks	Sow, 16 weeks	Bitch, 9 weeks	Goose, Rabbit, 30 days	Turkey, Duck, Peafowl, 28 days	Fowl, 21 days
	sep	*july*	*feb*	*jan*	*dec*	*oct*	*oct*	*oct*
1	3	10	28	22	4	31	29	22
2	4	11	*mar*	23	5	*nov*	30	23
3	5	12	2	24	6	2	31	24
4	6	13	3	25	7	3	*nov*	25
5	7	14	4	26	8	4	2	26
6	8	15	5	27	9	5	3	27
7	9	16	6	28	10	6	4	28
8	10	17	7	29	11	7	5	29
9	11	18	8	30	12	8	6	30
10	12	19	9	31	13	9	7	31
11	13	20	10	*feb*	14	10	8	*nov*
12	14	21	11	2	15	11	9	2
13	15	22	12	3	16	12	10	3
14	16	23	13	4	17	13	11	4
15	17	24	14	5	18	14	12	5
16	18	25	15	6	19	15	13	6
17	19	26	16	7	20	16	14	7
18	20	27	17	8	21	17	15	8
19	21	28	18	9	22	18	16	9
20	22	29	19	10	23	19	17	10
21	23	30	20	11	24	20	18	11
22	24	31	21	12	25	21	19	12
23	25	*aug*	22	13	26	22	20	13
24	26	2	23	14	27	23	21	14
25	27	3	24	15	28	24	22	15
26	28	4	25	16	29	25	23	16
27	29	5	26	17	30	26	24	17
28	30	6	27	18	31	27	25	18
29	*oct*	7	28	19	*jan*	28	26	19
30	2	8	29	20	2	29	27	20
31	3	9	30	21	3	30	28	21

These tables show when an animal served or an egg laid during the present month will give birth or hatch.

1999 UNITED KINGDOM AGRICULTURAL SHOWS cont'd

ROYAL SHOW, National Agricultural Centre, Stoneleigh, Kenilworth: 5th–8th July

ROYAL ULSTER Agricultural Society Balmoral Show, Balmoral, Belfast: 12th–14th May

ROYAL WELSH Show, Llanelwedd, Builth Wells: 19th–22nd July

ROYAL WELSH AGRICULTURAL WINTER Fair, Llanelwedd, Builth Wells: 7th December

SHROPSHIRE & WEST MIDLANDS Show, Berwick Road, Shrewsbury: 21st–22nd May

SOUTH OF ENGLAND Show, Ardingley, Haywards Heath: 10th–12th June

STAFFORDSHIRE County Show, Stafford: 26th–27th May

SUFFOLK Show, Ipswich: 2nd–3rd June ▶

Farmers' Tables

November									December								
Day of month	Mare, 48 weeks	Cow, 40 weeks	Ewe and Goat, 21 weeks	Sow, 16 weeks	Bitch, 9 weeks	Goose, Rabbit, 30 days	Turkey, Duck, Peafowl, 28 days	Fowl, 21 days	Day of month	Mare, 48 weeks	Cow, 40 weeks	Ewe and Goat, 21 weeks	Sow, 16 weeks	Bitch, 9 weeks	Goose, Rabbit, 30 days	Turkey, Duck, Peafowl, 28 days	Fowl, 21 days
	oct	aug	mar	feb	jan	dec	nov	nov		nov	sep	apr	mar	feb	dec	dec	dec
1	4	10	31	22	4	1	29	22	1	3	9	30	24	3	31	29	22
2	5	11	apr	23	5	2	30	23	2	4	10	may	25	4	jan	30	23
3	6	12	2	24	6	3	dec	24	3	5	11	2	26	5	2	31	24
4	7	13	3	25	7	4	2	25	4	6	12	3	27	6	3	jan	25
5	8	14	4	26	8	5	3	26	5	7	13	4	28	7	4	2	26
6	9	15	5	27	9	6	4	27	6	8	14	5	29	8	5	3	27
7	10	16	6	28	10	7	5	28	7	9	15	6	30	9	6	4	28
8	11	17	7	mar	11	8	6	29	8	10	16	7	31	10	7	5	29
9	12	18	8	2	12	9	7	30	9	11	17	8	apr	11	8	6	30
10	13	19	9	3	13	10	8	dec	10	12	18	9	2	12	9	7	31
11	14	20	10	4	14	11	9	2	11	13	19	10	3	13	10	8	jan
12	15	21	11	5	15	12	10	3	12	14	20	11	4	14	11	9	2
13	16	22	12	6	16	13	11	4	13	15	21	12	5	15	12	10	3
14	17	23	13	7	17	14	12	5	14	16	22	13	6	16	13	11	4
15	18	24	14	8	18	15	13	6	15	17	23	14	7	17	14	12	5
16	19	25	15	9	19	16	14	7	16	18	24	15	8	18	15	13	6
17	20	26	16	10	20	17	15	8	17	19	25	16	9	19	16	14	7
18	21	27	17	11	21	18	16	9	18	20	26	17	10	20	17	15	8
19	22	28	18	12	22	19	17	10	19	21	27	18	11	21	18	16	9
20	23	29	19	13	23	20	18	11	20	22	28	19	12	22	19	17	10
21	24	30	20	14	24	21	19	12	21	23	29	20	13	23	20	18	11
22	25	31	21	15	25	22	20	13	22	24	30	21	14	24	21	19	12
23	26	sep	22	16	26	23	21	14	23	25	oct	22	15	25	22	20	13
24	27	2	23	17	27	24	22	15	24	26	2	23	16	26	23	21	14
25	28	3	24	18	28	25	23	16	25	27	3	24	17	27	24	22	15
26	29	4	25	19	29	26	24	17	26	28	4	25	18	28	25	23	16
27	30	5	26	20	30	27	25	18	27	29	5	26	19	mar	26	24	17
28	31	6	27	21	31	28	26	19	28	30	6	27	20	2	27	25	18
29	nov	7	28	22	feb	29	27	20	29	dec	7	28	21	3	28	26	19
30	2	8	29	23	2	30	28	21	30	2	8	29	22	4	29	27	20
									31	3	9	30	23	5	30	28	21

These tables show when an animal served or an egg laid during the present month will give birth or hatch.

1999 UNITED KINGDOM AGRICULTURAL SHOWS cont'd

SURREY County Show, Stoke Park, Guildford: 31st May

TENDRING HUNDRED Show, Lawford House Park, nr Manningtree: 10th July

THAME Show: 16th September

THREE COUNTIES Show, Malvern: 15th–17th June

TURRIFF Show, The Haughs: 2nd–3rd August

UNITED COUNTIES Show, Nantyci Showground, Carmarthen: 12th–13th August

WESTMORLAND County Show, Lane Farm, Crooklands: 9th September

WOKINGHAM & READING Show, Spencer's Wood, nr Reading: 5th September

Dates of events listed here may change. Please check with local organiser/tourist board.

FINANCIAL OUTLOOK AND STOCK EXCHANGE FORECASTS 1999

The world economy as a whole will be in mild recession with few trading opportunities anywhere that could expand industries. Government money will be provided to sustain and expand the building industry, but credit-worthy buyers will be few and house prices will remain stationary or decline. The economic strength and importance of Great Britain will also decline. There will be a minor economic recovery, starting in July. The transport industry is indicated as the likeliest area for growth and profit, but building and retailing may have to lay off employees. Unemployment is likely to increase from August onward.

The year falls into two political parts. Between January 1st and early July there will be a period of planning measures to increase the prosperity of the citizens and to improve the economy of the nation. But no matter what measures are taken the results will be disappointing. Between October and the end of the year the Government will move all means at its disposal to support and help the financial institutions of Great Britain. The budget will favour the prosperous citizens.

You will have complete control over your own pensions savings and there will be no one to impose penalties for late payment of monthly instalments, or confiscation of all your contributions if you are unable to continue to pay into the pensions fund for one of many reasons. If you accumulate your yearly contributions and buy only once a year, you have the least trading expenses, i.e. just one charge instead of twelve charges if you buy monthly.

The London Stock Exchange
The London Stock Exchange will have a difficult time during the first five months. Competition will be very severe and the 100 shares index is likely to drop sharply during the first half of February. The demand for Government Stock will remain small and the interest offered will stay high. In the long run, and as an investment to keep towards retirement, Government Stock will prove safe and sound. You are likely to find that Government securities will be at their lowest price during the first half of

February 1999. The 100 share index is likely to rise steadily between the end of February and the middle of May, with shares of financial institutions and Government securities making most gains. Shares in engineering companies will be prominent during July and shares in retailers and manufacturers of consumer goods are likely to show good gains during September. The 100 share index should show a steady rise to the end of the year.

In the 1930s the sugar refiners Tate and Lyle sent each shareholder a 2lb packet of granulated sugar, additional to the dividend. One of the year's share recommendations is Associated British Foods, plc, who, among other items, produce Burton's Biscuits. Perhaps you will get a packet or two with the dividend. The other recommendation is Tesco plc. Both companies are sound and their shares are worth holding for years.

The Common Market was started on 18th April 1951, and it was founded for the benefit of its members and not the benefit of any specific member state. Great Britain never has had and never will have some special position in Europe. We need Europe, but the Europeans do not need us. Comparison between the horoscopes of Great Britain and of the Common Market shows that British retail goods like textiles and food are not essential to Europe and letting them be sold in Europe is looked upon as a concession to this country. Britain's financial services are looked upon as unnecessary and the social services mean and oppressive.

There is little interest in the London Stock Exchange and the only shares the Europeans would be interested in are shares in engineering companies and textile manufacturers. But although the horoscopes show that there is little interest in Great Britain, there is no hostility towards her either.

The Euro
On 2nd May 1998, eleven European nations agreed to abandon their individual currencies and have a common one – the Euro. This move means that – ultimately – these countries will merge into one nation, governed from Brussels. The horoscope shows a stable economy, but no great prosperity. The main anxiety is Europe's dependence on imported mineral oil, and there will be generous support for agricultural products that yield oil, e.g. rape seed. Comparing the horoscopes of Britain and the Euro shows that British textiles and agricultural equipment will be welcome in the eleven member states.

RAPHAEL'S TIDAL PREDICTIONS 1999
HIGH WATER LONDON BRIDGE (GMT)

	January						February						March					
Date	Day	Moon	a.m. h.m.	ht. m	p.m. h.m.	ht. m	Day	Moon	a.m. h.m.	ht. m	p.m. h.m.	ht. m	Day	Moon	a.m. h.m.	ht. m	p.m. h.m.	ht. m
1	F		0.41	7.0	13.03	6.9	M		2.07	7.0	14.30	7.2	M		1.05	6.9	13.32	7.1
2	Sa	○	1.32	7.0	13.53	7.1	Tu		2.49	7.2	15.12	7.4	Tu	○	1.52	7.0	14.16	7.3
3	Su		2.19	7.1	14.40	7.3	W		3.27	7.3	15.51	7.4	W		2.31	7.1	14.54	7.3
4	M		3.02	7.2	15.25	7.4	Th		4.05	7.2	16.28	7.3	Th		3.08	7.2	15.29	7.4
5	Tu		3.44	7.3	16.08	7.5	F		4.41	7.1	17.04	7.1	F		3.41	7.2	16.03	7.3
6	W		4.26	7.2	16.52	7.3	Sa		5.14	6.8	17.40	6.8	Sa		4.12	7.1	16.34	7.1
7	Th		5.06	7.0	17.33	7.0	Su		5.51	6.5	18.19	6.5	Su		4.43	6.9	17.04	6.9
8	F		5.45	6.6	18.15	6.6	M	☾	6.33	6.2	19.03	6.1	M		5.17	6.7	17.38	6.6
9	Sa	☾	6.27	6.3	19.01	6.3	Tu		7.24	5.9	19.57	5.9	Tu		5.54	6.4	18.16	6.4
10	Su		7.17	6.0	19.55	6.0	W		8.27	5.6	20.58	5.7	W	☾	6.37	6.0	19.00	6.0
11	M		8.17	5.8	20.55	5.9	Th		9.34	5.5	22.03	5.7	Th		7.31	5.7	19.55	5.7
12	Tu		9.25	5.7	22.01	5.9	F		10.45	5.6	23.10	5.9	F		8.38	5.4	21.04	5.5
13	W		10.35	5.8	23.06	6.1	Sa		11.51	5.9	—	—	Sa		9.56	5.5	22.21	5.6
14	Th		11.37	6.0	23.58	6.3	Su		0.11	6.3	12.43	6.4	Su		11.13	5.8	23.37	6.0
15	F		—	—	12.25	6.2	M		1.01	6.7	13.28	6.8	M		—	—	12.13	6.3
16	Sa		0.43	6.6	13.07	6.5	Tu	●	1.45	7.0	14.10	7.2	Tu		0.33	6.5	13.03	6.9
17	Su	●	1.25	6.8	13.49	6.8	W		2.27	7.3	14.51	7.5	W	●	1.19	7.0	13.46	7.3
18	M		2.06	7.0	14.30	7.1	Th		3.06	7.5	15.32	7.6	Th		2.03	7.4	14.28	7.6
19	Tu		2.45	7.2	15.09	7.2	F		3.43	7.5	16.10	7.5	F		2.42	7.6	15.09	7.8
20	W		3.25	7.3	15.49	7.3	Sa		4.21	7.4	16.50	7.3	Sa		3.22	7.7	15.49	7.7
21	Th		4.01	7.2	16.28	7.3	Su		4.59	7.2	17.33	6.9	Su		4.01	7.6	16.31	7.4
22	F		4.38	7.1	17.07	7.1	M		5.41	6.9	18.19	6.6	M		4.42	7.4	17.13	7.0
23	Sa		5.16	6.9	17.51	6.8	Tu	☽	6.32	6.6	19.15	6.3	Tu		5.28	7.0	17.59	6.6
24	Su	☽	5.58	6.7	18.40	6.5	W		7.35	6.4	20.24	6.2	W	☽	6.19	6.7	18.54	6.3
25	M		6.49	6.5	19.41	6.3	Th		8.54	6.3	21.41	6.2	Th		7.21	6.4	19.59	6.1
26	Tu		7.56	6.3	20.55	6.3	F		10.18	6.3	23.02	6.4	F		8.35	6.3	21.13	6.1
27	W		9.16	6.3	22.10	6.5	Sa		11.38	6.6	—	—	Sa		9.57	6.3	22.36	6.2
28	Th		10.38	6.4	23.23	6.6	Su		0.11	6.7	12.41	6.9	Su		11.20	6.6	23.49	6.6
29	F		11.51	6.6	—	—							M		—	—	12.23	7.0
30	Sa		0.26	6.8	12.53	6.8							Tu		0.46	6.9	13.12	7.2
31	Su	○	1.19	6.9	13.45	7.0							W	○	1.31	7.1	13.55	7.3

RAPHAEL'S TIDAL PREDICTIONS 1999
HIGH WATER LONDON BRIDGE (GMT)

Date	Day	Moon	a.m. h.m.	ht. m	p.m. h.m.	ht. m	Day	Moon	a.m. h.m.	ht. m	p.m. h.m.	ht. m	Day	Moon	a.m. h.m.	ht. m	p.m. h.m.	ht. m
			April						**May**						**June**			
1	Th		2.10	7.1	14.31	7.3	Sa		2.19	7.0	14.37	7.1	Tu		2.54	6.8	15.06	7.0
2	F		2.44	7.1	15.04	7.3	Su		2.48	7.0	15.04	7.1	W		3.29	6.8	15.40	6.9
3	Sa		3.15	7.1	15.33	7.2	M		3.18	6.9	15.32	7.0	Th		4.04	6.8	16.15	6.9
4	Su		3.44	7.0	16.01	7.1	Tu		3.49	6.9	16.01	7.0	F		4.42	6.7	16.50	6.7
5	M		4.14	6.9	16.31	6.9	W		4.22	6.8	16.35	6.8	Sa		5.21	6.6	17.28	6.6
6	Tu		4.46	6.8	17.02	6.8	Th		4.59	6.6	17.10	6.7	Su		6.04	6.5	18.11	6.4
7	W		5.23	6.5	17.38	6.6	F		5.38	6.5	17.48	6.4	M	☾	6.54	6.3	19.03	6.1
8	Th		6.04	6.3	18.18	6.2	Sa		6.23	6.2	18.33	6.1	Tu		7.57	6.1	20.11	6.0
9	F	☾	6.50	5.9	19.05	5.9	Su		7.17	6.0	19.29	5.9	W		9.15	6.2	21.33	6.1
10	Sa		7.48	5.6	20.07	5.6	M	☾	8.28	5.9	20.48	5.7	Th		10.28	6.5	22.46	6.5
11	Su		9.08	5.6	21.32	5.6	Tu		9.51	6.1	22.14	6.0	F		11.33	6.9	23.49	6.8
12	M		10.32	5.9	22.56	5.9	W		11.03	6.5	23.23	6.4	Sa		—	—	12.29	7.1
13	Tu		11.40	6.4	23.59	6.5	Th		—	—	12.02	7.0	Su	●	0.46	7.0	13.19	7.1
14	W		—	—	12.33	7.0	F		0.19	6.9	12.54	7.3	M		1.36	7.1	14.07	7.2
15	Th		0.50	7.0	13.21	7.4	Sa	●	1.08	7.2	13.41	7.4	Tu		2.26	7.3	14.54	7.2
16	F	●	1.35	7.3	14.03	7.6	Su		1.53	7.4	14.24	7.5	W		3.15	7.4	15.40	7.3
17	Sa		2.17	7.6	14.45	7.7	M		2.40	7.6	15.09	7.5	Th		4.04	7.5	16.26	7.2
18	Su		2.59	7.7	15.27	7.6	Tu		3.26	7.6	15.54	7.4	F		4.53	7.4	17.13	7.0
19	M		3.41	7.7	16.11	7.4	W		4.15	7.6	16.42	7.2	Sa		5.41	7.2	17.58	6.7
20	Tu		4.28	7.5	16.56	7.1	Th		5.06	7.3	17.30	6.9	Su	☽	6.30	6.8	18.46	6.4
21	W		5.17	7.2	17.45	6.7	F		5.58	7.0	18.19	6.6	M		7.21	6.5	19.38	6.1
22	Th	☽	6.11	6.8	18.37	6.4	Sa	☽	6.53	6.7	19.12	6.3	Tu		8.19	6.2	20.40	6.0
23	F		7.10	6.5	19.36	6.2	Su		7.52	6.4	20.13	6.1	W		9.25	6.1	21.53	5.9
24	Sa		8.16	6.3	20.44	6.0	M		8.58	6.3	21.25	6.0	Th		10.38	6.2	23.07	6.1
25	Su		9.32	6.3	22.05	6.1	Tu		10.15	6.3	22.46	6.2	F		11.40	6.4	—	—
26	M		10.53	6.5	23.23	6.4	W		11.24	6.6	23.48	6.5	Sa		0.02	6.3	12.26	6.6
27	Tu		11.58	6.9	—	—	Th		—	—	12.18	6.9	Su		0.46	6.5	13.04	6.7
28	W		0.19	6.8	12.47	7.2	F		0.36	6.7	13.00	7.0	M	○	1.24	6.5	13.39	6.8
29	Th		1.05	7.0	13.29	7.2	Sa		1.17	6.8	13.36	7.0	Tu		1.59	6.7	14.13	6.9
30	F	○	1.45	7.0	14.06	7.2	Su	○	1.50	6.8	14.07	6.9	W		2.35	6.8	14.49	6.9
31							M		2.23	6.8	14.37	7.0						

RAPHAEL'S TIDAL PREDICTIONS 1999
HIGH WATER LONDON BRIDGE (GMT)

			July						August						September			
Date	Day	Moon	a.m. h. m.	ht. m	p.m. h. m.	ht. m	Day	Moon	a.m. h. m.	ht. m	p.m. h. m.	ht. m	Day	Moon	a.m. h. m.	ht. m	p.m. h. m.	ht. m
1	Th		3.12	6.9	15.26	7.0	Su		4.11	7.2	16.21	7.1	W		5.06	6.9	17.14	6.9
2	F		3.50	6.9	16.01	6.9	M		4.48	7.0	16.56	6.9	Th	☾	5.48	6.6	17.59	6.6
3	Sa		4.28	6.9	16.36	6.8	Tu		5.27	6.8	17.33	6.7	F		6.37	6.2	18.56	6.4
4	Su		5.06	6.8	17.13	6.7	W	☾	6.11	6.5	18.16	6.6	Sa		7.42	6.1	20.10	6.2
5	M		5.47	6.7	17.52	6.6	Th		7.01	6.3	19.12	6.4	Su		9.01	6.1	21.34	6.3
6	Tu	☾	6.32	6.5	18.39	6.4	F		8.09	6.2	20.28	6.3	M		10.21	6.3	22.59	6.5
7	W		7.29	6.3	19.39	6.2	Sa		9.26	6.3	21.51	6.3	Tu		11.37	6.6	—	—
8	Th		8.40	6.3	20.58	6.2	Su		10.42	6.4	23.11	6.5	W		0.11	6.8	12.39	6.8
9	F		9.56	6.4	22.15	6.4	M		11.52	6.6	—	—	Th	●	1.07	7.1	13.29	7.0
10	Sa		11.06	6.7	23.27	6.6	Tu		0.22	6.7	12.53	6.8	F		1.55	7.3	14.13	7.2
11	Su		—	—	12.09	6.8	W	●	1.19	6.9	13.43	6.9	Sa		2.35	7.4	14.51	7.2
12	M		0.30	6.8	13.05	6.9	Th		2.09	7.1	14.30	7.1	Su		3.13	7.4	15.26	7.3
13	Tu	●	1.26	6.9	13.56	6.9	F		2.52	7.3	15.11	7.2	M		3.49	7.3	16.00	7.2
14	W		2.17	7.1	14.42	7.1	Sa		3.34	7.4	15.50	7.3	Tu		4.21	7.1	16.31	7.0
15	Th		3.05	7.3	15.27	7.2	Su		4.14	7.4	16.26	7.2	W		4.52	6.8	17.03	6.7
16	F		3.51	7.5	16.10	7.3	M		4.50	7.2	17.03	7.0	Th		5.24	6.6	17.41	6.5
17	Sa		4.35	7.5	16.52	7.1	Tu		5.27	6.9	17.38	6.7	F	☽	6.01	6.3	18.23	6.1
18	Su		5.19	7.2	17.33	6.9	W		6.05	6.5	18.18	6.4	Sa		6.44	6.0	19.17	5.7
19	M		6.01	6.9	18.13	6.6	Th	☽	6.47	6.2	19.07	6.0	Su		7.39	5.7	20.26	5.5
20	Tu	☽	6.44	6.5	18.58	6.3	F		7.38	5.9	20.07	5.7	M		8.48	5.5	21.41	5.4
21	W		7.34	6.2	19.53	6.0	Sa		8.38	5.7	21.16	5.6	Tu		10.05	5.5	23.00	5.7
22	Th		8.31	6.0	20.58	5.8	Su		9.43	5.7	22.31	5.6	W		11.21	5.9	23.59	6.2
23	F		9.34	5.9	22.08	5.8	M		10.55	5.8	23.41	5.9	Th		—	—	12.16	6.4
24	Sa		10.43	6.0	23.21	5.9	Tu		11.59	6.1	—	—	F		0.46	6.7	13.01	6.8
25	Su		11.45	6.1	—	—	W		0.32	6.2	12.47	6.5	Sa	○	1.28	7.1	13.42	7.2
26	M		0.15	6.1	12.32	6.4	Th	○	1.14	6.6	13.29	6.8	Su		2.09	7.4	14.21	7.5
27	Tu		0.58	6.3	13.14	6.6	F		1.55	7.0	14.10	7.1	M		2.47	7.6	14.59	7.6
28	W	○	1.38	6.6	13.53	6.8	Sa		2.34	7.3	14.48	7.3	Tu		3.26	7.6	15.37	7.6
29	Th		2.17	6.8	14.33	7.0	Su		3.12	7.4	15.25	7.4	W		4.05	7.4	16.17	7.4
30	F		2.56	7.0	15.11	7.1	M		3.50	7.4	16.00	7.4	Th		4.46	7.0	16.59	7.1
31	Sa		3.34	7.2	15.46	7.1	Tu		4.28	7.2	16.36	7.2						

RAPHAEL'S TIDAL PREDICTIONS 1999
HIGH WATER LONDON BRIDGE (GMT)

	October						November						December					
Date	Day	Moon	a.m. h.m.	ht. m	p.m. h.m.	ht. m	Day	Moon	a.m. h.m.	ht. m	p.m. h.m.	ht. m	Day	Moon	a.m. h.m.	ht. m	p.m. h.m.	ht. m
1	F		5.30	6.6	17.48	6.7	M		7.08	6.1	19.46	6.3	W		7.48	6.1	20.30	6.3
2	Sa	☾	6.20	6.2	18.47	6.4	Tu		8.16	6.0	20.59	6.3	Th		8.55	6.1	21.44	6.3
3	Su		7.24	6.0	19.59	6.2	W		9.32	6.1	22.19	6.5	F		10.15	6.2	22.57	6.6
4	M		8.38	6.0	21.19	6.3	Th		10.50	6.4	23.30	6.9	Sa		11.24	6.5	23.55	6.9
5	Tu		9.58	6.1	22.43	6.5	F		11.55	6.8	—	—	Su		—	—	12.18	6.8
6	W		11.17	6.5	23.54	6.9	Sa		0.25	7.2	12.44	7.1	M		0.43	7.0	13.01	6.9
7	Th		—	—	12.19	6.9	Su		1.11	7.3	13.26	7.2	Tu	●	1.22	7.1	13.38	6.9
8	F		0.49	7.3	13.10	7.1	M	●	1.49	7.3	14.03	7.2	W		1.56	7.0	14.11	6.9
9	Sa	●	1.35	7.4	13.52	7.2	Tu		2.23	7.2	14.35	7.1	Th		2.26	7.0	14.44	6.9
10	Su		2.14	7.4	14.28	7.3	W		2.52	7.1	15.05	7.1	F		2.55	7.0	15.16	6.9
11	M		2.49	7.3	15.01	7.2	Th		3.19	7.0	15.34	7.0	Sa		3.26	7.0	15.51	6.8
12	Tu		3.20	7.2	15.32	7.1	F		3.47	6.9	16.08	6.8	Su		4.01	6.8	16.28	6.7
13	W		3.49	7.0	16.01	7.0	Sa		4.19	6.8	16.45	6.6	M		4.35	6.7	17.06	6.6
14	Th		4.17	6.9	16.32	6.8	Su		4.55	6.6	17.23	6.4	Tu	☽	5.11	6.5	17.45	6.4
15	F		4.48	6.7	17.09	6.5	M		5.31	6.3	18.06	6.2	W		5.49	6.3	18.30	6.2
16	Sa		5.23	6.5	17.49	6.3	Tu	☽	6.15	6.1	18.57	5.9	Th		6.36	6.1	19.25	6.1
17	Su	☽	6.02	6.2	18.36	5.9	W		7.07	5.8	20.02	5.7	F		7.35	5.9	20.37	6.0
18	M		6.49	5.8	19.34	5.6	Th		8.17	5.6	21.23	5.8	Sa		8.54	5.9	21.54	6.2
19	Tu		7.49	5.5	20.51	5.5	F		9.44	5.8	22.36	6.2	Su		10.12	6.2	23.02	6.6
20	W		9.12	5.5	22.12	5.7	Sa		10.56	6.3	23.37	6.7	M		11.20	6.6	—	—
21	Th		10.36	5.8	23.20	6.2	Su		11.54	6.8	—	—	Tu		0.01	6.9	12.18	6.9
22	F		11.40	6.3	—	—	M		0.29	7.1	12.43	7.1	W	○	0.54	7.1	13.11	7.1
23	Sa		0.12	6.8	12.29	6.8	Tu	○	1.15	7.4	13.29	7.4	Th		1.43	7.2	14.02	7.3
24	Su	○	0.58	7.2	13.12	7.2	W		2.00	7.5	14.14	7.6	F		2.30	7.3	14.51	7.5
25	M		1.41	7.5	13.53	7.5	Th		2.44	7.5	15.01	7.7	Sa		3.16	7.3	15.40	7.6
26	Tu		2.21	7.6	14.34	7.7	F		3.29	7.4	15.49	7.6	Su		4.04	7.3	16.29	7.6
27	W		3.02	7.6	15.16	7.8	Sa		4.15	7.2	16.39	7.4	M		4.50	7.2	17.19	7.4
28	Th		3.44	7.4	16.00	7.6	Su		5.04	6.9	17.33	7.1	Tu		5.37	6.9	18.08	7.0
29	F		4.29	7.1	16.48	7.3	M	☾	5.55	6.6	18.27	6.8	W	☾	6.25	6.6	18.58	6.7
30	Sa		5.17	6.7	17.41	6.9	Tu		6.50	6.3	19.26	6.5	Th		7.15	6.3	19.55	6.3
31	Su	☾	6.09	6.3	18.40	6.5							F		8.14	6.1	20.58	6.2

The tidal predictions on pages 145–150 have been computed by the Proudman Oceanic Laboratory.
Copyright reserved.

TIDAL TABLES FOR THE BRITISH ISLES

The following time differences will, when applied to the standard port (London Bridge), give the approximate time of high water.

STANDARD PORT: LONDON BRIDGE

Secondary Port	Diff. H. M.	Secondary Port	Diff. H. M.
Scrabster	−5 09	Southwold	−3 50
Wick	−2 29	Aldeburgh	−3 05
Meikle Ferry	−1 43	Felixstowe Pier	−2 21
Nairn	−1 58	Clacton–on–Sea	−1 59
Lossiemouth	−2 05	Burnham–on–Crouch	−1 27
Fraserburgh	−1 33	Southend–on–Sea	−1 23
Aberdeen	−0 23	Sheerness	−1 19
Stonehaven	−0 13	Herne Bay	−1 25
Arbroath	+0 23	Margate	−1 53
Cockenzie	+0 46	Ramsgate	−2 32
Dunbar	+0 50	Deal	−2 37
Berwick	+0 54	Dover	−2 52
Blyth	+1 48	Folkestone	−3 04
River Tyne entrance	+1 47	Dungeness	−3 04
Sunderland	+1 49	Hastings	−2 57
Hartlepool	+1 59	Eastbourne	−2 51
Tees Bridge (Newport)	+2 04	Newhaven	−2 46
Whitby	+2 20	Brighton	−2 51
Scarborough	+2 29	Worthing	−2 39
Filey Bay	+2 45	Littlehampton (ent.)	−2 39
Bridlington	+2 58	Bognor Regis	−2 42
Grimsby	+4 13	Portsmouth	−2 38
Skegness	+4 33	Ryde	−2 38
Boston	+4 26	Ventnor	−3 05
King's Lynn	+4 51	Southampton (1st H.W.)	−2 54
Hunstanton	+4 36	Lymington	*−3 48
Wells	+5 01	Poole (entrance)	*−5 18
Cromer	+4 56	Bournemouth	*−5 18
Gorleston–on–Sea	−5 00	Swanage	−5 28
Lowestoft	−4 25	Lulworth Cove	+4 59

TIDAL TABLES FOR THE BRITISH ISLES

Continued:

STANDARD PORT: LONDON BRIDGE

Secondary Port	Diff. H. M.	Secondary Port	Diff. H. M.
Portland	+5 09	Solva	+4 49
Lyme Regis	+4 55	Fishguard	+5 45
Exmouth Dock	+4 50	Port Cardigan	+6 07
Teignmouth (app.)	+4 37	Aberystwyth	−6 11
Torquay	+4 40	Aberdovy	−5 41
Dartmouth	+4 25	Barmouth	−5 38
Salcombe	+4 10	Pwllheli	−5 48
Plymouth	+4 05	Caernarvon	−3 59
Looe	+3 55	Holyhead	−3 29
Fowey	+3 53	Menai Bridge	−3 09
Mevagissey	+3 53	Llandudno	−3 10
Falmouth	+3 35	Rhyl	−3 02
Lizard Point	+3 15	Hilbre Island	
Newlyn	+3 07	(Hoylake–West Kirby)	−2 58
Sennen Cove	+3 00	Southport	−2 55
St Ives	+3 35	Blackpool	−2 50
Newquay	+3 32	Fleetwood	−2 38
Padstow	+3 45	Morecambe	−2 33
Bude Haven	+3 57	Barrow (Ramsden Dock)	−2 28
Barnstaple	+4 30	Whitehaven	−2 30
Ilfracombe	+4 20	Kirkcudbright Bay	−2 25
Weston–super–Mare	+5 07	Portpatrick	−2 18
Newport (Gwent)	+5 17	Girvan	−1 58
Cardiff (Penarth)	+5 17	Ayr	−1 51
Barry	+5 10	Lamlash	−1 52
Porthcawl	+4 37	Greenock	−1 26
Swansea	+4 41	Oban	+4 17
Mumbles	+4 44	Gairloch	+5 17
Tenby	+4 25	Ullapool	+5 37
Milford Haven	+4 37	Belfast	−2 47
Little Haven	+4 47	Douglas (Isle of Man)	−2 44

*1st High Water Springs.

Conversion of Standard Times to GMT

Countries that keep Summer Time are marked with an asterisk (*)

EUROPE

GMT and Western European Time: the UK, Ireland, Iceland, and Portugal.

Mid–European Time (+1 hr): Albania, Andorra, Austria, Belgium, Czechoslovakia, Denmark, France, Germany, Gibraltar, Hungary, Italy, Liechtenstein, Luxembourg, Malta, Monaco, the Netherlands, Norway, *Poland, San Marino, Spain, Sweden, Switzerland, the Vatican, and the former Yugoslavia.

East European Time (+2 hrs): Bulgaria, Cyprus, Finland, Greece and Romania.

Russia, European (+4 hrs)

CANADA

Atlantic Standard Time (–4 hrs, * summertime kept in all states): New Brunswick, Newfoundland, Nova Scotia, Prince Edward Is, Quebec (eastern), Northwest Territories (easternmost).

Canadian Eastern Time (–5 hrs, * summertime kept in all states): Ontario (E of long. W 90°), Quebec (western), and Northwest Territories (portion W 68° to W 85°).

Canadian Central Time (–6 hrs, * summertime kept in all states): Manitoba, Ontario (W of long. W 90°), Saskatchewan (south–eastern portion), and Northwest Territories (portion W 85° to W 102°).

Canadian Mountain Time (–7 hrs, * summertime kept in all states): Alberta, Saskatchewan (except south–eastern portion), and Northwest Territories (W 102° to 120°).

THE USA

Eastern Standard Time (–5 hrs, * summertime kept in all states): Connecticut, Florida (greater portion), Georgia, Indiana, Kentucky (eastern), Maine, Maryland, Massachusetts, Michigan, New Hampshire, New Jersey, New York State, North Carolina, Ohio, Pennsylvania, Rhode Island, South Carolina, Tennessee (greater portion), Vermont, Virginia, Washington DC and West Virginia.

Central Standard Time (–6 hrs, * summertime kept in all states): Alabama, Arkansas, Florida (far west), Illinois, Iowa, Kansas (greater portion), Kentucky (greater portion), Louisiana,, Minnesota, Mississippi, Missouri, Nebraska (eastern), North Dakota (greater portion),

Oklahoma, South Dakota (eastern), Tennessee (western), Texas (greater portion), and Wisconsin.

Mountain Standard Time (–7 hrs, * summertime kept in all states): Arizona, Colorado, Idaho (except far north), Kansas (far west), Montana, Nebraska (far west), New Mexico, North Dakota (western portion), Oregon (far east), South Dakota (western portion), Texas (far west), Utah and Wyoming.

Pacific Standard Time (–8 hrs, * summertime kept in all states): California, Idaho (far north), Nevada, Oregon (greater portion), and Washington State.

Central Alaska Time (–10 hrs)

Hawaiian Standard Time (–10½ hrs)

AUSTRALIA
+8 hrs: West Australia
+9½ hrs: South Australia, and Northern Territory
+10 hrs: New South Wales, Queensland, Tasmania, Victoria

NEW ZEALAND: + 12 hrs

SOME OTHERS

Country	hours	Country	hours
Algeria	0	Korea	+9
Angola	+1	Kuwait	+3
Argentina (most of state)	–3	Lebanon	+2
Bahamas	–5	Madagascar	+3
Bahrain	+4	Malaya	+7½
Bangladesh	+6	Mexico (greater portion)	–6
Barbados	–4	Mauretania	0
Bermuda*	–4	Mozambique	+2
Bolivia	–4	Morocco	0
Botswana	+2	Nicaragua*	–6
Brazil* (divided into		Pakistan	+4½
3 zones, from E to W	–3,4,5	Peru	–5
China, coastal area*	+8	Samoa	–11
Cuba	–5	Senegal	0
Ecuador	–5	Somalia	+3
Egypt	+2	South Africa	+2
Ghana	0	Sri Lanka	+5½
Hong Kong*	+8	Syria	+2
India	+5½	Tanzania	+3
Iran	+3½	Thailand	+7
Iraq	+3	Trinidad	–4
Israel*	+2	Tunisia	+1
Jamaica	–5	Turkey*	+2
Japan	+9	Uganda	+3
Java	+7	Venezuela	–4½
Jordan	+2	Zambia	+2
Kenya	+3	Zimbabwe	+3

Lighting-Up Times for 1999

Day	Jan. h.m.	Feb. h.m.	Mar. h.m.	April h.m.	May h.m.	June h.m.	July h.m.	Aug. h.m.	Sept. h.m.	Oct. h.m.	Nov. h.m.	Dec. h.m.
1	16 31	17 19	18 09	20 02	20 52	21 37	21 51	21 19	20 17	19 09	17 04	16 25
2	16 33	17 21	18 11	20 04	20 54	21 38	21 50	21 17	20 15	19 06	17 02	16 25
3	16 34	17 22	18 13	20 05	20 56	21 39	21 50	21 15	20 13	19 04	17 00	16 24
4	16 35	17 24	18 14	20 07	20 57	21 40	21 49	21 14	20 10	19 02	16 59	16 24
5	16 36	17 26	18 16	20 09	20 59	21 41	21 49	21 12	20 08	19 00	16 57	16 23
6	16 37	17 28	18 18	20 11	21 00	21 42	21 48	21 10	20 06	18 57	16 55	16 23
7	16 39	17 30	18 20	20 12	21 02	21 43	21 48	21 08	20 04	18 55	16 54	16 22
8	16 40	17 31	18 21	20 14	21 04	21 44	21 47	21 07	20 01	18 53	16 52	16 22
9	16 41	17 33	18 23	20 16	21 05	21 45	21 47	21 05	19 59	18 51	16 50	16 22
10	16 43	17 35	18 25	20 17	21 07	21 46	21 46	21 03	19 57	18 48	16 49	16 22
11	16 44	17 37	18 27	20 19	21 08	21 46	21 45	21 01	19 55	18 46	16 47	16 21
12	16 46	17 39	18 28	20 21	21 10	21 47	21 44	20 59	19 52	18 44	16 46	16 21
13	16 47	17 41	18 30	20 22	21 12	21 48	21 43	20 57	19 50	18 42	16 44	16 21
14	16 48	17 42	18 32	20 24	21 13	21 48	21 42	20 55	19 48	18 40	16 43	16 21
15	16 50	17 44	18 33	20 26	21 15	21 49	21 41	20 53	19 45	18 38	16 42	16 22
16	16 52	17 46	18 35	20 27	21 16	21 49	21 40	20 51	19 43	18 36	16 40	16 22
17	16 53	17 48	18 37	20 29	21 18	21 50	21 39	20 49	19 41	18 33	16 39	16 22
18	16 55	17 50	18 39	20 31	21 19	21 50	21 38	20 47	19 38	18 31	16 38	16 22
19	16 56	17 51	18 40	20 32	21 21	21 51	21 37	20 45	19 36	18 29	16 36	16 22
20	16 58	17 53	18 42	20 34	21 22	21 51	21 36	20 43	19 34	18 27	16 35	16 23
21	17 00	17 55	18 44	20 36	21 23	21 51	21 35	20 41	19 32	18 25	16 34	16 23
22	17 01	17 57	18 45	20 37	21 25	21 51	21 33	20 39	19 29	18 23	16 33	16 24
23	17 03	17 59	18 47	20 39	21 26	21 51	21 32	20 37	19 27	18 21	16 32	16 24
24	17 05	18 00	18 49	20 41	21 28	21 52	21 31	20 35	19 25	18 19	16 31	16 25
25	17 06	18 02	18 50	20 42	21 29	21 52	21 29	20 32	19 22	18 17	16 30	16 26
26	17 08	18 04	18 52	20 44	21 30	21 52	21 28	20 30	19 20	18 15	16 29	16 26
27	17 10	18 06	18 54	20 46	21 31	21 51	21 27	20 28	19 18	18 13	16 28	16 27
28	17 12	18 07	19 55	20 47	21 33	21 51	21 25	20 26	19 15	18 11	16 27	16 28
29	17 13		19 57	20 49	21 34	21 51	21 23	20 24	19 13	18 09	16 27	16 29
30	17 15		19 59	20 51	21 35	21 51	21 22	20 22	19 11	18 08	16 26	16 30
31	17 17		20 00		21 36		21 20	20 19		17 06		16 31

Note: The times above are when *headlamps* on vehicles must be switched on in the evenings. *Front and rear position lamps* must be used between sunset and sunrise. These times are in GMT, except between 01.00 on March 28th and 01.00 on October 31st when they are in BST (1 hour in advance of GMT). They are calculated for London (longitude 0°, latitude N.51.5°).

Summer Time

Before 1981, the change-over from GMT to Summer Time and vice versa occurred at 02h. GMT on the dates specified. From 1981 onwards the change-over took place at 01h. GMT.

One hour advanced resumed:

1963. March 31st to October 27th
1964. March 22nd to October 25th
1965. March 21st to October 24th
1966. March 20th to October 23rd
1967. March 19th to October 29th
1968. February 18th until
1971. October 31st
1972. March 19th to October 29th
1973. March 18th to October 28th
1974. March 17th to October 27th
1975. March 16th to October 26th
1976. March 21st to October 24th
1977. March 20th to October 23rd
1978. March 19th to October 29th
1979. March 18th to October 28th
1980. March 16th to October 26th
1981. March 29th to October 25th
1982. March 28th to October 24th

1983. March 27th to October 23rd
1984. March 25th to October 28th
1985. March 31st to October 27th
1986. March 30th to October 26th
1987. March 29th to October 25th
1988. March 27th to October 23rd
1989. March 26th to October 29th
1990. March 25th to October 28th
1991. March 31st to October 27th
1992. March 29th to October 25th
1993. March 28th to October 24th
1994. March 27th to October 23rd
1995. March 26th to October 22nd
1996. March 31st to October 27th
1997. March 30th to October 26th
1998. March 29th to October 25th
1999. March 28th to October 31st*
Subject to confirmation.

Astrological Symbols, Abbreviations, Explanations and Classifications

ASPECTS

☌	Conjunction	0°
⊻	Semi–sextile	30°
⊥	Semi–quintile	36°
∠	Semi–square	45°
✳	Sextile	60°
Q	Quintile	72°
□	Square	90°
△	Trine	120°
⊡	Sesquiquadrate	135°
±	Biquintile	144°
▽	Quincunx	150°
☍	Opposition	180°

If two planets are in conjunction they have the same longitude (i.e. 0° difference of longitude). If two planets are in trine aspect their difference of longitude is 120°.

P	Parallel
T	Transiting

CLASSIFICATION OF SIGNS

Masculine	♈ ♊ ♌ ♎ ♐ ♒
Feminine	♉ ♋ ♍ ♏ ♑ ♓
Fiery	♈ ♌ ♐
Earthy	♉ ♍ ♑
Airy	♓ ♎ ♒
Watery	♋ ♏ ♓
Short Ascension	♑ ♒ ♓ ♈ ♉ ♊
Long Ascension	♋ ♌ ♍ ♎ ♏ ♐
Movable or Cardinal	♈ ♋ ♎ ♑
Fixed	♉ ♏ ♌ ♒
Common	♊ ♍ ♐ ♓
Fruitful	♋ ♏ ♓
Barren	♊ ♌ ♍ ♑
Double-bodied	♊ ♓ first half of ♐
Equinoctial	♈ ♎
Tropical	♋ ♑

MOON'S SIGNS

In each sign the Moon rules a different part of the body.

Aires	♈	head and face
Taurus	♉	neck and throat
Gemini	♊	arms and shoulders
Cancer	♋	breast and stomach
Leo	♌	heart and back
Virgo	♍	bowels and belly
Libra	♎	veins and loins
Scorpio	♏	secret members
Sagittarius	♐	hips and thighs
Capricorn	♑	knees and hams
Aquarius	♒	legs and ankles
Pisces	♓	feet and toes

PLANETS, HOUSES OR SIGNS

Sign	Planet	Sign	Planet
♈	♂	♎	♀
♉	♀	♏	♂ (♇)
♊	☿	♐	♃
♋	☽	♑	♄
♌	☉	♒	♄ (♅)
♍	☿	♓	♃ (♆)

If a planet is in its house or sign whilst the sign is rising or in the Ascendant, then the planet is the ruler or *Lord* of the horoscope.

PLANETS, SYMBOLS

♆	Neptune	☽	Moon
♅	Uranus	☉	Earth
♄	Saturn	♇	Pluto
♃	Jupiter	☊	Dragon Head
♂	Mars	☋	Dragon Tail
☉	Sun		
♀	Venus		
☿	Mercury		

"How To Attract Anything You Want Into Your Life, Be It Money, A New Car, Home or Lover!"

For centuries people have used the hidden power of their minds to achieve wealth, success, love and peace of mind. Instead of relying on luck or fate to bring them what they want, they rely on ancient occult secrets – secrets which enable them to turn failure into success, poverty into wealth, lovelessness into love and stress into peace of mind. These people are among the most successful and powerful in modern society. And now you can join them!

We are pleased to announce that we have just launched a brand new home-study course which is designed to introduce you to the **Secrets of the Occult!** This unique course, which consists of no less than eleven lessons, reveals all you need to know about the mysteries of modern magic. **The Secrets of the Occult** home-study course assumes that you have no previous knowledge of the subject and leads you, step-by-step to an excellent understanding of the most important ancient secrets. These secrets can help you to totally transform your life if you use them wisely. To give you a taste of what lies in store, here are just a few of the things you will learn ...

- **The Four Basic Laws which are central to practical occultism and which guarantee success if they are used properly.**

- **How changing the way you think can change the reality you experience in everyday life.**

- **How to speak 'magic words' for love, money, success or anything else you desire.**

- **How to leave your body and explore spiritual worlds by using a technique known as 'astral projection'.**

- **How to make and use a Magical Talisman.**

- **The Secrets of Forbidden Magic such as Voodoo, Sex Magic and other dark practices.**

All you need to make this course work for you is an open mind, access to these ancient secrets and the willingness to give them a try. Furthermore, you shouldn't think that occultism is dangerous or difficult. Our unique home-study course will show you very quickly that occultism is both safe and very simple – when you know how!

So there you have it. The portal of destiny is open ... step inside!

If you would like to receive our Secrets of the Occult FREE SPECIAL REPORT – including details of a special 'FREE BONUS OFFER' then all you need to do is complete the request coupon on the right and mail it to us today. Within a few days your requested information will be with you, and you will even discover how you can study lesson one of the course for FREE!

MAIN UNITED KINGDOM EVENTS 1999

For agricultural shows, see pages 137–42. Dates and venues of any of the events listed here are subject to change (please check with local organiser/tourist board). Several important events are not included because times/venues had not been fixed before going to press. Dates marked with an asterisk (*) are provisional.

ALDEBURGH FESTIVAL of Music and the Arts, Snape Maltings Concert Hall: 11th–27th June

BADMINTON Horse Trials: 6th–9th May

BBC GARDENERS' WORLD LIVE, National Exhibition Centre, Birmingham: 16th–20th June*

BBC PROMENADE CONCERTS, Royal Albert Hall: 16th July–11th September

BEVERLEY AND EAST RIDING FOLK Festival: 18th–20th June

BIGGIN HILL International Air Fair: 12th–13th June

BRAEMAR Royal Highland Gathering: 4th September

BRITISH ROSE Festival, Hampton Court: 6th–11th July

CHATSWORTH ANGLING Fair, Bakewell: 8th–9th May

CHATSWORTH COUNTRY Fair, Bakewell: 4th–5th September

CHELSEA Flower Show: 25th–28th May (RHS members only 25th–26th); tickets must be obtained in advance

COWES WEEK Regatta: 31st July–7th August

CRUFTS Dog Show, National Exhibition Centre, Birmingham: 11th–14th March

EDINBURGH International Festival: 15th August–4th September

EDINBURGH Military Tattoo, Edinburgh Castle: 6th–28th August

GOLF – The Open Championship, Carnoustie: 15th–18th July

GREAT AUTUMN ROSE Show, Harrogate: 17th–19th September

GREAT SUMMER FLOWER Show, Hampton Court: 6th–11th July (RHS members only 6th–7th)

HELSTON FLORAL DANCE: 8th May

HENLEY Royal Regatta: 30th June–4th July

IDEAL HOME Exhibition, Earls Court: 17th March–11th April*

LAWN TENNIS Championships, Wimbledon: 21st June–4th July

LLANGOLLEN International Musical Eisteddfod: 6th–11th July

LONDON INTERNATIONAL BOAT Show, Earls Court: 8th–17th January*

LONDON MOTOR Show, Earls Court: 19th–31st October

LONDON TO BRIGHTON Veteran Car Run, from Hyde Park to Madeira Drive: 7th November

LORD MAYOR'S SHOW: 13th November

MALVERN AUTUMN Show: Three Counties Showground: 25th–26th September

MALVERN SPRING GARDENING Show, Three Counties Showground: 7th–9th May

NOTTING HILL CARNIVAL: 29th–30th August

NOTTINGHAM GOOSE Fair: 7th–9th October

OLYMPIA INTERNATIONAL SHOWJUMPING Championships: 16th–20th December

OULD LAMMAS Fair, Ballycastle: 30th–31st August

OXFORD v CAMBRIDGE University Boat Race, Putney to Mortlake: 3rd April

ROYAL TOURNAMENT, Earls Court: 20th July–1st August

ROYAL WINDSOR HORSE Show, Home Park: 12th–16th May

ST HELENS Show, Sherdley Park: 31st July–2nd August

SPALDING FLOWER FESTIVAL and SPRINGFIELDS COUNTRY FAIR: 1st–3rd May

TOWN AND COUNTRY Festival, Nat. Agricultural Centre, Stoneleigh Park, Kenilworth: 28th–30th August

TROOPING THE COLOUR, Whitehall: 12th June*

TRUCKFEST, East of England Showground, Peterborough: 2nd–3rd May

NATIONAL LOTTERY – ZODIAC NUMBERS

Certain numbers relate to your astrological sign, and you might want to incorporate these into your Lottery selections. Use some of them along with your birthday and family numbers for a better chance of success. The Star Numbers in the left column relate to your zodiac sign and planet number. These could be the luckiest numbers of all!

ZODIAC SIGN		STAR		SUGGESTED LOTTERY Nos							
ARIES	March 21st – April 20th	5	1	11	15	24	28	33	40	43	44
TAURUS	April 21st – May 21st	6	3	1	17	28	29	37	39	42	47
GEMINI	May 22nd – June 21st	7	4	2	20	23	29	31	38	45	49
CANCER	June 22nd – July 22nd	8	10	3	18	21	25	26	30	35	48
LEO	July 23rd – Aug 23rd	9	6	10	19	28	33	37	39	42	46
VIRGO	Aug 24th – Sept 23rd	10	7	11	20	29	31	38	40	44	47
LIBRA	Sept 24th – Oct 23rd	11	8	12	21	30	33	39	41	43	48
SCORPIO	Oct 24th – Nov 22nd	12	9	13	22	27	32	40	42	46	49
SAGITTARIUS	Nov 23rd – Dec 21st	1	5	6	14	16	23	27	31	32	39
CAPRICORN	Dec 22nd – Jan 20th	2	4	9	15	17	24	28	30	32	43
AQUARIUS	Jan 21st – Feb 19th	3	2	10	11	16	25	34	37	40	45
PISCES	Feb 20th – March 20th	4	2	12	18	27	31	36	38	41	47

ALL THE LUCK IN THE WORLD CAN NOW BE YOURS
with this unique collection from
THE MAGICAL WORLD OF ALCHEMY

For hundreds of years Alchemists combined elements and universal energies to create powerful charms. Some were made to help you find a soul-mate for **eternal love**, others to **attract great wealth** to you. Many believers acclaim their powers, and now you too can put them to the test.

Jim 'Is it magic or belief that makes them work? Last month I won £282,000.

Believers say they became wealthy because of their charms, and that it can work for you too! In fact they are **GUARANTEED TO WORK ! ! !** yes all seven must bring you luck. Also you will receive with every order of each or all 7 charms … a **FREE** *CRYSTAL BALL* reading.

These unique items are valuable collectors pieces. However, you are invited to try them entirely at my risk. If fantastic good fortune does not instantly begin to bless you, simply return them for a no question refund. And as a gift from me you will still get to keep and enjoy your wonderful **FREE** CRYSTAL BALL reading.

ALCHEMISTS LUCKY MONEY MAGNET win a million. It's your time to be lucky with this fabulous wealth creating talisman. Career success, lots of money. Enjoy houses, cars, holidays. Prove it to yourself! Try it on pools, racing, lotteries, etc.

EGYPTIAN PENDULUM astonishing ancient knowledge and charm power at your fingertips. Allow it to swing over pools, racing, spot the ball and lottery coupons. Time and time again it will pick a winner for you.

AMERICAN INDIAN CHARM to feel close to nature's healing powers. Feel at one with mother earth and the universe. Let the great spirit guide you and protect you. Attain serenity and a calm inner strength and confidence.

CRYSTAL POWER CHARM a huge amount of cosmic energies are encapsulated within each crystal. Alchemists found its soothing vibrations can help bring spiritual and emotional harmony. This charm is also intended to attract great wealth to you.

AFRICAN CHARM used to persuade a troublesome person to see things from your point of view. Let enemies become friends. Often used as a talisman for protection from harm and to travel in safety.

ARABIAN ABUNDANT MONEY CHARM a most beautiful item, fashioned centuries ago by Royal magicians. Seen extravagantly dazzling in a casket of precious jewels. Some of the world's wealthiest people say they owe it all to this fabulous charm.

MERLINS SPELLS no experience required … simply focus your thoughts on these fascinating spell-binding words. Spells made to attract a soul-mate and true love, spells made to bring wins of huge amounts of money, spells and magic made to make your wishes come true.

SPECIAL ALMANACK READERS OFFER ! ! !

Send **only £5 each**, or select **4 charms for £15,** or the collection of all **7 charms for only £20.**
You will also receive with this order … your special FREE Crystal Ball reading about your life.

Don't miss this offer. Let your good luck begin. Make it happen. **Pull out this form and send it now.**

Send Cash/P.O./Cheque, payable to OCCALLABAR

or write your VISA/Access number. Expiry date:. . . . . Card number:. . . . .

Name . . . . .Address . . . .

. . . . .Post Code . . . .
Send to: OCCALLABAR, P.O. Box 194, Weston Super Mare, BS23 1ZA.

159